Police and the Community

Police and the Community

An Analytic Perspective

Robert S. Clark

New Viewpoints
A Division of Franklin Watts
New York I London I 1979

New Viewpoints
A Division of Franklin Watts
730 Fifth Avenue
New York, New York 10019

Library of Congress Cataloging in Publication Data

Clark, Robert S   1916–
  Police and the community.

  Includes bibliographical references and index.
  1. Public relations—Police. 2. Police administra-
tion. 3. Police—United States. I. Title.
HV7936.P8C57   363.2'0973   78-21610
ISBN 0-531-05405-5 lib. bdg.
ISBN 0-531-05615-5 pbk.

To Ciel, as always

CONTENTS

List of Figures   xiii

Preface   xv

Special Note to Teachers   xxi

Acknowledgments   xxiii

Part I   Analysis of Police-Community Relations   1

Chapter 1   Introduction   3

Chapter 2   Identification of Relevant Variables   5
The Use of Inference   7
Data Analysis   9
　Descriptive   9
　Inferential   11
Findings   13
　Statistical Presentations   14
　Other Presentations   16
Conclusions Based on Findings   16
　The Discovery of Alternatives   17
　Using Probability   17
Recommendations   18

Chapter 3   The Intelligent Use of Experts   19
What Can Be Done?   19
　Use of the Old   20
　Discovery of the New   21

Who Should Do It?   23
  Using Practitioners   23
  Parable of the Spindle   24

Chapter 4   Models and Modeling   28
Systematic Models   30
Sociological Models   32
Psychological Models   39
Politico-economic Models   41
Definitional and Other Models   44
Appraisal of Theoretical Models   47
A Return to Reality   50

Chapter 5   The Communication Model   51
What Is Communication?   51
  Why Is It Valuable?   51
  Communication Theory   52
The Route to Decision Making   56
Definitions   57
Basic Principles   58
Redundancy   62
Receivers   64
Two-Step Flow of Influence   70
Diffusion of Information   77
Communication and Thinking Patterns   78
Words   80

Part II   Psychosocial Contexts   83

Chapter 6   Interactions   85
What Is Interaction?   85
The Role Concept   87
The Concept of Personality   88
  Normal and Abnormal Personalities   93
  Application to Groups   96
Motives and Incentives   98
  Personality and the Social Order   98
  Conscious and Unconscious Motives   99
Symbolic Interaction   100

Attitudes, Values, and "Sets"   102
Alienation   103

Chapter 7   Confrontations and Conflicts   106
The Benefits of Conflict   106
The Community Confronts Itself   110
Tensions   112
Community Impact on Policing Systems   114
Levels of Conflict   115
The Importance of Being Black   118
The Quality of Life   122

Chapter 8   Sociopolitical Processes   125
Social Movements   127
Associations, Organizations, and Institutions   129
Social Force, Power, and Authority   133
The Elements of Power   135
Social Power in the United States   138
   The Search for Methods for Social Power   138
   Liberty   140
   Factions   143
   Pluralism   145
   Evolution and Revolution   145

Part III   Measurements   147

Chapter 9   Planning, Implementing, and Monitoring   149
What Can Be Measured?   150
Why Measure?   152
The Limits of Measurement   153
Planning As a Continuous Process   158
Planning Police-Community Relations   160
Plans for Action   163
Engineering Implementation   166
To Make an Omelet—Break Eggs!   167

Chapter 10   Evaluation   169
After-the-Fact Measurement   169
Real-Time Measurement   172

Research Aspects of Measurement   174
Organizing Evaluation Efforts   174
  Purpose of Evaluation   175
  Difference From Basic Research   177
  How to Lie With Evaluations   177
  Evaluation Design   178
  What Is Significant?   180
  Reporting on Evaluation   185

Chapter 11 Research   186
Research Into PCR   186
The Idea of Research   188
The Methods of Research   190
  Inference About Past Facts   191
  Prior Probability   193
  Hypothesis Testing   193
The Fallibility of Research   194
Continuous Renewal of Research   196
Research As Honest Inquiry   198
Inventories of PCR Knowledge   198

Part IV Administration   201

Chapter 12 Operations   203
A Systematic Approach   208
The View From the Top   211
"Hidden Persuaders"   213
Reaching the Community   216
  Functional Analysis   219
  The N-Square Factor   219
  Opinion Leaders   220
  Settling for Less   221
  Hoping for More   221
  Coming to Limited Agreements   222
Stop, Look, and Listen!   223
  Impervious Groups   223
  The Analysis of Tension   225
  Reconciling Dissidents   226

Chapter 13   Police-Community–Relations Units   229
Specialization and Generalization   229
Centralization and Decentralization   231
The Best of All Worlds   232
Basic Philosophies   232
Problems of Elites   238
A Review of the Field   240
  New York City Police Department   241
  Chicago Police Department   245
  Los Angeles County Department of Sheriff   253
  City of Los Angeles Police Department   256

Part V   Review and Recapitulation   261

Chapter 14   A Total View   263

Appendix A   The Nine Principles of Police of the
                London Metropolitan Police Force, 1829   267

Appendix B   A Model for PCR Program Development   269

Notes   271

Index   285

LIST OF FIGURES

5–1   The Flow of Communication   55
8–1   Types of Groups   131
12–1   Do We Agree or Disagree?   227
13–1   Police-Community Relations Control and Function   241
13–2   New York City Police Department, Deputy Commissioner in Charge of Community Affairs   243
13–3   Chicago Police Department, General Order, 16 April 1977   246
13–4   Chicago Police Department, Bureau of Community Services   250
13–5   Chicago Police Department, General Order, 22 April 1977   251
13–6   Los Angeles County Department of Sheriff   254
13–7   Los Angeles County Department of Sheriff, Special Services Division   255
13–8   Organization of the Los Angeles Police Department   256
13–9   Los Angeles Police Department, Organization of the Administrative Office-Community Relations   258
13–10   Law Enforcement Assistance Administration's Table of Organization of "One Form of a Well-Organized Municipal Police Department"   259

An orgy of avarice, hate, and violence was displayed on television, which clearly showed looters walking out of stores in broad daylight. Even the next day, the rage continued, with police capturing only a small percentage.

Community relations were demonstrated to be distinguished by contempt and violence within the community and by venom and hate toward the police. There is every indication that this condition is endemic everywhere in the United States, according to professional observers.

Growing attention has been given by government and universities to community relations and to the relations of communities with governments, particularly with the police, for a number of years. The Law Enforcement Assistance Administration (LEAA) has provided funds for this purpose since 1968. We have learned some little things, but the evidence indicates that we do not know what to do about the problem.

There is no reason to believe that community relations are any better today than in prior years, or that they will improve in the future. Indications are all to the contrary. It is claimed that the progressive extension of education and political awareness of the public has had the effect of pluralizing pressures on government, particularly on the police. Aside from general malaise, any group—or any individual for that matter—sensitive enough to perceive hurt, determined to press a cause, and knowledgeable enough to swing public opinion can successfully affect government today.

Police departments, whose success depends upon daily fluctuations of public cooperation, are peculiarly susceptible to such pressures. Constitutionally unable to correctly evaluate between factions, police reaction has been to try to insulate itself from such biases, to interpret them all as without merit, because of their obvious motivation in the self-interest of estranged fragments of society to the detriment—or danger of detriment—of the nonmilitant majority of citizens.

Progress in education and political awareness has more than magnified the number and intensity of incidents adverse to police and government. The increase in mass-media coverage has let loose a flood of information into every home, resulting in a demand for ever-improving police performance, even from those not directly involved in complaints. Peccadilloes and irregularities of officials are no longer relegated to the back pages of newspapers. The lurid details now come into the home, in living color television, reminding all that *"something* should be done about it."

The crime problem, serious as it may be, is only one of the facets involved. There has always been a litany of charges of arrogant police behavior, "cover-ups," mis-, mal-, and nonfeasance in office. Bruised feelings arising from government official versus citizen confrontations are a permanent state of affairs.

In recognition of all of this, and more, the LEAA, as stated, has distributed hundreds of millions of dollars. This is in addition to the annual bill for crime, which is alleged to run anywhere from $5 billion to $50 billion, depending on the authority cited. All of this appears to be directly related to the conditions involved in police and community relations.

The thought and effort, as well as treasure, devoted to attempts at resolving some of these matters have been great. The literature is growing at an enormous rate. There has been little success, however, at organizing the available information into coherent approaches to the entire subject of police and society.

It is appropriate to set forth the list of objectives of this book:

1. To foster a continuing examination of society and government, particularly the relations between individuals, communities, and police.
2. To explore all discernible options in police-community relations.
3. To discover and describe the existing organization and administration of police-community relations and the processes involved.
4. To identify variables connected with legitimation of police and policing methods and with other aspects of police-community relations.
5. To outline, however crudely, the critically relevant variables of police-community relations and how they might be measured.
6. To specify realistic, rigorous methods of evaluating programs in police-community relations and to encourage their use.
7. To encourage the development of the communication skills necessary to successful police-community relations. This, under the assumption that although communication may not necessarily ameliorate, without communication no amelioration is possible.

The objectives formally stated, we must consider how to attain them. The usual textbook commences with a discussion of general statements and then describes particular cases as illustrations of the application of the theoretical generalizations. However, the state of knowledge of criminal justice has not reached a point of theoretical validity, such as to permit a straightforward presentation of either police or community action. Actually, there is almost no acceptable theory in either field.

Perforce, the device that is used in this book is to reach into collateral disciplines more firmly based in theory and applied knowledge. These associated bodies of knowledge are used to provide parallels and generalizations that are here submitted in the hope that they will aid our

understanding of police and community and their relations. This joinder
has resulted in a number of working hypotheses for which there has not
been sufficient research to determine acceptance or rejection. But at least
the discussion has commenced.

Whether this approach can be described as elegantly eclective or,
pejoratively, grab bag, we confess we do not know. In any case, this is
what is done: Anthropology and history are scanned for useful data. Psychology, sociology, political science, and economics are searched for apt
models, concepts, and methodologies. From this review, we have come to
the belief that there is much to be gained by seeking among the literature of group dynamics and communications research that can aid in
preparing a coherent text on the subject of police-community relations
that has, to this date, consistently evaded the practitioners in the police
and community most concerned.

There is, of course, a great need for the collection of organized knowledge about police and community. Classes on the subject in schools and
colleges struggle with the elements as police and community people have
presented them. These "elements," however, have appeared in different
sets with cyclic changes in orientations. We have had formal approaches
recommended, reaching for "sensitivity" as a desirable police quality,
followed by a cycle of "tough cop" proclamations. At various times in the
past we have placed the responsibility on the community—varying that
with placing it on the police, or on "outside agitators," or on the mass
media, or on the "multiversity," or on racism, or on reverse discrimination, and on and on.

Too much of the literature, even scholarly writing, has been politicized
by those overeager to present the point of view that favors one group
or another. Can one book tie together the manifold case histories, the
ruminations of experts, and the small body of research? If it can be done,
it would aid the serious student to understand—a little bit better—the
startling and unexpected consequences of well-intentioned intervention in
police-community relations. That is what this book tries to do.

The method used is defined by the book's divisions: Part I, "Analysis
of Police-Community Relations," tackles the conceptual conundrums of
behavioral-science analysis. For clarity it is divided into five chapters:
Chapter 1 points out the truism that the problem in police-community
relations, at bottom, is to discover the behavioral variables involved. Chapter 2, "Identification of Relevant Variables," is devoted to the most difficult problem of scientific research: the identification of factors that "make
a difference." Chapter 3, "The Intelligent Use of Experts," discusses that

important problem of modern administration. Scientific inquiry involves so many subspecialties, requiring long and arduous training before mastery, that there is probably no one person so omniqualified as to be able to do any substantial piece of research without the use of trained experts in several learned specialties, from programming to computers and on to statistics, research design, interviewing, psychology, and others. Chapter 4, "Models and Modeling," reviews one of the basic analytical tools and describes how such models can be used for better comprehension by practitioners and consumers of police services, as well as by community workers and opinion leaders. Chapter 5, "The Communication Model," concentrates on the model that appears most adaptable to practitioners' use to facilitate decision making in police-community relations. This model is explained in detail, because of the potential it presents for immediate and direct use, even by the tyro.

Part II, "Psychosocial Contexts," goes into the fields treated by both psychology and sociology, particularly by their progeny, social psychology and group dynamics. The treatment, analytical yet on an elementary level, explores "Interaction" in Chapter 6 and then, on an applied level, zeroes in on specific types of problems faced by practitioners in Chapter 7, "Confrontations and Conflicts." Chapter 8, "Sociopolitical Processes," backs off a bit to cover basic concepts involved in crossing the line between political science and the other behavioral sciences.

Part III, "Measurements," is a review of fundamentals. It does not go so far as to say, "If you can't measure it, it doesn't exist," but it notes the firmness with which modern scientific inquiry tries to pin down ideas quantitatively. Chapter 9, "Planning, Implementing, and Monitoring," discusses the present-day importance of measurement and its limits as the measurement concept applies to the administrator's main problems: planning, implementing, and monitoring to assure proper performance. Chapter 10, "Evaluation," mulls over the thankless task of reviewing performance and comparing it with goal attainment or the failure thereof. It considers the current wisdom that "evaluation is the name of the game" and estimates the limitations of that approach. Chapter 11, "Research," ends this section by trying to explain the place of research as a continuing resource, past, present, and future.

Part IV, "Administration," goes into what is actually done. Chapter 12, "Operations," reaches for the "view from the top," as to the place of police-community relations in the thrust of government effort, and what police-community relations really is to society at large and to the leaders of community and police management. Chapter 13, "Police-Community–Relations Units," picks out the specialized ways in which community relations have been handled within departments by divisions, given a variety of names but generally called police-community units, as examples of what is actually done in practice.

Finally, Part V, "Review and Recapitulation," in Chapter 14, "A Total View," restates the highlights, as they have been treated, in an attempt to rationalize the subject of police-community relations in a way that will be functionally useful to the practitioner. His job often is to forecast the future, and his main difficulty is to weigh the odds. Thus some options are presented, with the probable eventualities of each.

SPECIAL NOTE TO TEACHERS

The materials from which this book springs have been used for a number of years in a course on police-community relations. They have been well received by students, who contributed substantially to the development of the course.

As a text, the organization of the book calls for a full semester's work at the college level. If the term is shorter, say a quarter or ten weeks, a teacher may find it advisable to skim through some of the chapters. Chapters 5, 11, and 12 provide much detail that could be omitted. Each of these chapters, actually, could be the subject for an entire course.

Here, at Florida International University, we have found that this text has served not only to acquaint students with the complexities of police and community, but also to persuade students to pursue other courses in criminal justice and the behavioral sciences with an analytic and research orientation.

R.S.C.

ACKNOWLEDGMENTS

No mere acknowledgment can express my debt to the many police departments and community organizations that have assisted in the research and writing of this book. However, I must mention, with gratitude, the officers who gave unstintingly of their on- and off-duty time. Particular obligation is acknowledged to the police departments of New York City, Chicago, the Los Angeles Department of Sheriff, and the Police Department of the City of Los Angeles.

I am deeply grateful to the departments of psychology, anthropology, and sociology, and all the members of the faculty, of Florida International University for their aid in preparing all stages of the manuscript. I must single out, for special thanks, Professors Carlos Brain, Ralph G. Lewis, and Jo-Anne Segura-Miller, as well as Professor Harry S. Diamond of California State University at Los Angeles and Professor Arthur Niederhoffer of John Jay College of Criminal Justice, City University, New York, for their constant encouragement, advice, and support. All errors and omissions, of course, are my own.

R.S.C.

Part I

Analysis of Police-Community Relations

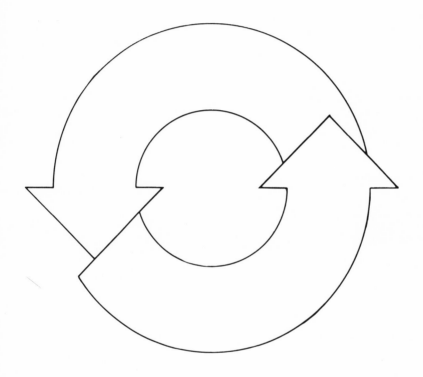

Chapter 1

INTRODUCTION

The law has no power to command obedience except that of habit . . .
—Aristotle, *Politics*, Book II

Four presidential and numerous local commissions have studied police and community relations, and it is the subject of countless speeches, articles, books, and studies.[1] For most people, the *police are the government,* with millions of contacts between police and citizens occurring daily.

It is highly significant that President Jimmy Carter in his State of the Union Message of 1978 stated, "To some persons the government has come to seem like a foreign country." The government and all its agents are estranged from the people.

Despite the time, money, and effort given to remedies, the malady remains. We do not know the cure, but we are relearning some ancient wisdoms.[2]

Enforcement by police usually demonstrates a low probability of detection of crime and of apprehension of offenders and a high probability of inciting resistance to, and even hatred of, the police.

Education in law observance offers higher probability of encouraging compliance.

Engineering a self-sustaining communication system can result in extremely high levels of law observance with a minimum of social costs.

The engineering of human behavior is not necessarily a concept out of operant conditioning. The building of a paved highway will far more surely persuade motorists away from a nearby rocky road than any amount of either enforcement or educational effort. Engineering human conduct calls simply for finding easier paths for desired behavior. The problem is to analyze human behavior for the variables involved in discovering these easier paths.

This, however, is not an easy task. It calls for a rare combination of research skills, deep human insight, and long police and community experience. No book can provide all this.

The following pages merely review some of the fundamentals of each of these areas, in sequence. A new generation of research-trained professionals will have to flesh out and apply these basic ideas.

Chapter 2

IDENTIFICATION OF RELEVANT VARIABLES

It is easier to discover a deficiency in individuals, in
states, and in Providence, than to see their real
import and value.
                    —Georg Wilhelm Friedrich Hegel,
                              Philosophy of History

This chapter discusses the concepts and terminology of science as
a preliminary to a more intensive analysis of police-community
relations.

The importance of identifying critically relevant variables is
stressed, as it is at the beginning of every analysis. It is pointed out
that in great measure this calls for creative guesswork. The forms in
which this guesswork, or insight, is best put are discussed, for much
of the scientific approach to inquiry is simply following certain
procedures that have been found to be very productive of useful
information.

An analytic inquiry into the nature of things today calls for an approach
quite a bit different from the way such inquiries were conducted in times
past.[1]

Briefly, *analysis* can be said to be definable as the separation of a subject of analysis into constituent parts or aspects.[2] The purpose of this
separation is to try to understand the particular characteristics that are
relevant to the concerns of the investigator. It is true that on occasion
when a complex substance is separated into parts sufficiently minute, it
may lose its original character—the whole, as it were, being something
more than, or at least different from, its parts.

In this vein, water, separable into hydrogen and oxygen, two gases, is
clearly something quite a bit different from its gaseous "parts." No
amount of examination or testing of the two gases, oxygen and hydrogen, at room temperature would enable one to understand the nature of
water as it affects, say, the hull of a ship passing through it at high
speed, or of the same water being absorbed by the digestive tract and
functioning as an all-pervading ingredient of the human body.

Thus it is not relevant to hydrodynamics to separate water into such parts as its two constituent gases. For the purpose of discovering the relevant variables of water as it affects the ship's hull, our efforts at analysis would be more fruitful if we were to consider such other parts, or variables, as the water's density, its viscosity, its tendency to form into waves, its idiosyncrasies when it flows, its resistance to displacement by the ship's hull, and so on. If, on the other hand, we are investigating the nature of water as a nutrient, necessary to body function, we may be interested in a different set of variables, such as its ability to pass through thin membranes, that is, its ability to diffuse by osmosis, its ability to dissolve many minerals and absorb a number of gases and release them as temperature goes up or pressure goes down and so on.

The wave formation of water is not ordinarily of critical interest to a physiologist inquiring into arteriosclerosis; but water's ability to carry globules of fat and on occasion deposit them on the walls of arteries will be of intense interest to him. These attributes appear to be not only relevant, but critically relevant variables, that is, absolutely necessary to the understanding of the formation of all sclerotic coatings on arterial walls. Much of the physiologist's inquiry may be devoted to identifying such critically relevant variables as "parts" not only of water, but of the problem of arteriosclerosis as well.

In police-community relations the first task of research is to try to identify equally critically relevant variables relating to our inquiry about police and community and their relations with each other.[3]

In all studies having to do with human behavior, the identification of *critically relevant variables* is difficult. There appear to be so many variables involved in human behavior, each with its concomitant effect, and there are so many interacting relationships among the variables that it is not easy to say with any degree of authority that *this* variable is critically relevant and this other variable is not.

Generally, policing arrangements are designed to encourage normative behavior in a community. In modern countries formal policing arrangements involve government agents who enforce bodies of law—specific prohibitions and permissions for individuals and organizations—that are devised in one place—the legislature—to be applied in another—the community. Thus one might be tempted to the obvious conclusion that the informal, internally accepted normative rules and the formal body of law are two critically relevant variables. One might suppose that any differences between the two sets of norms might be especially critical, as they might engender role conflicts. Of course, that supposition would be founded on the guess that role conflict is relevant to police-community relations.[4] A supposition founded on a guess hardly seems scientific, but there is no other way to start an inquiry into the factors connected with the matter under discussion. Of course, we reach for a wise judgment in this matter: We compare with reality—we look for empirical verification of our guesses. We try to use reasonably accurate logic in deduction, when deduction is appropriate. The method of identifying what may be critically relevant variables requires the careful formulation of guesses, called inferences, that are constantly checked and rechecked with reality and stand all subsequent investigation.

When we consider the different kinds of role conflicts, or the differing intensities of a single type of role conflict, we are reaching for a kind of measurement [5] that will involve some kind of comparison with a standard, which brings in other concepts that will be left to Part III of this book. Merely to distinguish between variables at this stage is quite enough.

It really is a creative act to envisage a critically relevant variable. There is no way to *prove* your choice, although there are ways to indicate the probability that your choice is relevant. This process of determining the most probable critically relevant variables is really the entire process of scientific inquiry. But it all starts with a guess.

Of course, empirical inquiry may reveal that some of the suggested variables are not as important as others. Perhaps the differential biology of different peoples is more critically relevant than role conflicts. We can try to investigate that possibility. There are any number of attributes or phenomena that might be inferred to be important in police-community relations.

1. Personality characteristics of the police.
2. Educational level of the police.
3. Human-relations training or ability of the police.
4. Climate (for example the lowest average temperature in the country).
5. Cultural traditions of the people of the community.
6. Average age of neighborhood residents.
7. Occupations of neighborhood residents.

The Use of Inference

Inference is the process of making reasonable guesses from something known or assumed. Experience has forced searchers after new knowledge to the conclusion that the future is never certain knowledge to humans. However, experience has also shown that we can often calculate the probability associated with some eventualities.[6] For some events, the probability may be very high, such as finding the floor underfoot when one steps out of bed, but it is definitely not of the order of absolute certainty.

Other events are possible, but not highly probable, such as your getting up to bat in a baseball game and pointing to the place on the outfield fence where you will send the ball on the first pitch, and then actually doing it and rounding the bases for a homer. Not so likely, you will agree, but still possible, and, of course, it has happened.

There are a number of ways to describe degrees of probability. Usually, however, it is done in the form of "so many chances of success out of so many possibilities," that is, a ratio, "one chance out of two" or "$\frac{1}{2}$." If one prefers, it can be written in decimal form, .5, or in percentage form, 50 percent.

All of these expressions are ratios and indicate the anticipation that out of a given number of such events, the probability will be that one-half of them will be favorable.

Thus we may anticipate that a juvenile who enters a certain training program has a 50 percent chance of being "rehabilitated," in that he has that chance of not being caught up again in the criminal justice system after successfully completing the program. How do we get such probable figures? Usually they are calculated from past performances by counting the number of juveniles who have been in the program but have never been arrested again and dividing that number by the total number of juveniles who have been treated by the program.

Thus the *inference* that such a program is successful with 50 percent of its accepted cases is often made. It satisfies the definition given: "a reasonable guess from something known or assumed."

Of course the inference will have more useful meaning if it is compared with the ratio of "successful" juvenile cases that have not had the benefit of that program. It may be that 50 percent of juveniles who are not so treated remain out of the criminal justice system thereafter. In that case, it would be reasonable to infer that the program had no discernible effect on rehabilitation.

Another inquiry might reveal more about the actual dynamics of the program. It may be that although the training program had something to do with the subsequent absence of re-arrest of the youths, that *something* is not a return of the youths into the path of "righteous conduct" but rather, it could be the scene of an informal "teach-in" as to how to avoid re-arrest by being more clever about future violations and avoiding detection!

This points out that the probabilistic correlation that resulted in inference does not say anything about actual causation. It merely is a reasonable guess that a pattern from the past will be repeated.

Probabilistic inference—that is, inference acknowledged as a guess, based on identifiable reasons, and put in ratio form—is the ultimate rationale of scientific inquiry.[7]

Scientific inquiries about police-community relations are not concluded with reference to authority, religious or secular. They are not concluded with appeals to self-serving interests. Nor are they concluded with appeals to tradition, custom, taboo, or general practicality. It may be startling to realize that not even irrefutable logic is sufficient to sustain a scientific inquiry in police-community relations, for that logic may be based on incorrect premises. No, the scientific use of inference, based on empirical facts, sustained by a tentative theory explaining those facts, and put in probabilistic form, is the route to take if one desires to retain a scientific orientation.

Data Analysis

Descriptive

Data is just information. Information can be of any kind, but not all of it is useful in the form it is first collected. Actually, some data cannot be made useful no matter what one does with it. When that happens, it usually is because someone went out and collected information without any plan or specific purpose, hoping to come upon something that could be turned to good use.

That does happen, occasionally. If we are lucky and observant, almost anything can happen. In the long run, however, we come upon only the things we've been on the watch for. It's that we have a particular question or problem on our mind, and in the vagrant turn of our gaze something catches our eye, tugged by the aptness of the bit to the riddle that is puzzling us. Some of the greatest discoveries of our civilization have been made that way, but if we want to go about information gathering in an organized way, we act quite differently.

We must remember that when the information comes in, it will be in "raw" form. It may be the "counts" on the juveniles in a training program as described previously; it may be scores on an intelligence test of these same youths; it may be answers on a questionnaire—the list is endless, but ordinarily you will plan for your data in advance. It does not stop there, however.

You must also consider what you will do with those raw scores after you obtain them. Will there be only a few of them? Or will there be hundreds of bits of data, perhaps thousands? In the latter case, you must evaluate different ways that the data might be handled.

If there are many, many scores, maybe the best way to try to grasp them will be to make a graph of them. If that's the case, you must make sure the information will be arriving in a way that will be adaptable to that kind of graphic analysis. Even if the data are to be very few, or in such cases as can be easily understood as to their meaning and thrust, you might consider the advisability of tabulation and make a trial run to see if the data, as you expect them to come in, tabulate to make sense. If it appears that there is some difficulty, modify the kind of data you collect, or the collection methods, or the way in which data is presented so that you will not be faced with a completed data-collection project—costing much time, money, and effort—that cannot be used.

In other words, if you are going to take a lot of trouble doing an inquiry, plan the entire project in advance, in as much detail as possible. Take a course in research or at least read a book about it,[8] so that you can avoid problems, rather than try, tediously, to get out of trouble that you need not have gotten into in the first place if you had prepared yourself.

When the problem is scientific research about police-community relations, another way to undertake an inquiry is to first get the advice of an experienced research scientist about every phase of the inquiry, as proposed. Undoubtedly, he will make sure that the kind of measures you decide to use are adaptable to the kind of analyses that are most appropriate—or, if there is an incompatibility that is irreconcilable, you can be given the various options that are open to you and the likely risks or consequences of each. In any case, you will probably be best advised to remember that data collection should be made as routine and undiscretionary a task as is reasonably possible. This is to minimize the incursion of unwanted errors, caused by carelessness, bias, or personal inclinations.

If the assistance of an electronic computer is to be sought, the people in charge should be consulted as to the forms in which the data must be put to make it acceptable to the machine for the kind of analyses you may require.

As a last comment, it usually is advisable to consider very seriously the use of graphic displays [9] at every opportunity, for your own understanding and to convey the thrust of the data and to summarize the data.[10]

Inferential

We discussed inference earlier as being more or less "educated" guesses as to the future, with the result put into numerical form such as four times out of five, or ⅘, or 80 percent. Sometimes that may not be possible. It may not even be possible to say, "Well, it appears to have between a 60 percent and 80 percent chance of happening." Nevertheless, the effort of putting a numerical figure on the probability has a salutary effect on your understanding.

This probabilistic attitude to all events is valuable in the identification of critically relevant variables in inquiry oriented around hypothesis construction and testing. The first step, ordinarily, is the careful description of a specific problem. This may be the attitude of a given community toward a police department. The problem, specifically, is that the community's attitude interferes with police operations, say, because the public is not assisting the police in criminal investigations.

The problem defined, the next thing to do is to try to focus on a hypothetical solution to the problem or at least an aspect or phase of the problem. This is tantamount to the identification of *critically relevant variables*. Often the hypothetical answer to the subproblem would be put in the form: If A . . . then B. . . . For instance: If A (police department telephone number is publicized), then B (community individuals will report more criminal information to the police).

Granted, not all of the main problem can possibly be resolved by such a simplistic device. Many police managers might be of the opinion, however, that it would help. That is, if the hypothesis is accepted.

By "accepted" is meant that the results—once the police number is installed and publicized and *enough additional information comes in to be "important"*—indicate that the hypothesis was correct.

Actually, those words must be "operationalized" before we can really say we have a workable hypothesis that can be tested. That means we must be specific.

Regarding the A variable:

1. Exactly what number will be publicized.
2. How many and what kind of facilities will be provided to receive the calls.
3. Exactly how will the number be publicized, by what media, how many times, for how long a period.

Regarding the B variable:

1. "Criminal information" must be defined exactly; for example, "the total of all calls giving complaints of crime plus all calls giving information about specific criminals."
2. Exactly how the calls will be recorded must be stated and totaled.

In addition, one final decision must be made: We must define and state how much of an increase from the previous state of affairs would be considered "important" enough to accept the hypothesis. Thus, we might arbitrarily decide that because the installation of phone exchanges and the assignment of personnel will cost $1,000 per week for the period of the operation of the project, there should be an increase in the number of such phone calls of, say, 100 percent.

Presumably we do have a record of phone calls with criminal information made for previous time periods to use as a comparison standard.

How were the above decisions made? The police manager would act entirely on his own experience, supported by whatever empirical records he may have at hand that corroborate his inference that more such citizen participation would assist the police department in its operations. Whether this is a factor in "improving" community attitudes is another inference, with, very likely, not so much empirical evidence to support it. In that sense the project would be a "pilot project," and one of its main functions would be to gather more information about how critical the A and B variables are to community's attitude toward the police. If there is a good response and, say, the phones ring 100 percent or more than they did before the publicizing of the police complaint number, the hypothesis would be accepted. That is, it could be inferred with a certain degree of probability, which could be calculated, that publicizing the phone number is associated with increased calls providing criminal information.

We still would not know for sure whether the community attitude has changed until we actually appraise the attitude both before and after the publicizing of the telephone number. If this appraisal indicates a "significant" increase in positive feelings toward the police department, we might infer that the publicizing of the number was related, perhaps critically, to the change in community attitude. As far as the logic of it goes, on the face of it, we could not tell whether the change in the community's attitudes involved only those citizens who actually participated in telephoning the police department, or whether informal lines of communication revealed to the community as a whole that the proposal was made in good faith, the number was valid, and the *reports* that the project had greatly improved flow of criminal information to the police department had the effect of changing the attitude of the community.

It's quite complicated, quite open to several interpretations, and obviously calls for further investigation. It is, however, better than being completely in the dark about what to do, and how to do it, to try to improve police-community relations.

Findings

The "findings" of an inquiry are the objective statements of the patterns discerned in the data. Sometimes findings are phrased in very general terms, for example, "It appears that the use of radio cars for patrol tends toward a lessening of the personal, friendly contact situations between citizens and police officers that were more frequent when foot patrol officers covered beats in this sector."

Such impressionistic statements of findings are very common, and if they are all that can be elicited from the data, that is the end of the matter.

Findings, of course, can be more lengthy, involving many such impressionistic or descriptive statements, and, in fact, many a book of science has been constructed in large part of such comments, along with some of the specific data that gave rise to the descriptive findings.

Anthropological studies are often of this nature, with such well-known examples available as Margaret Mead's books, Konrad Lorenz's popular *On Aggression,* Oscar Lewis's *The Culture of Poverty,* and many others. Traditional geology has been of such descriptive character, as well as the older psychological and sociological works. Today, however, most scientific inquiries reach not only for precise descriptions, but also for numerical statements proffered to indicate efforts at measurement along the dimensions considered critically relevant to the inquiry.

In police and community studies we have such familiar examples as James Q. Wilson's *Varieties of Police Behavior,* Lewis Mumford's *The City in History,* Michael Banton's *The Policeman in the Community,* the Knapp Commission *Report,* and the American Bar Association's *The Urban Police Function.*

The trend in recent years, however, has been to try to identify the critically relevant variables more particularly, to establish a reasonable measure for such variables, and finally to actually measure the various chosen variables and consequences, always endeavoring to find the relations, if any, between them.[11]

This has resulted in a growing reach for quantification. That is, there is a constant effort to particularize not only the variables conceived to be important, but also to devise reasonable ways to measure the magnitudes of these variables. Of course, measuring a variable, however conceived, that is not critically relevant is an exercise in futility. Thus it is of prime importance, prior to any measurement that is credible, to identify whether or not the variables are important to the phenomena being studied.

A growing number of people in the field feel, however, that the act of operationalizing inquiries into specific measures is itself helpful in identifying critically relevant variables. This has led to the increasing use of measures and of large quantities of data in numerical form. These masses of data involve, on occasion, thousands, even tens of thousands, of items. It is impossible for any human mind to encompass such hordes of numbers and make any sense out of them without specific orderly techniques. These techniques are developed under a branch of study called *statistics*.[12]

Statistical Presentations

Statistics was developed, originally, as a technique for handling the enormous quantities of data accumulated by governments regarding their populations: birth, mobility, occupations, illnesses, injuries, and death. It was found that analysis of these huge masses of data was necessary to discern the patterns implicit in them.

Analysis of the distribution of ages of individuals in the population showed that there were more young people than old people. That *finding* could have been expected without special techniques. But the discovery that the average height of men was about five feet eight inches could not have been expected, except in the most general way, and further, that the average height of women was some three inches shorter was another discovery of statistical analysis. The fact that the average height of freshmen at Harvard increased from five feet eight in 1890 to five feet ten inches by 1940 could not have been discovered until reasonably exact records were kept and the necessary computations made.

The fact that the income of the average family increased from 1890 to 1977 from one specific dollar amount to another specific dollar amount is another fact of importance to economic planning that could not have been known until the data were recorded and the calculations completed.

Such discoveries could not have been made unless rather precise records were kept for long periods, and methods devised, and used, that would produce the results. Data processing methods, as now used, were the direct result of the necessity of keeping data records and using them to assist decision making in a wide variety of administrative problems.

Some of the analyses that have been found useful determine certain "indexes," which, while not fully describing the data, mark out certain characteristics that give the thrust of the data in general terms. Thus the "average" height of freshmen at Harvard and of the "average" family are *indexes* that give an idea of the generality of the heights of those college students and of an American family, respectively. These indexes are used because they have been found useful in presenting information to people. Not many people have the time or energy, let alone the inclination, to wade through masses of records to discover patterns by accretion of impressions over long periods of time. It is simpler, faster, and probably more accurate to calculate an "average," use it as an index of the entire mass, and proceed from there.

By the same token, the *maximum* value of a series of figures is often useful to know, as well as the *minimum* of that series. Thus a frequency distribution will often be prepared, either in tabular or graphic form, to easily determine the maximum and minimum frequencies to be encountered in a mass of data. Other indexes that have been found useful are: *arithmetic mean* (one of the "averages"); the *range,* which is simply the maximum minus the minimum magnitudes, and the *dispersion* of the data around the arithmetic mean by any one of several indexes; and various other indexes, all of which are studied in courses on elementary descriptive statistics.

As far as the ordinary police manager or community leader is concerned, however, they cannot be expected to become experts in the use of statistical analysis. That is a full-time job in itself. However, statistical presentations, although they involve a number of assumptions that sometimes are not revealed or easily comprehended, are a most convincing way to present information.

Often people are overly impressed with figures and the sometimes intricate complexity of statistical analyses. That should not daunt either police officer or citizen. The purpose of such presentations is to make certain swirls, patterns, or points in the data clear to the understanding of those who are most concerned. If the statistical presentation does not do this, it is faulty, and explanations should be demanded of those who made the presentation. It is important not to be overawed by technique or by technicians. The function of both is to serve the people whose values are most involved, not to make decisions that will affect their lives now and in the future.

Other Presentations

In view of the possible abuse of statistical presentations by uninformed persons, one must always consider the probable utility of other ways of understanding the results of an inquiry and of presenting the findings to the public or other concerned people.

A well-written discussion of the problems, the approaches, and the results obtained is often far more comprehensible to lay people than any amount of numerical data. True, it is subject to its own kinds of abuse: It is conducive to the substitution of judgment by the analyst in place of the proper decision maker. That is, the values of the persons who make up the presentation, whether it is in standard English, a slide series projected on a screen, or a motion picture, can all, unaware, intrude and distort the facts and findings. If a reasonable degree of skepticism is retained, however, it is easier to guard against this kind of conclusionary presentation than when the bias is hidden behind a maze of numerals.

Conclusions Based on Findings

Conclusions are "operations of the mind," as lawyers say, and not statements of fact. It may be difficult for the student to appreciate the importance of doing everything possible to separate *findings* from *conclusions*.

Findings are summaries of facts based on the data. Thus, a given police-community relations program may call for a set of procedures to be followed in an attempt to increase the feeling of friendship toward the police department. Whether this increased feeling of friendship is actually accomplished is to be determined by questionnaires issued to an appropriate sample of 500 members of the community. The data, then, will consist of the original questionnaires and the entries as made by the members of the sample. This data included a question that was answered "Yes" by 300 respondents and "No" by 200 other respondents. Findings, as summaries, would include the question: "Do you think the police are doing a good job?" The 300 affirmative responses and the 200 negative responses would be the *finding*.

It would *not* be correct to say that the public approved the work of the police by a figure of 3 to 2. The finding, when correctly stated, is a summary of the actual data, not a guess as to what the data mean. The leap toward a conclusion—that the majority of the public approved the police—could be stated, if so desired by a researcher, but it should be clearly labeled a *conclusion*, as it is a judgment and not an objective finding.

The objective finding is almost invariably much narrower than any conclusion based on it. The finding restricts itself to the actual facts, with nothing added on either side of a pro or con judgment, nor any guess as to past, present, or future. It should be as value free as human effort can be.

A conclusion, on the other hand, is a judgment and is properly included only when the findings of objective fact upon which it is based are clearly stated.

The Discovery of Alternatives

One of the important reasons it is necessary to clearly separate findings from conclusions is to facilitate the discovery of alternatives. Every police-community program is a reach for better relations between police and the community. Thus any given program is only one of many ways to try to skin the cat. A clear statement of the *facts* relating to a given program is necessary so that careful evaluation can be made of exactly what the program is accomplishing and whether it is on a line toward the ultimate goals of police-community relations programs.

Mingling findings and judgmental conclusions leaves an evaluator in perpetual doubt as to what he is doing and where the program is going.

In the last example, which attempted to discover the community's attitude toward a police department program, this point is brought forward. To incorrectly conclude that the community does have a favorable attitude toward the police would blur the possibly correct conclusion that although the police are regarded highly, this particular program is not.

The opposite error, to conclude that the community has a certain attitude toward the program, whereas it really is expressing an emotional attitude about the entire police department, would also remove from consideration facts that would be important to a decision to modify the program or to couch the research in different terms to identify more accurately exactly what the opinion of the community is concerning which specific characteristic.

Using Probability

Probability has been discussed a bit, and all we want to do here is to reiterate the importance of singling out all findings, and the conclusions based on findings, and presenting them in probabilistic form, rather than as ultimate verities, certain to exist or not to exist, or to fail or to succeed.[13] In a scientific sense, nothing in life reaches such final certainty. It is better judgment to state the degree of probability.

If we are ignorant of the probability involved, there is no damage if we admit our ignorance. If we do admit such ignorance one can begin to suspect we have the beginning of knowledge, because our ignorance is more notorious than our knowledge of the recondite, diffused subject of police-community relations.

Recommendations

Recommendations are often given in the report of an analysis of police-community relations programs and procedures. They are in the nature of judgments and should admit the personal elements of the judgment in the formal statement of the recommendation. The open admission of the tentative, unproved nature of the recommendation is truly representative of the fact of the case, and in so presenting and admitting the tentative nature of the recommendation, credibility is enhanced and an open, frank tone is established, which is refreshing in formal documents.

The need for ultimate verification of any recommendation before it is sent forth as fully sustained by the data and findings of the report is an obvious and necessary part of intelligent effort at improvement.

Thus the way is opened to further inquiry as to action taken on recommendations and the continued inquiry to determine whether amelioration has or has not become a fact.

Chapter 3

THE INTELLIGENT USE OF EXPERTS

An expert is one who knows more and more about
less and less.
—Nicholas Murray Butler,
Commencement Address, Columbia University

In this chapter we discuss the various ways experts and their
knowledge can be used by community leaders and criminal-justice
administrators. Although the findings of experts are not by any
means predetermined, what is mandated, in part at least, is the way
each expert will look at a problem and the resources each expert
will bring to bear on its solution. We are all prisoners of our own
language and our training, and specialists in any field appear to be
no exception.

Experts must be used judiciously. Then their differing orientations,
providing an ever truer picture of nature's reality, will be useful
to those who make the decisions affecting the fate of people and
communities.

What Can Be Done?

It is important to realize that there are only a few things that can be
done and a whole lot of things that cannot be done. The major problem
is to identify one group and to avoid the other. There is one reliable way
to begin: discover how much is already known. The beginning point in all
investigation is to find out *who* knows the thing you want to know, and
then get him to tell it to you.

This is the basic technique of practical detective work everywhere, except in fiction. In real life, there are a great number of people and places
that have stored up great banks of knowledge either about the things
you want to know or about things very much like them. The first job
is to find those people and places.

Where? An expert is like gold: He's where you find him. Even if the
information is in such an obvious place as a book, unless you are something of an expert in bibliographic research, you are going to have to
ask someone, in this case a reference librarian, where it is. Of course

everyone knows something. When the question involves problems in police-community relations, however, *you want to know everything available.*

There really is no way the average person, whatever his education or experience, can ever acquire all the knowledge of all the experts that could possibly be of use to the development or implementation of police-community programs. Knowledge and learning is too specialized in this day to permit all skills to be acquired by one person in a single lifetime.

Police-community relations calls for skills as a negotiator, as a crisis intervenor; there are innumerable clerical tasks, from filing, classifying, indexing, typing, and other secretarial arts to research design, sample design, polling techniques, questionnaire development, rumor analysis, behavioral sciences, computer programming, statistical analysis, and on and on.

Thus the key to successful performance is for the practitioner and scholar to reach, constantly, for a centralist position, involving broad areas of comprehension of the objectives and the sub-objectives of an entire program of police-community relations, and to search persistently for ever more qualified experts to perform the various technical tasks demanded.

Use of the Old

If you are working in the community—or in a police department—undoubtedly there are people who have been faced with problems similar to yours. Find them. Find them, by asking everyone you can think of if they know of anyone who has information about what's worrying you. It is surprising how much information you can turn up in this manner. It is surprising, too, how helpful people will be, often when it is not in their personal interest to help you and even in derogation of their interest.

Use your best interviewing techniques. Remember you came to them for their help. A proper respect for their knowledge is often a good background for obtaining their cooperation in helping you.

An even more reliable source of information at the beginning of an inquiry is printed matter and the storehouses where it is kept, libraries. It would be difficult to mention any subject that is not discussed, at least in part, by the accumulation of the ages contained in libraries. However creative a new idea may seem to its originator, a careful search will undoubtedly discover someone else who had a similar idea, though perhaps in regard to another use. Too, there are similar arrangements, methods of approach, of implementation, of review, of evaluation—a good library is a fund of old material that can be put to good use.

The experts, living and dead, who have contributed so generously to the libraries, by putting their dreams, thoughts, and experiences in writing, should be fully used. Some books are the product of years of thought and experience. Libraries are treasure-houses of expert information.

However, although there are enormous banks of knowledge contained in various libraries and in computer-data storage banks, tracing through their labyrinths is a difficult task, calling for considerable training merely to locate knowledge that has already been accumulated and is awaiting the taking. Thus a constant search for all relevant library materials, for input, is needed in all police programs from every field for critical examination and recommendation as well as for monitoring guidance by experts so that ever more refined examination will result in more apt recommendations.

Discovery of the New

Of course, each new program requires something new. There is no project or any kind of effort, really, that is so similar to what has gone before that it can be said to be "on all fours."

The time is new, certainly. The conditions, invariably, are different in some particulars. The critically relevant variables, however defined, will almost certainly reflect new constructs.

Thus the problem is not merely discovery of the new—rather it is finding new ideas that will be *useful.* That is where luck is so important, but that is not to say that luck will happen as often to each person or under each circumstance. The evidence seems to indicate that there must be an organized effort to increase the probability of "lucky" breaks. Primarily, this is reachable by orchestrating the interplay of various expert concentrations on the subject problem. Operations research is the older term often used for this effort.

However, at the inception of the reach for really new approaches, one should be careful not to become involved too soon in quantification. The act of quantifying locks thinking into the present state of affairs, which is all to the good when you want to get started on the project but is overly burdensome when one wants ideas to fly. Problem solving, discovery of innovation, if you will, should not be sought by a dogmatic and sterile process.

There is an *attitude* for dealing with complexity and uncertainty that can be acquired, utilizing the focused specificity of experts in various disciplines. This attitude involves a coordination of solution techniques and the strengths of human problem solvers. The strengths of human problem solvers may have little to do with their technical expertise, although that is always relevant. The basic attitudinal reach, particularly in police-community relations, is in exploiting differences in cultures and values in the expert advice you seek.

Two adversaries, faced with open-ended problems [1] of human relations, can arrive at very different but equally valid solutions, because they start with different sets of values.

It has been said that the subject of values and value theory is the problem of problems. For it is a person's value system that ratifies his model of reality.

Appreciation of choice of actions and reactions must pass through a filter of values before coming to rest in decision, in human relations. Thus every effort at resolving problems should begin with a reexamination of the basic value systems of researchers and practitioners, as well as of the subjects of the inquiry: the community and the police. That is a fair beginning.

Then we consider that a truly systems approach to innovative problem solving does *not* start with quantification, but rather considers a sequence similar to this series of questions:

1. What exists now?
2. What is desired?
3. Can what is desired be made to exist?
4. Need *anything* be done now?
5. What is to be done—if anything?
6. How to do it?

Most of systems analysis has been concerned solely with the sixth question: How to do it? Rarely has deep thought or vigorous effort been given to a review of the preceding questions. The central thrust of this book concerns questions 1 through 5. There, it appears, lie the greatest hopes for ameliorative developments.

The last question is treated only on a surface level because it is in large degree technical in nature, subject to quantitative approaches and engineering know-how. This book reaches for theory and analysis, rather than specific programs that are germane only to their unique situations of time, place, and people. To the extent that space allows, however, a number of specific programs from various parts of this country are presented in the last chapter.

Who Should Do It?

Using Practitioners

Of course we want to know the opinions of all knowledgeable experts, but knowledge is not the sole province of thinkers, scholars, academicians, researchers, and specialists. *Practitioners* are the greatest potential source of information. They control the huge mass of experience in other communities and other police departments. Their knowledge, however, is often so situation-bound by the uniqueness of their private experience that it may be difficult to apply their conclusions to the problem at hand.

It is important, therefore, to obtain from them the *reason* for their opinion. Without the reason, we shall have learned at best only the appropriate decision in a specific situation without any chance of transference to other situations. The *reason,* then, becomes as valuable a part of the knowledge obtained from the expert as his opinion.

This is a fault that is no greater than those found in other sources. Each source has constraints that prevent certain things and channels that facilitate the transmission of other facts and relationships. Thus a psychologist will tend to see police-community matters as problems in psychology, resolvable by psychological methods, that is, by investigations of personality and psyche using the various instrumental techniques with which he is familiar. A sociologist is equally conditioned to see sociological implications and resolutions. Generally he will see climaxes and denouements in social behavior as sequences in interactional patterns. His assistance in problem solving will be in terms of quite different concepts, hypothetical solutions, and instrumentation.

As to police-community affairs, the person in charge will ordinarily be either a community leader or a police manager. As a matter of professional responsibility, the police manager is always on the scene. With government funding involved, often he will be the project director, and, in any case, his position is institutionalized, independent of any one individual, the role position that is always filled.

It is incumbent, then, for the police manager always to take a prime interest, to match the primacy of his role, in using all the empirical evidence [2] he can bring to bear on the situation, and to collect as much as possible from other practitioners elsewhere. In that sense, most frequently the police administrator will come to have a central role in the entire problem of community relations and be in a position to examine all the different orientations the various concerned individuals, experts, and practitioners can provide. He cannot very well avoid this responsibility. The police department is his "baby"; he is also intensely concerned with the community, his client. He is in a position to exert more influence on the identity of the experts to be consulted, the practitioners, and the entire mix of assistance and resources that will be applied.

In effect, he becomes the generalist on the scene, the person in control of all phases of an inquiry or a program.

This control of research inquiry and all programs founded thereon is mandated in the police administrator by the responsibilities of his position and requires him to have at least some understanding of the subject matter of each of the various experts he may consult,[3] so that he may best choose among them and better use the results of their consultation.

It is appropriate to repeat here a story that is probably apocryphal but has been retold for at least two generations of public administrators.

Parable of the Spindle

It appears there was a restaurateur in Miami Beach, Florida, who had a very successful business preparing and serving food during the tourist season to swarming customers anxious to obtain a good meal.

Unfortunately, however, he had numerous troubles with his employees. There was a constant stream of arguments and clashes between the cooks and the serving staff. The waitresses were often in tears; the cooks cursed loudly in several languages; too often the soup was cold and the beefsteak burned. As a result, customer complaints mounted, many refused to pay their bills, and many others were so unhappy they never returned.

Discussing his problem with a customer, the restaurateur discovered that he was speaking to an eminent visiting sociologist who became interested and offered to help. The sociologist returned the next day, with his notebooks, and carefully observed the patterns of sociological interaction and the implications that were involved. After five days of this survey research he told the owner that over the weekend he would complete his report and submit it to him the following Monday.

Monday came, and so did the sociologist's report. It was a formidable piece of work, of many pages, filled with learned discussion and many citations to other learned authorities. To make the story short, the sociologist had come to the conclusion that there was an ongoing sentiment of social and labor unrest that filled restaurant workers of all kinds. The unions wanted to organize the workers but the existing state and municipal laws, which required various police identification cards and investigations, hampered unionization efforts. Because there were two unions involved, one concerned mainly with waiters and waitresses, the other with cooks, but not exclusively so, there also as a conflict of interests that exacerbated the situation. The recommendations of the sociologist, recognizing these sociological factors, pointed out that the absolute necessity of obtaining union cooperation in settling the differences between the factions might take some negotiation with the national or perhaps even the international offices of each union. The report brought out an interesting sociological factor, the "peer pressure of union organizations," which forecast that the desire of the unions to present a united front would, in the end, result in a resolution of this internal squabble.

"This is all very well," thought the restaurant owner, "but it doesn't really help very much." He felt completely helpless as far as the union was concerned. He was, after all, the owner of a single restaurant, caught up in a problem that involved state laws and union jurisdictional conflicts that were possibly nationwide. This was too much for him, especially in view of the present slowdown in business.

He continued to discuss his problems with his customers, however, for whatever heart ease there was to be had that way. One day a customer asked him how things were going. That set him off. Glad at the chance, he poured out his troubles, the words rushing in a torrent of complaint. Responding to the restaurant owner's appeal, the customer revealed he was a psychologist.

"Perhaps I can help," he said. "Since I am a psychologist, let me investigate the psychological aspects of this situation. There may be a simpler solution."

Of course the businessman gave him permission, and this expert, too, studied the matter all week long, and left on Friday, promising to have his report the Monday following.

The report of the psychologist was even more impressive, but of course it took a different tack. This report was filled with fascinating case histories of each of the employees, with analyses of the basic drives and motivations of each. Profound explanations were included of how conflict and aggressive behavior was the natural result of frustration in the employees' job roles. His analysis clearly showed that the probable basic cause for the trouble was the fact that the waitresses were mainly young women who directed their disapproval at the older men, the cooks, in a reflection of their resistance to parental control. "A variation of the Electra complex," as the psychologist put it. The solution he suggested: to hire either older waitresses or younger cooks.

By this time the restaurant owner was thoroughly exasperated. In desperation at the constant bickering between waitresses and cooks, he seized the spindle file—a gadget like a short knitting needle set in a metal base— and slammed it down on the counter where the prepared dishes were placed by the cooks.

"Look," he said to the assembled help. "You waitresses! You write out your orders on your pads, tear off the sheet, and pin it onto this spindle. Don't you dare talk to the cooks! Just write down your orders and spindle them. And don't say a word!" he warned them.

Turning to the cooks, he pointed his finger at them. "You cooks! You take the order slips from the spindle, fill them, and then return them to this countertop, with the order slip underneath each plate. And, that's all!"

He glared around. "I don't want to hear any of you talking to each other. Shut up—use the spindle instead of talk!"

And, so the story goes, everyone lived happily ever after—without shouting and screaming, no tears, no arguments. Unnecessary communication was suppressed; necessary communication was facilitated and objectively confirmed by the written food orders on the spindle.

The entire story, whatever its truth, aptly illustrates how differing conclusions can be the result of different approaches. The story could have been extended interminably by bringing in even more experts, each with his own orthodoxy.

The intelligent use of experts, then, is to call for help, certainly—but also to carefully weigh the probable areas of concern of each specialist, as a human being and as a virtuoso in the orientation involved. Include in this appraisal the presumptions and assumptions implicit and explicit in each discipline. Add to this the assumptions and bias inherent in all human inquiry. Finally, try to retain a judicial overview of all problems and inquiries without becoming embroiled in controversies as to the *truth* or *validity* or even the success of programs or projects.

The wisest position for the generalist—and that is the only role worthy of a scholar of police-community relations—is to realize that his job is to maintain contact with all phases, at all times, that the battle for understanding is continuing, and that the ultimate resolutions are still in doubt.

This brings us to the investigative use of models of reality drawn along one or more organized sets of concepts, or constructs, the better to identify and comprehend the critically relevant variables in a given situation, the topic of the next chapter.

Chapter 4

MODELS AND MODELING

Words are but wise men's counters, they do but
reckon by them; but they are the money of fools.
— Thomas Hobbes, *Leviathan,* Part I, Chapter IV

Police-community relations is a complex, real situation, difficult to comprehend.

In this chapter we discuss one of the techniques that has been devised to assist in understanding complex, real situations. This is the use of models, or simulations.

This involves imitating life in a simplified form so that we can better observe and comprehend the articulation of various parts and processes.

Just so, a model airplane can simulate the wings, motor, fuselage, rudders, and tail parts of a transatlantic jetliner. Its wings, rudder, and other parts in the airflow undergo aerodynamic pressures very like its large counterpart, affected by the same critical variables as to the relationship and shape of its parts.

By studying the actions of the model plan either in actual flight or in a wind tunnel much can be learned about how the large plane will act without risking the multimillion-dollar full-sized jet and the lives of its human operators.

The same modeling principle is more abstractly used when we state that an apple will fall a distance that is measured by the model equation:

$$s = \tfrac{1}{2}\, gt^2$$

This is a mathematical model and is an approximation of how far nature's forces will induce the apple to fall in a given time. It enables us to obtain a reasonably accurate prediction of the apple's future behavior.

In the same way, models of the reality of *you,* of other *people,* of the *community,* and of *police* can be devised, using various assumptions as to the relevant critical variables as conceived by psychologists, sociologists, economists, jurists, and many others.

Complex social mechanisms [1] such as the relations between government and the public have so many variables, known and unknown, of infinitely fine gradations of magnitude, as to present an insuperable problem to the analyst trying to obtain a grasp of the relationships contained. In short, police-community relations (PCR) appear to be infinitely complex.

How can such perplexing real situations be simplified so as to permit penetration of understanding? The use of models as a device to clarify meaning of complex mechanisms is older than history. The sundial is, simply, a model. A model of the *rotation* of the earth, under the sun. Interestingly enough, it was so used even before it was known to be such—and was presumed to model the movement of the sun across the sky at various times of the day and of the year.

This model served a useful function, that is, it had *meaning* to the people who used it, even though the premises upon which it was constructed were entirely erroneous. The sundial, constructed to provide an analogue of the apparent movement of the sun and its shadow, provided useful information for millennia despite the lack of general understanding of the true mechanics involved in the reality.

There are many other such models of reality that can give useful information, whether or not we comprehend the true relationships.

The slide rule, among other artifacts, is a model of the relationships numbers have with each other when they are multiplied. A map is a model of the spatial relationships between geographical locations and other features, such as roads, intersections, cities, bodies of water, and other features. It is not a perfect replica of the geographical reality, of course. For instance, the distances scaled off between marks on the map will give only approximations of actual distances. Often, however, that will be sufficient to provide very valuable information. A police command without maps of its district would be under a severe handicap. Mathematical equations, too, are models, for presumed relationships, such as the distance a falling body will travel in a given time interval, $s = \frac{1}{2}gt^2$, the Newtonian proposition that was so radically modified by the later equation by Einstein, $e = mc^2$.

A sentence can be a model of presumed relations: "If a police team patrols more aggressively it will make more arrests and incur more civilian complaints." Of course, this prediction may not turn out to be true. As long as it is used, however, it is used as a proposed model of reality.

Another relationship that could be hypothesized would be, "Increased monitoring information given to the public will result in a proportionate increase in public satisfaction with a given police department." Though in sentence form, such a statement really expresses a mathematical relationship: quantitatively proportionate. Specific units by which such a relationship might be measured need not be stated but can be left to the investigator's choice. In some cases, a new, and specific measure of "monitoring information" and of "public satisfaction" could be devised.

Different points of view may provide different models. Each of the scientific disciplines has developed its own set of ideas, concentrating on the particular aspects of reality that are of concern to them. Many of these specialized disciplines can provide interesting and useful insights into police-community relations.

Thus we find sociological models that try to explain this subject in terms of *norms, status, roles,* and so on. Political-science models will use such ideas as *factions, state's rights versus federal rights, separation of powers,* and others. Legal models lean toward seeing matters in terms of guilt or innocence; religious models usually seek the interpretation of sin and grace as they are relevant to the study. There are any number of others, including economic models, Marxist models, democratic models, authoritarian models, each with its own particular slant on things.

Systematic Models [2]

It has on occasion been found useful to look very broadly at the entire process that is the subject of concern. Police-community relations, insofar as it becomes the subject of concentrated inquiry, is the study of a social problem. In turn, we might comment that a social problem is a condition, or a way of behavior, that is regarded by a substantial number of people as not being acceptable.[3]

Social problems then are, at bottom, human and subjective with political overtones. If police-community relations are not seen as a problem by a good-sized group of people, well, then, they are not a social problem, no matter how displeased a small group may be. Too, there is a hint—or more than a hint—that to fit into the classification of a social problem there should be some hope of solving, resolving, or at least ameliorating the problem. Centuries ago the state of being poor was considered not a social problem but rather a condition of life, fated by the laws of God and nature.

As noted on page 22, a systems approach calls for answers to a series of questions, and most efforts in police-community relations have been snagged on the technical question: "How to do it?"

The problem has been that administrators feel themselves blocked by a set of constraints which demand a tortuous path between opposing dilemmas: Constitutional requirements versus demand for crime controls. Staying within the Constitution limits the freedom of action crime-fighters feel they need.

A philosophy of humanism that argues against the use of negative therapy, behavior modification techniques, and operant conditioning; an economic system that encourages people to "make a buck," versus a tax system that denies that opportunity; a verbal morality at the highest ethical level versus a "get ahead" normative system that says "anything goes as long as you don't get caught!"—all of these present difficult, even impossible choices.

But a complete systems analysis should consider the prior, more fundamental questions, particularly the question, "Need *anything* be done now?" Going past that, it is remarkable how practically all effort is concentrated on massing technical, analytical positivists to discover the "How to do it" rather than acknowledging the subjectivity of the descriptions of "What exists now."

Without going into that rather recondite analysis now, it will be sufficient here merely to point out that *all* of the questions are supposed to be treated by a "systematic model," even if the answers are unavailable.

Perhaps the hiatus in approaching a truly systematic model results from the obsession some systems analysts have for defining their task as the quantification of a system without bothering too much to determine whether they have identified the proper system.

One would think that the first and major problem in the proper use of a systematic model would be to explore the ramifications of the different systems within systems that might provide the proper subject of subsequent analysis. Perhaps it would be accurate to say systems overlapping systems, or *under*-systems and *over*-systems.

Once the system is properly identified, one can then study—and even try to quantify—inputs and outputs of that system. In that sense, the effort in this book to view police and community relations in a broad view of groups of people with various "policing arrangements" in pursuit of norm compliance is a reach for a more "systematic model." The details of particular policing arrangements may vary. The features of each community provide their unique patterns and ornaments. Invariably, however, we find "groups of people composed of individuals who are faced with subgroup mandated prescriptions and proscriptions." This is the generalized "system."

Of course, even a systematic model must come to halt somewhere and say, "Here is where the system begins, as far as my inquiry is concerned." Each student, the reader included, can make this halt wherever he pleases. This is the "systematic model" that will demonstrate the inputs and outputs that will be quantified.

In quantified analysis, the internal processing of the prescriptions and proscriptions would include all the policing arrangements that sanction and monitor behavior. To maintain the analogy with the computer model, which is one of the outstanding applications of systematic modeling, the "central processing units" for sanctioning and monitoring would include all the social structures, formal and informal, that act to perform those functions.

The individual police manager, or community leader, will select the specific boundaries of the system, or systems, he chooses to study, to set up a program for, or to report on. As he chooses, the system can be as small as a police organizational unit of a large geographical area or the entire police department, or a study of systems within systems of national ideal norms and policing arrangements enclosing state and local structures. The choice is his.

Sociological Models [4]

The various behavioral sciences—as all sciences—have developed sets of concepts and terminologies that have been found useful to describe the particular phenomenon in which they are interested. The use of sets of concepts and terminologies can expedite the construction of a model of police-community relations that will describe that phenomenon in sociological terms and provide, hopefully, the same kind of insights for police and community that such models have for the study of urban development and expansion, crowd behavior, and social movements.[5] Perhaps the special value of the sociological model is to provide insight into ethnic immigration and emigration.

The concepts and terminologies involved include, as a core, *norms, statuses, groups, associations, institutions, authority, power, class, caste, race,* and *skin color,*[6] as a sociological event.

All these words have ordinary dictionary meanings, but in sociology they have particular emphases that encompass different usages. Thus, *norm* means *expected behavior* and can be applied to individuals or even groups; norms are found in every society and in every group that has lasted any period of time whatever. Norms, then, are a part of every culture and subculture.

Social relations, when repeated, appear to fall into patterns that follow rules. There are benefits granted to those abiding by the rules and penalties for those violating the rules. Because it is expected that the rules be complied with, that is, that the standards of the norms will prevail, there is little occasion to admonish or otherwise penalize noncompliance. Whether we comply or not, it is expected that we will, and the action of norms as instruments of social control is all-pervasive and seldom noticed until brought to our attention by a violation.

The surprising thing about norms is that there may be many, many violations without the norm of proper behavior being changed. The norm is not an "average," statistical or otherwise, nor is it what is most frequent. It is simply what is considered "proper," appropriate, and thus expected.

Whatever we may think of the behavior of politicians or community members, no matter what proof there may be of deviance, the norm of appropriate behavior for government officials and people in general is honesty. That is the expectation. As to policemen, the same is true. We care not if improper behavior is frequent or if it is rare. We expect proper behavior, that is, the norm established for police actions of all kinds.

Stability and predictability to life are given by normative behavior by all members of society. In fact, without normative behavior there would be no society, merely a chaotic noninteracting mass of people. People have expectations as to what other people should do and what they should do themselves. They know what to expect and what should be done. There are rules of *do* and of *not to do*. The rules are implicit in the notion of being anyone or doing almost anything at all. Ordinarily, it does not require forethought—it's just the "natural" thing to do. Any other kind of behavior, in most situations, would be just too silly and confusing for words.

Some norms are written down, particularly so where infraction might be subject to severe sanction such as the criminal or traffic laws. Other norms are known mainly by observation and repeated performance, such as conventions, fashions, customs, and etiquette.

There are a number of ways norms can be listed or classified. Some are prescriptive, some are proscriptive. A classification that cuts across this is *communal* and *associational,* that is, pervading an entire society or found only in certain smaller groups. Thus kissing as a greeting between women or between women and men is widespread throughout our society, but the slapping of hands in lieu of a handshake is normative only among young people, usually black, and almost invariably among men rather than women. Still another classification scheme tries to exhaust the list with three branches: *laws, folkways,* and *mores.*

Laws, generally, can be said to be those rules whose strict compliance is required and enforced. In modern urban society they are enacted by a political entity as a legislative act.

Folkways, the practices of the folk, are practically synonymous with customs and are the norms that are customary in a community. There is no law in Germany that requires one to sleep on a three-part mattress. Nor is there a law in the United States requiring a mattress be all of one piece. It is merely a customary matter in each. In the same vein is the eating of three meals a day, attending church and school functions, watching television, drinking water from a cup, sipping soup from a spoon, writing from left to right, eating popcorn at the movies, wearing jewelry, combing hair in certain styles, and saying "Good morning!" rather than some other salutation.

Mores include more than folkways in that they imply a moral imperative, such as many deviations from sexual behavior norms. It is against our mores to be cruel, especially to the weak or helpless; to be insulting to one's mother; or sacrilegious. Too, mores subsume, to most people, proper ways of thinking and feeling if there is a moral constraint contained. To admit to belief in communism as a way of life would be grossly offensive to most of the members of police departments throughout this country today. The feeling was even stronger, it appears, in the 1950s at the height of the cold war.

Student communities where liberal philosophies verge farther toward the left than usual, some toward the Chinese version of communism, were considered by many police departments as being traitorous and deserving of short shrift. Enforcement of norms is as varied as the norms. Those that are proscribed or prescribed in formal laws have penal sanctions allotted to each that carefully spell out the behavior that is condoned or condemned. Ridicule, perhaps even more effective as a sanction, is more usual for those norms that are classed as folkways or mores.

Social disapproval may be a milder policing procedure, from a raised eyebrow to ejection from a meeting. On the other hand, social approval may encourage compliance, which may range from awards of money or prestige or just a smile and a nod.

Often associational norms—the rules governing a part of a community—

may be in direct conflict with the norms of the larger society. Thus a college fraternity may expect a new candidate to steal a traffic sign; a youth gang may demand that an initiate commit an assault or a burglary. Too, normal behavior under brutal ghetto conditions may mandate carrying a knife and an attitude of readiness to use it. Because the average person is affected by the normative structures of the people closest to him, affectively and proximally, we can find frequent instances of such violation of society's standards. It would probably be impossible for an individual to withstand the enforcement procedures that demand he comply more strictly with the norms of his closely bound associational group—which he encounters every day and which monitors him most carefully—than with those of the wider, distant society, which provides only occasional surveillance and policing.

It is interesting to note that greater intensity of sanction, either of approval or disapproval, does not provide a linear increase in compliance. However logical it may appear that a five-year sentence is half as punitive as a ten-year term, enforcement of a norm by the latter is not twice as effective. In fact, it may be less. Certainly there is no determinable simple relationship between severity of enforcement and compliance. Mere ridicule may be more effective as policing than a large fine or even incarceration. This, certainly, is an area that requires more research. The need is great.

We dress in conformity to fashion, lest we be ridiculed. We keep appointments, we do not put spinach in our hair, although there is no law prohibiting such an action.

With innumerable groups enforcing countless different subsystems of norms, there appears to be manifested a group need for a unifying overset of norms applicable to all the individuals in all the subgroups, especially in regard to forbidden behavior. Because of a lack of constant personal attention, which maintains customs, folkways, and mores, these criminal laws, proscribed behaviors, are enforced by formal policing arrangements.

In one sense the criminal laws and formal policing strengthen group ties and cohesion, unifying the entire American society. However, the inevitable conflict between these laws and various associative norms sets subculture against subculture and both against the larger society. What is commonly accepted usage in many communities, from suburban housewives to detective squads, becomes the subject of shocked comment when displayed by mass media for the delectation of other communities.

Nationally accepted norms, in short, are quite different from community norms. The communities meant are all those called communities of interest. Throughout a complex society, no homogeneous culture or normative patterns exist other than the most broadly accepted types of behavior —not enough to maintain an individual as a functioning person. The individual is literally forced to accept the life-sustaining norms of his associational community. Aberrant though such norms may be—he has no choice.

People, then, do not conform in a functional way with society's norms, nor even to those that are most commonly consensual—rather they conform only to the norms of their communities of interest, to the devil with any conflicts with the norms of other communities or even with state or federal laws! When, however, the individual is confronted with conflicts between the norms of two of the communities to which he claims allegiance, he is in a quandary.

Some physicians believe that such conflicting demands are responsible for a large part of the incidence of mental illness. Sociologists see such conflicts as being prime causes of civil demonstrations and riot behavior. To just about everyone, however, it appears that just as certainly as norms provide stability and order, the conflict between norms provides instability and conflict.

We see that the use of only one sociological concept, that of "norms," can give us a reasonably useful, if partial, view of the relations between community and police. We can go on from there to bring into our discussion a number of other sociological concepts.

Status is another sociological concept relevant to our topic. *Status* refers to the fact that certain norms as complied with by an individual are often specially patterned around roles. The norms attached to the position of police officer are different from those attached to schoolchild. Different behavior is expected from each. It is a useful analytical tool and can be used, among various other ways, to indicate a differential in prestige attached to each norm complex, that is, position.

It is expected that children will obey their mother, that the mother will decide what the children will have for breakfast. Obligations, prerogatives, rights, duties, privileges, and perquisites pertain to statuses.

A police officer who sees his status as demanding instant obedience to his order to "get off the corner" or "pull over to the curb" is going to view noncompliance in a different light than would a man speaking to his neighbor.

Inadvertently to mistake another's status is often to call for an apology: "I'm sorry, Officer, I did not see you were in a police car."

Role is another concept that denotes the behavioral aspect of status.

Role is what one does in the status occupied. Of course, the interpretation of the role, as played by one individual, will vary in details from that of another. Insofar as this is relevant to the model being constructed, we are verging toward the individual view of personality and performance, which is the concern of psychology. This overlapping area is often called social psychology.

In a sense a status is an *institutionalized* role, meaning that it has become regularized and standardized in the community. Thus we are introduced to the sociological idea of *institutions,* which, although subject to some ambiguity in the literature, can be said to be an *organized procedure.*

Institutions are established ways of doing things. All the procedures for the formal implementation of the idea and use of police departments, including police district station houses, uniformed police, and so on, constitute the institution of formal policing in the United States. The institutions of banking or public education, or social welfare are all established procedures. A single event is not a procedure, but it may be a precedent for a procedure. The precedent, if repeated often enough to become established, may become an institution.

Such institutions may appear to be norms, in that they are expected behavior. They differ from norms, however, in that institutions are supported by specific communities of concern, especially formal associations. It is important, nevertheless, not to confuse institutions with associations. Government is an institution, but any particular government, say that of the United States, is an association. The institution of journalism is supported by many associations, such as the Associated Press, the Los Angeles Times, the St. Louis Post-Dispatch, the Miami Herald, and many others.

Still another sociological concept that has been found valuable in constructing models of community and police is that of *force*. There has been difficulty in defining force in a sociological sense. There is some agreement, however, in viewing *force* as meaning the actual limitation of the social choices of an individual or group. Thus, placing a person in jail limits his choice of possible changes of location. Levying a monetary fine limits his use of his money. Banishing him, excommunicating him, ostracizing him, all reduce the individual's social choices. Executing him, of course, eliminates all social choices whatever. A community that withdraws public support from its police has limited the choices of that department in the performance of its functions, and a community that discharges a chief of police limits that chief's police choices even more drastically.

This brings us to consideration of the influence that can be exerted by the *potential* use of force—otherwise named *power*. Power, seen as the possibility of the application of manifest force, exerts profound influence on individuals and groups, without actual application of force. The latent force implied in *power* can guide and constrain actions within a family, a community, or a police department. The power to exact obedience by the ultimate application of force influences by its known existence, usually without ever being transformed into force itself. Power is, perhaps, the most often cited analytical tool in the current discussion of police-community relations and is of the most obsessive concern to participants on both sides.

A last concept useful to our foreshortened summary of a sociological model is that of *authority*, which has been described as the power that attaches to a given position or status. If the position is part of an association's pattern of statuses, it is supported by the same bonds that support the association itself. Denial of that authority would be denial of that association's bonds. Of course, the association can be as informal as a family, as diffused as a community of learned scientists, a geographically circumscribed community, a formally organized corporation, or a police department.

Such institutionalized authority governs the choices made by most of us, whatever our position or status and in relation to any of the choices that are meaningful to us. However rebellious or freedom-loving we may be, in a civilized society we are caught up in a matrix of norms, groups, statuses, associations, and institutions, all in a position to use social force on us by limiting our choices. The potential of force—that is, social power —everywhere impacts on us, and institutionalized power, authority, is what we are talking about in this book.

There seems no escaping these influences. Despite "turning-off" or "turning-on," social power wreaks its way. Refusal to abide by the sanctions that enforce norms imports but little; even "anomie," meaning "lack of norms," eventuates into a *comparative* lack of norms. There still remains, in the individual, uncountably more norms that are obeyed than are defied. The structure of society itself provides the mold we cannot escape, nor can we avoid the prohibitions of normative policing arrangements.

All of the sociological concepts listed above are quite obviously useful in discussion about the relationships involved in a community. If, in addition, they are useful in providing understanding, predicting consequences, or supplying valuable generalizations—why not use them?

There are, of course, many, many other sociological concepts and a host of generalizations, theories, and research studies in the literature.[7]

Reference to the literature and to experts in developing programs, policies, or procedures in police-community relations have often been found useful.

Does it help to view the police, say, as institutionalized authority with power—that is, the potential—for limiting the social choices of citizens? If so, we can use this approach, as many scholars have. That would be one of the possible sociological models—as a partial image of reality.

There are other ways of looking at community and police, other models, as we have called them. The psychological approach, which opens the door to a large number of psychological models, is one.

Psychological Models

Psychological models, as analytical tools, are concerned basically with the individual—his mind and his behavior. There is, however, a study called crowd psychology in an overlapping discipline, social psychology,[8] which addresses the individual in a group situation.

The subject is a large one, with many researchers and scholars in the field who have concerned themselves with such concepts and their manifold complexities as assimilation, influence and resistance to influence, survey and opinion research, the induction of attitude and action changes, the diffusion of information and innovation, legitimate and coercive power, leadership, and so on.

Even without delving into the fascinating intricacies of each of the above concepts, their relevance to the community in its relations with government are quite clear. Some of these ideas will be used in developing social-psychological models of police-community–relations programs in later chapters. The social-psychological model is persuasive to many practitioners and scholars.[9] Again, however, it is only a partial picture, as all models are. Valuable not because it presents any absolute truths but rather as an analytical tool.

Moving further away from a sociological orientation are the more purely psychological views that dig deep into the depths of the individual's personality and its development from earliest childhood, through adolescence to maturity, and finally old age.[10] These topics are undoubtedly relevant to our own subject, because much crime and disorder concerns adolescents and youths when they are still in the process of personality formation, as many scholars claim. Psychology also deals with the determinants of behavior and attitude, motivations, stress reactions, and pathological aspects of personality in relation to crime, alcoholism, and drug addiction.[11] Here, too, we find the psychic and behavioral aspects of certain brain disorders.

All of these themes appear to have a connection to our own subject. Thus psychological models concentrating on these factors explain much that might otherwise be inexplicable, and the promise is that even more understanding will be available in the near future, as new theories and new findings are made.

Basic psychoanalytic propositions, such as the id, the ego, and the super-ego, have provided much insight into the presumed development of personality, from infancy to maturity. Only the shallowest definitional presentation is possible here. The *id* is a construct, that is, a set of concepts, used to represent the presumed existence of innumerable, and partially understood, instinctual drives that are present at birth, that know and care nothing about the real world or about morality, and seek only their own gratification.

The *id,* the pleasure principle of life, calls for gratification by a primary process, the forming of a mental image of the object desired, as in hallucinations, wishful thinking, and dreams. The effort to gratify the instinct is called wish fulfillment.

The *ego,* or reality principle, is the part of the personality that progressively develops an ability to perceive and to organize and store knowledge, to initiate problem-solving behavior, such as that necessary for wish fulfillment. Its reality-oriented performance is called the secondary process.

The third part of the personality in the psychoanalytical model is the *superego,* or "moral principle," which is concerned with what it has learned to value as "good" or detest as "bad." It incorporates the conscience and the entire set of values learned first from parents, later from peers and the organism's whole experience. It can be seen as evaluating all thoughts, its own and others, as either good or bad.

This particular psychoanalytical model gives a partial view of reality by viewing the personality as built up of these three organizing principles. The id is the biological aspect; the ego is the psychological aspect per se, as individual reactions in coping and in combining thought and behavior; and, finally, the superego, which concerns social aspects. Stated in another way, the personality is seen as constituted of three types of thought and behavior: selfish, rational-coping, and socially effective.

Again, we must ask ourselves if such models as these can be used to build a view of police-community relations that will be useful to the practitioner or scholar. We shall continue with these and other approaches, in later chapters, but we can see now that in citizen-police conflict situations on the street, role-conflict models immediately come to mind when we note that some police officers may not enjoy the role of enforcer against people with whom he might otherwise like and identify. As well, we can see the role-conflict churning in the usually law-abiding motorist, now resentful at being demeaned in the eyes of his family by the officer who gave him a traffic citation. Countless other critical police-community situations fit into the schema presented, from rebellion against parental substitute figures to solving the problem of getting "wheels" for a Saturday-night date by jumping the wires on a tempting Cadillac parked on a lonely street.[12]

Politico-economic Models

We can discuss political and economic models [13] together for two reasons:

1. Much political structure and process is designed with a view to economic consequences. This is a variation on the slightly tongue-in-cheek comment that "Government is a system for taking money away from one group and giving it to another" and "Politics is the art of deciding *who* gets *what!*"
2. Much of economics is constrained by political decisions. True, economics is concerned about "making a living." But making a living today is a matter of the flow of money, a political invention.

Economic models, of course, because of the importance of scarce resources, can be helpful in almost every study in modern life.[14] In a worldwide view of police and community there would probably be quite different models for countries with different economic systems. There are many models, of course: capitalist, communist, collectivist, socialist, syndicalist, and others. All, however, are concerned with the production, distribution, and consumption of material wealth.[15]

Communist, socialist, and fascist economies are termed collectivist, with each providing increasing amounts of economic activity in the private sector.

Capitalism, itself, though generally providing an even larger private sector, may—and does—have varying amounts of government regulation, depending on the country and the time period studied.

The impact on police-community relations in a capitalist society springs from the existence of the institutions of private property and freedom of contract. In an aside, it should be noted that in many communities in the United States dissatisfaction with government-provided police has provoked a private police, which are believed to be better. Not only do banks, rail-roads, communication companies, and many other large businesses employ their own police—with a very specialized police-community relations ensuing—but also there are a number of very large companies that supply police services to other organizations. Burns and Pinkerton, two very well-known outfits that have been providing private police for years, have been joined recently by a number of other companies. Private policing is an active area of entrepreneurship. Interestingly, new customers are presented with an economic model displaying the economic factors that substantiate their claim of being able to do more and better policing, for less money, than government police.

In economic models, the common denominator is money. All inputs and outputs are translated into dollars, and the balance indicates the benefit. Analysis of cost/benefit is only one subbranch of economic models, but this factor is of rising importance to police and city managers everywhere, pressed as all are with inflation and eroded tax bases.

Economic models are of even greater importance now that most large communities have come to depend on credit financing. It is one thing to have a *capital* budget on a credit basis—it is an entirely new game when the *expense* budget depends on the state of the money market and the price of money.

Inflation has brought the cost of a single radio car, with a two-man team, to approximately $125,000 per year, when calculated on a 24-hour-day basis. That one glaring budget fact, together with its ramifications in other rising costs, has changed the points of view of both police and community leaders from "Let's hire sufficient police to do the job" to "How can we keep the payroll down!"

Increasingly sophisticated use of economic models is one way the future must travel.

A short comment about political models, insofar as they are separate from economic implications, should be sufficient.[16]

Aristotle's comment that "Equality consists in the same treatment of similar persons" has not been bettered in the two thousand years since it was uttered. It is the basis of American democracy.

As a people, we have not produced the great minds whose ideas have conquered a world, but we have taken the ideas of the world's best, and Aristotle was one, and gone as far as any other country in making dreams come true for the many.

Patriotic self-praise in the third century of existence of the longest-running constitutional republic in the world is not really chauvinistic, but merely congratulations based on a successful implementation of the ideas of theorists of a score of nations on freedom and equality, cemented by the sweat and blood of the descendants of a hundred more.

As Walt Whitman wrote in 1855, "The United States themselves are essentially the greatest poem . . ." [17] Political models in this country are concerned with vested interests, factions, lobbying, and influence peddling in one sequence and personal liberty, privacy, and constitutional rights in another series. Technical matters, such as the separation of powers, checks and balances, the federal system, states' rights, are all brought into contention, and police-community–relations people are right in the middle of these matters on a national stage. We have repeated investigations of our Central Intelligence Agency and bewail the fact that all through history no one has yet been able to discover effective restraints or organizational controls for the "secret police." But that's just the point. That is not a failure of our political model: No people have yet discovered that grail of police organizational science. The only surprise is that the American political system hasn't yet solved that conundrum, as it has so quickly solved so many others in the relations between men.

We expect everything of the American political system. It has come through, triumphantly, time and time again. De Crèvecœur's delight in the enormous, limitless opportunity for freedom in the mid-eighteenth century has been repeated by hundreds of millions since. The first years of the first President saw a rebellion, which was quieted without serious harm. Stupid errors, such as the confirmation in slavery of black Americans, have been met by the system and after long, unrelenting effort are in process of being overcome. Our country, the United States, has been a party to foolish actions, but also to many more inspiredly noble ones. We have never ceased to hold up the lamp beside the door for millions of refugees from other political systems—and that lamp still burns brightly, still lights the path to freedom for beggars and paupers and turns them into citizens and presidents.

All of these attributes are part of the basic machinery available to community leaders and police agencies.[18] There is an abiding faith in this country, in the American system. That is, perhaps, the strongest force, and the greatest asset, working for those in police-community relations. Perhaps it was best said in *Democratic Vistas* by Walt Whitman in 1871:

> Political democracy, as it exists and practically works in America, with all its threatening evils, supplies a training-school for making first-class men. It is life's gymnasium, not of good only, but of all.[19]

Definitional and Other Models

There are a number of orientations that tend toward definitions of objectives or values as a basic starting point. These can be grouped together as definitional models. The most ancient of these in current use, the *religious model,* defines certain behavior as "sin" and other behavior as either merely permitted or as having special "grace," such as compassion, piety, and charity.

Such a predetermined definition of goals, when used to devise models of police and community, reveal interesting insights that are not as out of date as one might believe.

The *Living New Testament,* a 1971 version of the Bible, cites in Romans 13:1: "Obey the government, for God is the one who has put it there." It goes on: "There is no government anywhere that God has not placed in power."

The same section in another contemporary English version, *Good News for Modern Man,* is given as: "Everyone must obey the state authorities, because no authority exists without God's permission, and the existing authorities have been put there by God."

Actually, the King James version of the same section is not that much different: "Let every soul be subject unto the higher powers. For there is no power but that of God: the powers that be are ordained by God."

With that definition of legitimate power in the minds of a large section of the public, it can easily be appreciated that civil disorder and attempts to change power balances by ethnic and other minorities are going to meet strong disapproval.

As to attitudes toward police that are sanctioned by Holy Writ, the *Living New Testament,* Romans 13:4:

> The policeman is sent by God to help you. But if you are doing something wrong, of course you should be afraid, for he will have you punished. He is sent by God for that very purpose.

The World Bible Society edition:

> Whoever opposes the existing authority opposes what God has ordered; and anyone who does so will bring judgment on himself. For rulers are not to be feared by those who do good but by those who do evil. . . . if you do evil, be afraid of him [the man in authority] because his power to punish is real. He is God's servant and carries out God's wrath on

those who do evil. For this reason, you must obey the authorities, not just because of God's wrath but also as a matter of conscience.

Again, the authorized King James version, despite its poetic lyricism, says much the same thing, Romans 13:4:

For he is the minister of God to thee for good. But if thou do that which is evil, be afraid: for he beareth not the sword in vain: for he is the minister of God, a revenger to execute wrath upon him that doeth evil.

It must be understood that models are not used by only the scientific-minded. The various religious models are used as a natural model for thought and feeling about police-community relations, as well as many other aspects of everyday life, by those who know and accept such religious mandates. Whether a model is conceived as merely a tool for analysis or whether it encompasses all that is known or believed about the reality involved, the method and the effect are much the same: Thought is guided by the model, as a surrogate for the real world.

The consequence of using a model is often acceptance of the real world very much as that model articulates it. No politician, police manager, or other person interested in understanding community can ignore the religious models, accompanied by public opinion, that are so powerful, the nominal secularization of government and mass media notwithstanding.

When we add concepts from other religious tenets, such as, "Let the punishment fit the crime" (Exodus 21:24, 25) versus compassion for even the worst criminal; against "gay power" (Genesis 38:10), as contrasted with tolerance for others, in the Book of Ruth, and the elevation of charity above all virtues, in Corinthians 13:13, and dozens of other examples that might be cited, we can readily see that religious models can, and do, lead to public preconceptions as to what community relations are all about.

Another definitional model is known as the legal model.[20] Such a model defines by civil and criminal law the rights and duties of community and police. Often there is a tendency toward a simple dichotomy between guilt or innocence in reference to alleged violations of specific statutes, which spell out in multitudinous detail overt manifestations that are identifiable by observers as lawful or unlawful.[21]

Legal models, applicable to police-community relations throughout the country, have leaned heavily on constitutional law and Supreme Court decisions in individual cases.[22] The changes in police procedures under this pressure have been great. "Improvement," however, is hard to find, whether we search among police-community relations, criminal apprehension and conviction, or the general administration of justice.[23]

It appears that mere legality has not accomplished legitimacy either for community or police, nor for their practices or procedures. Every civil demonstration, every "stop and frisk" incident easily becomes a crisis. There is no agreement as to what is legitimate for either police or community.[24]

Since the legal model underpins the entire structure of the criminal law, it is the rock upon which police matters stand as upheld or founder dismally when rejected by the highest appellate court.[25]

There are any number of other models, many of them definitional, which can be dealt with rather summarily, now that the pattern of models and modeling has been made explicit. There are a number of Marxist models that view all social problems as simply a matter of the exploitation of labor by the nonproductive baser elements in society.[26] Ever present is the secure knowledge that this battle [27] must end with ultimate victory for labor and the accession of the proletariat into control of all means of production and wealth as a historical imperative.

Democratic models [28] are easily devised in this third century of our existence as a constitutional republic,[29] with ideals of democracy that extend from a Jeffersonian acclaim for the good sense and judgment of the average person, once he is well informed, to the equal opportunity promised by practically all American idealists,[30] to the more conservative "most good for the most people," to the "of the people, by the people and for the people" government of Abraham Lincoln.[31]

The definitions of democracy are many, but in the United States they rarely move very far from a central core of faith in the "American ideals of freedom," which is quite a bit different from the way other countries would define democracy.

Each national administration tries to put its logo on this idea, from Square Deal to New Deal to Fair Deal to The New Society, without really affecting any fundamentals. The new administrations tend to continue the most popular innovations of the past and also try for their own brands. But when the new is put into practice, it doesn't really differ much: "law and order" or "America, love it or leave it" or "consumerism." They all reach for individual rights.

Each proclaims democracy, and though each announces a brand-new path, everyone knows there won't be that much change—and, sure enough, we're all Americans again right after the inauguration.

In this picture of the "democratization" of the American people it is amazing that we do not have political assassinations by repulsed political parties, but only by the mentally unbalanced. These unhappy occurrences are not really political in nature, but the result of aberrant individuals.

Our political battles are, in the main, battles of slogans for economic power—but there is not a sign of any fundamental change in the patterns of power. Our institutions remain, a few faces change, that is all.

We, as a people, as every police-community manager soon comes to feel, respond to the most idealistic of slogans and the most pecuniary of interests. Appeals to self-interest seem to have an inordinate degree of success in community and police matters, as they do, to some degree, in all other phases of American life.[32]

The net effect is in the opinion of some, a dollar democracy—not the worst of all possible worlds, perhaps, but to the idealist, not the best.

Nevertheless, in this real world, self-interest is a factor, though never the entire answer. The weights given to various elements in the democratic model depend on the particular views of the involved theorist or practitioner.

Appraisal of Theoretical Models

From the point of view of the practitioner, either in community or in police work, the use of models, although they provide some valuable insights, appears to have most value in "palaver rather than performance." That is, models provide a common vocabulary, expedite communication—but what to do about it?

There is, however, another use: to assist in the preparation of persuasive applications for grants of funds to support programs. Funding authorities have no more to guide them at this state of the art of police-community arrangements than have the practitioners. In ignorance, funding must be mainly on the basis of rational hope. What could be more reasonable under the circumstances than a hope based on an expectation of useful programs, founded on learned disciplines, which can express in coherent form a model that is referable to a reality. Unfortunately, evaluation of the program in police-community relations is usually in terms of the same model, and, of course, it is found to be "successful."

The result has been billions of dollars in funding, with many hopeful expectations satisfied by the attainment of many short-term goals. Basic problems, however, remain unresolved, perhaps not even stated, as yet.

This is not mere denunciation of the well-intentioned efforts of practitioners and scholars. It is the considered opinion of the most thoughtful
and knowledgeable people in this field.[33]

Perhaps, behind this lowered estimation of the success of community-
police programs and efforts is the thought that there is a great goal, a
grand objective somewhere out there. Is it something like: The object of
police-community relations is not merely to smooth troubled waters, to
keep from "making waves," as they say. No, perhaps the real achievement
envisioned, the Ultima Thule, is a final resolution of all the problems
that government has always had with society.

When royalty was supreme, social life was a matter of slowly but inexorably pressing people to comply with the rule of God and King, and
often they were the same. The *Truth* was known; *The Right Way* was
known; the problem of government was simply a matter of sweeping the
corners to bring unenlightened marginal individuals into the mainstream
of social life. Those benighted souls were few in number, an insignificant
proportion.

At the outbreak of independence in this land, as we sense the surging
perception of *liberty* in the accounts of those who then lived, the arch-
enemy of kings, *The People,* quickened in the womb of this continent.
The concept was born, alive and kicking, demanding nourishment. After
all, these early Americans were the sons of Englishmen who had executed
a king in 1649. Now they were confirming their right to liberty from all
human sovereignty, as the Englishmen had not done. They did not need a
Great Protector; they needed neither High Church nor Low. They were
united in their freedom—and they seized great gobs of it, in land taking
and land stealing, in forest raiding and corporate plunder, in bounty
hunting, in gold rushes, all in an intoxicating draft that titillated the
world. There was endless freedom in every way, for everyone. Don't like
your neighbor? Move out and stake out all over again. There was never
any closure, always an open door beckoned; and millions all over the world
noted the invitation and swarmed to the new country.

Now—some people say it is different. They say there is closure now.
Whatever there is in the land, that is all there is going to be. There must
be sharing. But sharing implies that those Americans who have collected
perquisites and material goods are now called on to surrender some of
them to others. Ah, but that is not the America they were promised. The
late call for a moral imperative—it's nice to share; it's godly to share—is
seen as a fraudulent plea. In short, it is not American, it's not comple-

mentary to the right—and duty—of each individual to be free to struggle for what will be his. The result they say is a "fragmented" society.

Not so! It might be better described as a "ganging up" society. Instead of the ideal being the image of an individual struggling against man and nature, we are showing signs of a society that has become painfully aware that in a democracy there is strength in numbers. People now combine into constituencies that can exert social and political power. That power is used to obtain material goods, in the last analysis the ultimate measure of success and the best reason for liberty.

The very first Americans wanted what we would call today "a piece of the action." That's what Americans still want. It does not, and probably will not, change things to call on a new version of ethics: "Let us share." This is not so thrilling a tenet as "Let us pray—and then go out and get ours!"

"Constituencies" are the factions the Founding Fathers dreaded—but with a vengeance. There is only so much money in the pot, we are told. Therefore, we are admonished, it is better to split the pot with all the players. But, of course, that is not why we came into the game, is it?

In poker, that situation would call for a strong bluff, if you play it honest; and it would call for dealing from the bottom of the deck, if you do not have such scruples.[34]

That is the situation, it appears, put in simpler language than most scholars are accustomed to. For individuals and groups, the rational way out is to join in "gangs" and try to loot the pot. If it's a zero-sum game, let's get going and get the biggest slice we can.

That is the societal problem facing police-community relations, it appears. It isn't that a unified society is now fragmented. It is that a society of individuals is faced with a new phenomenon: "gang up or go without." [35] If you are not a part of a coercive power group,[36] from Black Power to Gay Power to Woman Power to . . . —you name it— . . . Power, you can focus on your own interests only on occasion, obedient to mass-media hoopla on one side or the other of rather narrowly drawn issues, from civilian review boards to mass meetings or parades by various groups considered obnoxious by other groups, ranging from renascent Nazis to anti-homosexuals to homosexuals; electrical blackouts; mass looting by unemployed, later discovered to be employed freebooters.

To the outsider—the lonely individual—police and community seem to be sparring with each other constantly, rather gently at times, more roughly at other times, with neither side, thankfully, trying for a knockout blow.

If that analysis has any validity, is there any reason to fault a police-community program in a single department that tries to "cool it, without killing it?" Contain, without control, just to try to get through the day, so that everyone can get a little rest overnight until tomorrow brings its new crisis. Robert K. Merton's advice to "Seek middle-range theories" is persuasive to every practitioner.

A Return to Reality

Regardless of whether the policing arrangements we have in the United States today are really merely "holding actions," without anything better in view, the immediate problem to police managers and community leaders and activists is no less than critical.

A knowledgeable public presses for action—sparked by repeated television "documentaries" that come on more like indictments; by exhortative editorials in newspapers; by our current electoral habits of not voting an officeholder in, but rather of voting someone out of office; and by a general malaise, loss of faith, and simple disgust with government and government officers, police included, but not the worst of the lot.

The revulsion is, in great measure, fully returned. The public is seen by many police officers as a great beast, ungrateful for their sacrifices in blood, which in recent years have reached unprecedented proportions.

What can we offer to resolve some of these dilemmas? As far as modeling is concerned, there is at least one type of model that leans sedulously away from the implicit and almost invisible values and prejudgments of most of the learned disciplines: the series of communication models that leads so quickly to decision making in a reasonably objective manner, with the possibility of implicit values being ultimately revealed. In the same way all "buy and sell" orders can be summed and translated into a rising or a falling market by the ultimate consequence on the market tape.

That is, the communication model is based not on a single learned discipline restricted by definite boundaries, but rather on the basic processes immanent in every aspect of police and community relations. This is the topic of the next chapter.

Chapter 5

THE COMMUNICATION MODEL

To do good and to communicate forget not.
  —*The Epistle of Paul to the Hebrews,* 11:16

The *communication model* is discussed in detail as being potentially more useful than some other models in providing assistance to managers of police-community relations. Ultimately, the information that is available at the time a decision is made is the only rational basis for decision. Therefore, the circumstances and processes by which that information becomes available, if understood, should help determine the value of the information to the decision-making process for community programs.

What Is Communication?

Why Is It Valuable?

In the preceding chapter the use of models was discussed at length, including the fact that models constructed within the frame of reference of specific theoretical constructs have often been found useful and perhaps essential to understanding. Too, they are a convenient symbolic language with which to communicate to others.

Here we give special attention to only one model, *communication,*[1] because it appears to have great advantages in practical decision making in the field of police and community management. It is one thing to arrive at a subjective feeling of insight and comprehension. It is quite different to arrive at a decision that offers reasonable promise of accomplishing a specific objective.

It was in this vein that the Parable of the Spindle was related in Chapter 2. However rich the understanding of the sociologist and psychologist in that little story, the restaurant operator was not aided in developing a consistent plan that would ameliorate the situation. The solution he stumbled on—the use of written communications between the contending parties and the use of the spindle as the clearing point for these communications—may seem ridiculously simple, and, of course, it is. It may not provide a profound understanding of humanity or the dynamics of communication, but, in the story at least, it was a quick and ready solution.[2]

Communication models often have that happy serendipity: They frequently provide quick answers to difficult questions. If the answers suffice, it is all to the good. If they prove to be insufficient, well, we certainly have a lot of other models to work with, as well as an abundance of specialized techniques both for discovery and for analysis.[3]

If, however, a communication model works well, we can use it, get our answer, and go on to the next problem. There are no guarantees, however, for there is no mechanistic simplicity to anything human.

Nevertheless, it is helpful to isolate concepts. A way to represent some of the elements basic to communication is:

TRANSMITTER	CHANNEL	RECEIVER

That is, idealized communication consists of a single transmitter of signals and a channel to carry the signals to the receiver.

Questions remain: What characteristics of the transmitter are critically relevant? We must ask the same question about the other two elements.

Communication Theory [4]

Classical theory in communication consisted of the analysis of the distribution of signs, that is to say, defined sets, or "stationary" statistical distribution of coded signs. These theories, based on the assumptions of statistical theory, were found to be quite well adapted to problems that arose in telegraph and telephone systems. Later this theory was adapted to television and other, even more heavily laden, channels of information. There is even relevance to cryptography.

However, problems in social interactional communication involve changes in the signal statistics of indeterminate nature. That is, the set of signs and their distribution will change from situation to situation—that is, the vocabulary, the gesticulatory emphasis used in formal statements within a police organization, reports and such are quite different from that used in an informal community group. Street situations, too, present entirely different sets of signs, with different distributions of the kinds and numbers of the various words and phrases.

Of course this is not unique to community problems. Any physically controlling factor in the social field will result in changes in the statistical structure of the communication stream.

Thus, "nonstationary" statistics are the mathematical tool of choice in learning situations, economics, various hot-gas problems involving changes in the velocities of particles of plasma, as well as human behavioral and police problems. All involve questions of the relative instability of data distributions.

In all of the nonstationary problems the time vector must be taken into account, for over a sufficiently long period of time, fluctuations will be averaged out and escape observation. The longer the time span, the more detail of changes will be lost. In time-averaged observations, the more information will be lost.

The constraint imposed by the necessity of observing and allowing for the time dimension is only one of a number of conditions encountered by the communication stream. Another is "noise," which is undesired physical disturbance that interferes with identification of the signs. Thus there must be a matching of the sign stream to an appropriate channel used for transmission. The concept is quite obvious and is even a universal principle in human behavior. It applies to real situations when the receiver is required to respond instantly.

Concepts such as "information rate," "channel capacity," "noise," and even "redundancy" are not easy to acquire, nor are they simple to apply.[5] Since they have been precisely defined mathematically, and in this form can be applied directly to technical problems under clearly defined conditions, they can be used to solve communication problems. It is almost too easy, however, to use these terms metaphorically and descriptively. Such use by analogy has been criticized. We should not, nevertheless, be kept from such use if it is helpful. True, we cannot describe a physical reality in its entirety, but applied mathematics is necessarily approximate, too. If the description we use does not jibe exactly with reality, it is also true that the mathematics does not either. And the fact that the description does not exactly fit the mathematical concept matters not a whit.

What does matter is whether or not we can speak of reality usefully in any way at all.

The use of models of any kind is always an exercise in approximations, providing analogous descriptions, not reality. Therefore, the objection of imprecision can be overcome by refreshing the spirit of inquiry by recalling, humbly, that we are not creators of the fruits of inquiry. We only till the garden, and whatever we harvest will merely be preliminary to making the effort again and again.

Continuing, then, in a nonmathematical description: When noise disturbs the signals, the information they carry to the receiver is not perfect.

The event becomes one not of absolute recognition but of interpretation. The signs have been modified and the issue is: What were the *probable* signs that were transmitted. It is now a matter of weighing the evidence, in the light of all past and present evidence.

After estimating all the evidence, the decision is an inference—a guess —of a lesser or greater degree of probability.

That is the logic of the situation, and its close parallel with managerial decision making is clear. The process may be described mathematically, and herein may be the ultimate power of the communication model.[6]

Communication, under the constraints of reality, involving errors in perception of the situation, of encoding, of transmission, of decoding, and of recognition of the message, is essentially a process of inference, and a number of logical and mathematical approaches have been seen to be appropriate and useful.

On page 55 is a diagram of a more detailed model of the communication process.

Note that two sources are included, one supplying information, the other destroying the information. The information content of one (noise) signal is x-y, and the stream of noisy signals is a stream of the differences between the stream of output signals minus noise, and the total information content is:

$$(x_n - y_n)$$

The mean rate of information is the average of all possible x's and y's. That is, multiply by the joint probability density of $p(x,y)$ dx dy and integrate over the ranges of x and y values.

It is important to distinguish between the communication process as diagramed, which illustrates the ongoing process, and any description of that process by an observer, which, perforce, is *after the fact*.[7]

Analysis of the signals and the channels whereby they are carried is always a posteriori and describes what was, at best.

Thus *speech* is an articulatory process that produces sounds. The speaker (transmitter) may use the sounds to monitor his own performance,[8] but the sounds are chiefly *coded* signals carrying a message to communicate to the receiver.

The specific speech signals appear to be of great variety: words, syntactic structure, syllabic rhythms, other acoustic qualities, and minute acoustic clues. If the speaker is within view, facial expressions, such as pouts and grimaces, and the movement of eyebrows and eyelids will be included in a stream of signals along a different channel. Both streams of signals elicit all of the past experience of the receiver, his knowledge of

The Flow of Communication

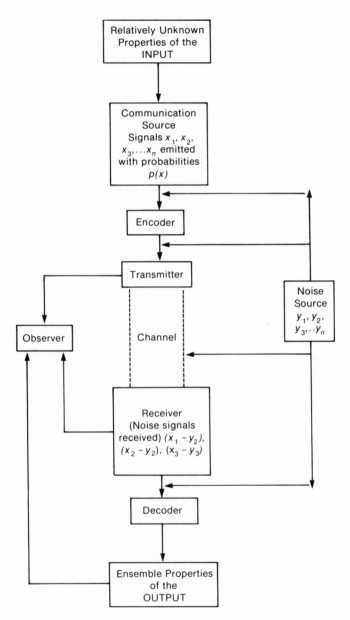

Figure 5–1

the subject of the message, his like or dislike of the topic or the speaker or even of the place of occurrence of the communication.

Contextual clues of all kinds are involved as signals travel along every perceptual channel available to the receiver and are translated or decoded according to the recognition level, conscious or unconscious, of the receiver.

The intelligibility of such communication, then, is a most chancy thing, difficult to predict. Mathematical assessment of the information content of a message has only a remote relation to the message that is recognized.

The degree to which the message contains confirmatory signals is called the *redundancy* of the message and will be a factor in assuring consistency in receipt of that message. Whatever else it does, redundancy adds to the intelligibility of the message.

All other things being equal, the more highly redundant the message, the greater the weight of evidence on the side of a reliable interpretation. Mathematical proof of this is quite straightforward, even obvious [9]—but it may not be obvious that the redundant signals need not be sheer repetition, but any and all confirmatory signals by whatever channel. As long as the redundant signals are perceived by the receiver, recognition and intelligibility will be increased. It is well to note that the redundant signals need not have been emitted by the human transmitter. The very location of the receiver may convey signals corroborative of the message he receives. The internal or external ambience impacting on the receiver may make the difference between lack of comprehension and complete clarity.

The Route to Decision Making

It must be understood at the outset that communication is not synonymous with *influence*. Both are relationships, true, but they are not of the same kind. Communication is the transmittal and receipt of messages of varying degrees of perception, comprehension, and influence, depending on factors other than, or at least in addition to, the actual content of the message.

Nevertheless, without communication of some kind, influence cannot be said to exist, not, at least, in contemplation of the communication model of reality.

Decision making is the critical function of managership and calls for a choice among alternatives. Whether that choice is made on a rational or other basis, inevitably, such choice is made by de facto performance. That is, there are cognitive and motor aspects of decisions. As far as the observer is concerned, the motor performance—whether accomplished by the nominal decision maker or by other people or things—is the important thing. Presumably such choices are subject to influence that is conveyed by a communication channel.

Choice implies discrimination between two or more alternatives and appears to be one of the simplest and most basic attributes of living things. Now, discrimination between alternatives is a definition of information.[10] Sequenced choices between only two options constitute, in a chain of such choices, as much information as one desires to convey. The amount of information being directly proportional to the length of the chain. Actually, life is not required to store information or to transmit it. A teletype machine communicates with another of its kind. A stack of punched cards stores information, which can be input to a computer, which will comply with the instructions contained in the stored information. A series of pluses and minuses or of alternating digits, 1, 0, 1, 0, 1, 0, 1, 1, 1, 0, 0, 1, constitutes information that can guide a decision. Each one of these digitary physical signals relieves doubt by directing a decision in each case.

Of course the total number of options in the above series is 2^n from a binary set of alternates. But sub-decisions can be reduced to a coupled set of only two. Thus this model appears consonant with reality. The sequence of decisions, it will be noted, is the message that can convey a decision of larger and more thought-filled character than each tiny binary decision. That more complicated message is the sum of the individual digitary decisions, and the sum of the binary decisions is called the information content of the message. As it affects decision making, it is the means of exerting influence.

Definitions

It is arrogant to try to set down hard definitions in any behavioral study. The concepts are not fixed, the terminology could hardly be more diffused. Nevertheless, a student has a right to expect a firm base to a discussion, not to mention Voltaire's dictum: before we discuss let us define our terms.

The following series of definitions is offered in the hope that their intrinsic circularity will not be too disturbing.

ALPHABET: a set of physical signs used for communication.

BIT: the smallest possible information unit, e.g., yes or no, + or –, 1 or 0, in a set of binary signals. In a set of twenty-six possible signals, say, the English alphabet, a bit would be any of the letters in that set.

CHANNEL: the means, physical or other, by which a message is transmitted.

ELEMENT: an item distinguishable from its background.

INFORMATION: logical instructions to select among alternatives.

MESSAGE: a set of signals containing information.

RECEIVER: the (human) receiver of a message.

REDUNDANCY: an excess of confirmatory signals over that barely required to constitute a message.

RELATIONSHIP: a statement about two or more elements.

SIGN: having a coded meaning.

SIGNAL: as a noun, is a physical item in a message indicating a choice. As a verb: to transmit.

TRANSMITTER: the (human) sender of a message.

Basic Principles

A *message* implies the transmission of *information*. Of course, information is a many-sided concept, but the fundamental aspect that is of concern to police-community relations is the semantic one—that is, the *meanings* involved. Without meaning being included in the transmission of information there really is no point.

The use of *signs* of various kinds to represent different meanings is a common feature of all communication. For ordinary human speech, the scheme of signs includes a vast array of vocal sounds. For written intercourse, the signs include letters, letters joined into words, words, in turn, linked in sentences. These are the two bases of communication. However, speech, at least when the speaker is in view, provides a slew of visual clues for the receiver: gestures, grimaces, body stance or movements, head inclinations or movements, also many sign events more remote from the human source, such as colors or other surroundings. Writings, too, are on a medium, or channel, which can provide signals that convey meaning: color of print, of page, of book covers, illustrations, photos, diagrams, graphics. Even the lighting of the room, it has been thought, may be a factor, as well as surrounding noises and experiences just prior to reading or just after.

The receiver of the message, to correctly translate the meanings involved, must have previous knowledge of the meaning corresponding to each sign. If there is any difference in his set of assigned meanings from that of the message source, his "reading" of meaning will be different from the message sent, even if every sign has been correctly received and perceived.

Examples are almost too obvious to mention, but one that is often encountered in regard to government is the use of the word "democracy," which means different things to different people. On the international level we often read of the American democratic republic. Now, as it happens, the name of East Germany is really Deutsche Demokratische Republik, which translates to German Democratic Republic. But the peoples in each country would probably see little similarity in their governments, and each would deny that the other is "democratic."

Semantic confusion, because of a difference in the meanings assigned to the message signs, is ubiquitous unless we restrict the message alphabet to only the most commonly used terms with universally understood meanings. The avoidance of ambiguous terms is mandatory in low-error communication.

Another way to reduce errors in message comprehension is, as previously mentioned, by the use of redundancy: the repeating of signs. This may be the entire message, or, more economically, only certain of the signs and other signs that confirm the meanings intended. Nevertheless, many messages will be misinterpreted.

Not only will messages be perceived that were not sent, but many messages will be sent that are in contradiction to the intentional signals that are transmitted.

Thus, there must be a screening process used by the message source to filter out unwanted message signs and to maximize intended signs. Particularly is this true when the message sender has attitudes adverse to the receiver. One may be quite aware of the importance of suppressing aggressive signals but be completely unable to do so. Many "bloopers" have gone out over national television and radio, usually with humorous consequences. In a more serious vein, the British Navy, at one time, included in its penal code the punishment of lashing for "scowling or glowering in the ranks." Signs of hate and detestation are often compulsively revealed, a useful thing for community- and police-relations people to remember.

Screening out all unwanted signs can be a difficult, and sometimes an even impossible, task. That granted, communication necessarily entails the selection of the signs that best represent the intended meanings. That is the coding process. The signs selected are chosen not only for their assigned meanings, but also for their potential for transmission and reception.

Please note that the signs one would select to be transmitted by speech would not necessarily be the same as those that would be encoded for writing. The degree of formality or other circumstances will also affect the specific set of signs selected.

Such modifications will be in consideration of conventions of politeness, as well as in recognition that speech permits many varieties of inflection, emphasis, and timing that are not available to the written word. On the other hand, print has the advantages of various sizes of type, format, and layout, underlining or italicizing, visual paragraphic indications, and the opportunity given the reader of going back to recheck a prior signal. There are graphic displays without number and even moving pictures with color and sound added, providing one of our most intense communication media channels.

All messages, after being encoded, are transmitted via *channels* of various kinds and qualities. Of course, the channel selected must be one that is available. The stream of sound that is speech is transmitted via a channel consisting of waves of alternating compressions and rarefactions in the intervening air, produced by a complicated anatomical structure involving human lungs, diaphragm, larynx, and throat moving in coordinated conformations. There is a time dimension to speech. Each signal is sent out in sequence, and gradually its intensity dies away until it can no longer be identified as a signal. Even when that speech signal is converted into electrical impulses and transmitted over a wire or over an electromagnetic carrier wave, it retains a time dimension in that the signals are eventually reconverted to air sound waves that are heard in sequence and implacably die away.

Of course, modern technology makes permanent records of speech, either by differentially grooving a vinyl disk, by patterns of varying density on optical film, or by more or less permanently magnitizing small areas on magnetic tape. These records are not speech—merely records of speech that can be converted into speech.

Print and handwriting, however, are signs marked on a convenient substance, usually paper, though clay, cloth, wood, stone, and metal have been used. The time dimension of such communication is different from that of speech. In speech the time variable is fixed by the transmitter in a time sequence that is unalterable by the receiver. The written word is read and comprehended sequentially in time, but the receiver has the power to stop, go back to a prior signal, skip, stop again, compare different parts, or even other writings, muse, calculate, and perhaps reach new understanding.

In speech, the receiver's attention must march in time to the transmitter's beat, else he loses the sequential pattern that is an integral part of the meaning symbolism.

One is tempted to wonder whether this acceptance of pause, by written words, may inhibit the *influence* of writing, as compared with the power of speech to influence. The inexorable march of the spoken word does not permit the kind of critical comparison and reach for objectivity that writing allows. The charismatic and powerful influence of talented speakers on human emotion and behavior is a common refrain in the histories. It is not absent in modern times, either. The influence of Adolf Hitler, Martin Luther King, Jr., Huey Long, Daniel Webster, William Jennings Bryan, and hundreds of clergy and lay preachers, as well as outstanding lawyers and orators, is acknowledged everywhere. It is only to be expected that this phenomenon will be utilized by commercial interests and advertisers. Perhaps the most persistently persuasive pleas delivered by the spoken word are those selling wares in living rooms all across the land, carried by television channels.

Much of the unrest of segments of the public appears to have been encouraged, if not incited, by mass media, particularly television. Given equal time, much of the backlash from the more extreme manifestations of unrest has received coverage in the media as well. News is news, whichever way it goes—but the consequence is polarization and division in the community.

Each channel, whether direct speech, telephone, radio, television, or any of dozens of others, including graphic means, has its own characteristics, which affect the communication and the consequences of that communication.

Thus face-to-face speech, for example, by a citizen and a police officer, implies the possibility of an immediate response by both parties to the communications between them.[11] What that response will be is a function of the particular circumstances. But the danger signals are up. Will the consequences be exaggerated or minimized by the danger signals? Will they call for more informal or more formal styles of communication? Will spoken communication best be left to another time, and the burden of communication be taken over by fiats and billy clubs?

These hazards, interestingly, do not so easily reach a crisis when a remote channel that does not imply immediate reaction is used, for example, a phone call to a potential defendant for whom an arrest warrant has been issued to allow him to have his lawyer present when he surrenders to the police. Or even the service of a warrant of arrest, implying a mere ministerial action on the part of the police at the time of service, with action of serious consequences to occur later, when the arrestee will have aid of friends, family, and counsel, is an event in which the face-to-face communication is far more predictable and therefore less tension inducing.

What channel, then, should be selected? Most of the time in community situations the choice will be obvious and inevitable. It would serve a useful purpose, however, for police and community people to frequently review the various options available. Perhaps a different channel would be more serviceable? Perhaps a short television talk by a leading figure would be more valuable than a general meeting, where two-way conversation would quickly deteriorate into a complaint session or petty squabbling. One can turn that suggestion around: Would it be better to have the meeting? Would the airing of the topic let off a little steam, discover what the major complaints are and who are the leading figures in the community?

It is important that the decision in this case should not be any ideological or knee-jerk response. The variables of the fact situation in the community and all other groups must be carefully weighed. It would be rather foolish to try to use only one solution for every problem. The use of the communication model includes self-admonishment always to explore the options.

Redundancy

In common parlance, *redundancy* has a negative, even pejorative, connotation.[12] It means, of course, that something is present that is not necessary and should be eliminated.

In human communication, however, redundancy is a valuable quality whereby it becomes increasingly difficult to make an undetectable mistake.

Redundancy is built into communication in many ways. In addition to formal rules of spelling, pronunciation, syntax, and so on, there are habits of usage and of performance, ranging from the kind and styles of vocabulary appropriate in a given situation to footnotes, headnotes, and summaries. Speech, as was noted previously, uses gestures, grimaces, postures, body stance, exclamations, breath holding or expelling, and the entire spectrum of the actor's art.

Always, the specific situation and the ambience will contribute signals pertinent to the message. For instance, a motorist calls a police officer by a number of different possible signals: "I want some information," or "I am being held up by a robber. Help me!" or "My wife is pregnant. Can you clear a way?" [13]

In addition to the vocal appeals, other signs will ratify or deny the message: presence or absence of an armed man or of a pregnant woman in the car; the tempo and manner of arm waving through the car's open window; the time of day or night; the quality of the neighborhood—all will provide additional evidence that assures recognition of the message by the officer.

One often hears annoyed comment, "But I've already given that order!" or "I've told him what to do, why doesn't he do it?" Much of this emotional reaction is pointless. What is called for often is simple redundancy. If an order is expected to be obeyed it must be reinforced by an organized program of redundance confirming that order: printed, read aloud, report requested, questions asked about the order, follow-up orders, observation, orders to others to monitor performance, and on and on. One repetition avails little.

It is well known that maritime tradition calls for the helmsman to repeat the orders given him: "Hard starboard, helmsman!" "Hard starboard, sir." The feedback ensures accuracy; additionally, the bridge officer is right there to watch and monitor.

In police-community relations, where there are large numbers of people involved on all sides of every event, the necessity for redundancy—confirmatory signs—in every effort at communication is manifest.

It is an interesting experiment for the student to cover the bottom half of a line of type with the edge of a sheet of paper. It will be noted that the message will still be recognizable. The bottom half of print is not necessary to recognition, but it confirms it. It is interesting, too, that the bottom half of a line of print, when the top part is concealed, is perhaps recognizable, too, though probably with not as great a degree of ease. One might say that a line of print carries the message at least twice, and in so doing, makes the receipt of the correct message more certain.

The opposite is noted in most computer programming languages. Even though great effort has been put into devising "natural-like" programming languages, such as COBOL, FORTRAN, and others, neophyte programmers are continually exasperated by the irritating habit of the computer to reject long run-streams, sometimes involving hundreds of punched cards, for failure to close a single parenthesis or to skip a tiny space.

We do not expect our communications to be taken exactly and literally. That is inhuman. We, as humans, emit countless confirmatory signs with every message. We expect that the gist of those signs will assure message content received. If, as transmitters, one of those signs is contradictory, our intention is for that sign to be ignored. Thus if ten signs, each an assurance of the validity of the other and of the message, are sent, but one sign is, by reason of noise, reversed in symbolic content, we expect the nine correct signs to carry the message correctly to the receiver. The receiver, too, in most cases, will follow that intention.

Receivers

A sign is not received isolated from all other indicia. It is not only a part of a sequence of signs but part of a complex situation. The information-bearing elements that constitute the sign may include not merely the objective sound or form of the word or phrase but also a vast set, all of which may be necessary for the receiver to recognize the sign. In this sense, information is what is recognized as the meaning of the entire set and may include not only what is projected as the intended information-bearing sign, but also who and what is recognized by the receiver: the speaker's appearance, the surroundings, which may be necessary to recognize him and his objective, and the whole fabric of the situation.

Once a sign is recognized, the receiver has taken part in a communication event. From that time on he is a different person. His state of mind has been changed, all his responses thereafter will be determined, in part, by the fact of his recognition of the sign.

These changes are complex and multitudinous and reveal themselves in many ways. A subsequent recognition of the same sign may be facilitated; it may also change what would otherwise have been the receiver's response to a different sign.

The very act of communication has established a relationship of some influence on the receiver, as soon as recognition at either conscious or subconscious level is established. Whether this "influence" will be along the lines hoped for by the sender is not determinable merely by the message content of the sign.

The agreement as to the meaning of the alphabet of signs between sender and receiver depends in great measure upon which alphabet is being used. Ordinary language signs are complex, rarely with singular, definite meaning allotted to a sign. At best, the meaning will be described or discussed in terms of other words tail-chasing in a perpetual circle. There is no end to this in a final, absolute understanding or agreement, but only an intuitive residue. We hope we understand what the other chap wants us to understand.

In formal sign systems, mathematics for example, we accept the idea that we do not need to know what the signs mean, but only how they are related. We do not know what a "point" is or a "straight line"—we need only follow the rules of mathematics and the body of theorems follows inexorably. Most people, however, feel they have an intuitive understanding of "point" and "straight line" and of many of the other terms in mathematics.

All sign usage in human communication is similar, depending on the *relations* of each sign with another sign. No sign has meaning in isolation, but only in its connection with another sign.

The point is that a sign does not mean anything in itself, but only to signify something to someone. Without being operationalized by *use*, it is nothing. Thus the meaning of a sign refers to the use made of it by a human being in a particular set of times and places. Necessarily, the meaning of a sign is slightly different for each person because of their diverse histories of exposure to the sign.

Thus a sign is always part of a *working* system of other signs in use by specific users. No one can be absolutely sure of the meaning of a sign produced by another. However, by continuing his reception of signs he can extend his probability of understanding and so learn more.

At the first perception of a sign there is no implicit critical faculty operating to deny the perception, however "incorrect" it may be. In fact, the perception is partially "correct" however it may differ from what is later determined to be "more correct" or perhaps even be denoted "reality."

A description an observer gives of what he "recognizes," then, is not "reality," but, at best, what he "sees." The phenomenon itself, however accurate the description, is a different thing entirely.

Most of us believe we can recognize certain attributes. Certain of these are physical in nature, such as smoothness, hardness, colors, or even such qualities as boxlike or streamlined.

Of course we cannot recognize these attributes unless they are attached to material objects. We can see and feel a "smooth" wall, a "hard" mattress, or "red" dresses on boxlike or streamlined figures. Such attributes have an invariance: The same redness or smoothness is recognized as a quality of many different objects. Such qualities of invariance have been called *universals.* The recognition of the common property of many objects—the redness, the smoothness, the universals—depends on someone responding to that concept stimulus, which in turn will depend on his particular past history.

The recognition of such universal signs implies classification of a recognized sign into an existing class of such signs. It involves a mental process that is called *recall.*

The class of universals includes literally thousands of familiar invariants, or attributes, that innumerable objects may have in common, although each is different from the other: square, round, flat, curved, in description of physical objects; good, bad, fair, treacherous, loyal, in classes of abstract universals; and even past, present, and future, as temporal universals in common usage.

Recall is the bringing of past experience into the conscious level of thought for present use. Such recall is constantly occurring, as we recall the assigned meanings of signs or recall prior events similar to the present. Recall can be compared with retrieval of information either in an electronic computer or in a paper bound memory bank, such as a library, card index, or writing record.

In recalling and extracting concepts from memory one may summarize, abstract, and form classes of classes of universals. One can and does invent (or discover) new classes in infinite combinations and complexity.

Signal recall operates to bring in, by association, a host of subliminal operations triggered by the sign itself or by any of the collateral circumstances attending the reception by the receiver. Such associations extend the classes and abstractions set off by the sign as part of past experience and are applied in recognition of the sign and inferences about the sign and about its implications.

Thus, we recognize the meaning of sentences even when some of the words are not heard or are not visible. We recognize expected sequences of letters or words. We may infer, correctly or incorrectly, the meaning of missing sentences. We are not barred from inferring by reason of a possibility of a mistake (as is a computer). We infer, whether we plan it or not. It is as natural a transaction in mental processes as is recognition itself.

In opposition to our ability to recall—is our ability and necessity, really, to screen in or screen out signs and meanings to fit our preconceptions as to what such signs or meanings might be. Regardless of whether this process can be identified as the effort to make a cognitive whole of the reception, to make it dovetail with what we already "know," or whether it is conceived as a separate and distinct process, the phenomenon is ubiquitous.

The entire process can be summarized by the term *decoding* and is characterized by a *filtering*, or *selectivity*, that is characteristic of human decoding processes.

The meanings attributed to the signs by the receiver, changing his state, often induce *adaptive reactions* in him, either to respond, to defend, to attack, to flee, or to make another observable response that fits into the taxonomies devised by one behavioral scientist or another.

Thus, the working system of sending signs and responding signs is different with each pair of senders/receivers, with many possible bypaths. The sender's sequence of signs, sent off with a goal in the mind of the sender, may find itself way off track, as each sign is responded to by other signs by the receiver, which in turn set off other signs.

Each sign can be responded to by an unlimited number of response signs. As an officer at the scene of an accident may indicate a person, using the words "Hey, you!" the individual may respond by taking off at high speed or by other signs, such as, "Who, me?" or "Why pick on me?"[14]

It is said that the word *kangaroo* means in the Australian aborigine language "I don't know," as it was the response given to Captain Cook when he pointed out one of the animals to a native, or so the story goes. The expected association was: the "name" of the animal, as later travelers would say, "What name belong him?"

The set of associations brought into play depends, again, upon the "sign" that triggers that array. Often called psychological expectancy or psychological set, the phenomenon is familiar in everyday life.[15]

When someone questions, "What did you do?" the receiver of the question is in a different psychological set depending on whether the questioner is his girl friend, his spiritual counsellor, or his mother. In each case, the answer might be quite different.

There would appear to be a possibility here of mathematical analysis of response sets. The literature, however, does not reveal much persuasive application of analysis to ordinary language. There has been some work, however, in the statistical analysis of responses to defined alphabets of signs, as well as binary analysis on a microphysiological level of neural responses, which appear to be of an on-or-off binary character.

As far as present application to police-community relations, communication consists of noisy signals that are evidence of a sender's messages. These are intercepted, decoded by noisy mechanisms in the receiver, which affect the receiver's prior hypotheses concerning possible messages from a prior probable set of messages.

Recognition, then, can be said to be the assignment of credence from a prior hypothesis to a posterior hypothesis. That is, a sign is recognized by a process of inference, progressively ascertained guesses, rather than with the clicking certainty of a key fitting a lock.

It is as if the brain operates on the entire *ensemble* of signs, as sequenced, triggering an ensemble of hypotheses likewise sequenced.

Although semantic associations undoubtedly aid in recognition of signs, it appears that associations of the sounds of speech and the syllabic patterning and the syntactic flow are more important in identification of signs.

Thus we find it possible to listen to and understand one speaker when surrounded by the noisy chatter of a party. That speaker's voice is picked out by acoustic clues, in the main, and by relying on the abundant redundancy supplied by the speaker's voice and other visible signals, the receiver is able to follow him and understand him with an ease that is not duplicable by a microphone pickup and electronic reproduction equipment.

Of course, the more familiar the signs, the speaker, the surroundings, the gestures, the more easily are the signals interpreted. We recognize relatively large patterns of familiar signs, and meaningful sentences are far easier to identify and remember than phrasing patterns that are unfamiliar to us.

Statistical communication theory has suggested many areas calling for experiment, but thus far there has not been very much forthcoming that is useful on a level that can be adapted to police-community relations. However, it has been stated that the human organism has a definite limit for reception of information, which is a minute fraction of the content of the physical signals that reach human sensory organs. The physical signals in human communication transmission are estimated to be of the order of millions of bits per second, but humans are limited to receipt of perhaps several hundreds per second. The redundancy of the signal production is enormous.

We are limited by our reaction time when faced with multiple choices of signals, which has been measured as of the order of one-half to one-tenth of a second and increases with the logarithm of the number of choices.

Actually, the physical capacity of the sense organs is estimated to be millions of bits per second. However, the *perceptual* rate of information intake depends on how quickly one can discriminate between signs and react to them, and this is more nearly in tens of bits per second.

Thus perception of visual images in printed English is estimated to be about fifty bits per second, and that of auditory speech signs is only a few dozens of bits per second. Signs are disseminated by producers with the abandon of spawning salmon, but the signs that result in acute perceptions are much fewer in number. The redundancy of available signs may constitute a valuable assurance of accuracy in communication.

The "survival value" of those signs that are consummated in perception consist not only in their amplitude, clarity, and uniqueness, but also in the kind and nature of the background "noise," which interferes, and with the "acceptability" of the surviving signals to the receivers.

Generally, however, the sense organs and nervous system take advantage of the multidimensional redundancy, and communication, however, modified, does occur.

It is important not to overlook the fact that the recognition of signs depends as much on the receivers' perceptions as on the nature of the signal itself. These perceptions are not merely of details but of entire patterns or invariants, which has the effect of squeezing signs into classes of similar signs. Thus we recognize and comprehend words whether they are shouted or whispered, sung or mumbled. The properties of the signals that are perceived as invariant, despite the differences in these quite different signals, it has been suggested, are due to our unfelt imitation of heard speech with our own vocal organs, and it is this muscular sensation we recognize.

It is as though perception of speech is almost synonymous, and simultaneous, with the production of speech. This hypothesis is evidenced, it is held, by some well-known experiments in which a subject is fitted with headphones that are muffled so that he can hear his own speech only after it has been recorded on tape and played back to him about a quarter of a second later. With the acoustic environment changed, most subjects stutter violently or demonstrate other vocal disabilities. They cannot talk well unless they hear themselves properly!

The human organism can perceive from the slenderest clues, but it does need certain significant ones. Perhaps the critically relevant ones are temporal? It does seem, according to the evidence, that the important signs that attain perception will be different with different people or even on different occasions. Recognition depends on complex psychophysiological structures at each end of the transmission line, complicated by a multitude of physical factors in between, all overladen with probability factors at every stage of the process.

The receiver, in accomplishing the near-miracle of recognition, summarizes the entire process of human thought organizing, comparing, setting up relationships, forming generalizations, identifying universals, associating and developing more complex details, while seeking invariants—all to facilitate communication.

It is time to consider the relationship of communication with influence, how influence starts and flows from one person to another.

Two-Step Flow of Influence

The "two-step flow of influence" [16] is a hypothesis that has received much attention from scholars of communication. In effect, it envisages most innovation as being adopted by people only after the new has been socially validated by persons of legitimacy to the people or group that is to be influenced. Usually the legitimizing process on these ideas is performed by individuals from the group. There is, however, evidence that respected individuals from a wider group can produce the legitimizing effect. This is in line with the concept of community of interest as developed in Chapter Two.

The point is that not only have modern communications systems enabled messages to be conveyed by and to thousands or millions of people at once, but rather that these millions are *constantly* exposed to mass communications. Their area of attention and concern is created and commanded by mass communications. Charles Horton Cooley wrote of this as long ago as 1909, when he commented that the basis of *consensus* was in the establishment of standard patterns of communication.

Since then, evidence has accumulated overwhelmingly of the validity of the concept of communities of interest, in which norms and a common set of values and attitudes are acquired by people at some distance, as well as by neighbors. Some people far away become more intimate and more "in tune" by far than neighbors and, in some cases, than relatives. Concepts of kith and kin must necessarily be changed by police to comply with the new concept of *normative* kith and kin. Plaintive, even pitiful, claims of relationship to figures in the mass media are common contemporary phenomena.

The neighborhood folk-oriented community fiction of local political figures, promoted for obvious reasons, is valid only as it becomes a self-fulfilling prophecy, because some people act on it as though it exists.

The coordination of values and norms is effected over wide areas, first by dissemination of the information that other sets of values and norms exist, then by repetition, so that they are made familiar. To this is added an improved transportation system, so that every community has people who have been north, south, east, and west of any given location hundreds and thousands of miles away. The influence of the mass media then operates in a number of complex ways, of which the current research concentration on the two-step flow of influence is perhaps an oversimplification.

The evidence indicates that the mass media pervasively familiarize the public with ideas and norms, which diffuse on an informational level throughout society as in recent years, in regard to civil rights, the rights of blacks to employment opportunities, sexual mores, women's rights, and many others. Then an individual who has "influence" with a group, by his acceptance and assent with the innovative patterns, persuades a new group to comply. Sometimes "controllers" of the flow of influence are local personages, but ever more frequently they are at a great distance, but have attained a special communication relationship with the individual they influence. This has been observed to be due to a "connection," for example, prestige in a common occupation; an honored leader; the showing of large numbers of people apparently similar to the group being influenced who have accepted the innovation; or famous or charismatic disseminators of general opinion, such as television commentators, clergymen, and national figures.

Of course, none of the above vitiates the impact of face-to-face relations on influence. People *are* influenced by those with whom they come in contact, with whom they have direct, primary relations. The shared communications, which are their structure, the decision, and the networks of people to accept or reject an idea—all of these are the interpersonal processes that intervene in mass-media influence. Mass society, in a communication sense, is far from anomic and disorganized, but it is structured, today as never before, about communication channels and complexes.

The acceptance of individuals as "legitimizers" of the new, that is, as having "influence," is in some respects identical to the psychological process called "identification" or acceptance as a "significant other." This process is said to describe the power that respected national union leaders have to direct boycotts of businesses or products and to convince persons to resist or submit to police. Certainly the effect is large.

Whether or not anonymous information can have this effect to any significant degree has not been determined quantitatively, but it seems likely that there is some diffusion of influence by this means. Especially may this be so, in that some individuals may be more susceptible for conscious or subconscious reasons. In any case, the claims of such ethologists as Konrad Lorenz and the belief of molecular biologists that behavior in compliance with influence will have a parallel effect on people close to each other, either physically or in any other communication sense, must be granted. Thus teenage girls often accept innovative styles and fashions that eventually percolate to older women.

It does appear, however, that leaders of opinion and influence in one area of social conduct may not have such influence in other areas. However, the two-step process of influence, as modified by mass-communication-developed interactional patterns seems to be a common occurrence.

Of course, in a bureaucratic situation, innovation can be mandated to a considerable degree, and compliance can be assured via the internal enforcement system of the bureacratic system. Even here, however, the two-step flow of influence can be demonstrated to make itself felt. Those new procedures that are validated by admired leaders will be more thoroughly and accurately instituted. Those that are scorned by significant leaders will be faultily performed, if at all.

The value of all the above to community and police managers is quite obvious. It emphasizes the value of being the subject of favorable messages by respected leaders and the mass media.[17] A police chief who has the most popular newspaper on his side has a good part of his work in police-community relations done for him. Granted that newspapers do not elect presidents they way they used to, they still control much of the information that gets to the public, especially since they review and comment on television news reports.

Of course, television reaches larger numbers of people—and with a particularly brilliant, vibrant style. The individual message, however, is often very short, for the television stations are under some constraints regarding "equal time" and the expense of production necessitates appealing to the largest Nielsen rating, rather than those parts of the community of interest and the police that are most concerned with specific issues in police-community relations. With a continuing program, an innovative leader in police or community might change this.

Campaigns to reduce racial prejudice, to cooperate to "support your local police," to report crime, or "to make this community a garden spot," all can be studied with a view to analyzing the pragmatic effect of the two-step flow principle. This can be important for this reason: Those who hope to have an impact on human behavior will have to become students of the two-step flow of influence. This involves the search for opinion leaders. Not those who merely proclaim themselves to be such or even those believed by other people to be such—though both the above examples tend to become self-fulfilling prophecies—but those who are identified by an empirical objective study of the facts of the flow of influence in field situations.

Opinion leaders are not a single class of persons who exercise their influence in the same way, and are thus easy to pick out of a card catalog or listing of "important" people. No, one must untangle the networks of interpersonal communications.

This expands the original communication model and reaches past simple, primary face-to-face communication, as the core of interactional patterning, toward the larger society and the resultants of its immersion in the multi-media. The old view of "Who has said what to whom . . . and what has been the effect?" which implied that the major initiative was with the sender of the communication, is too simple. It does not contain all the relevant variables. It omits the power of selection that the receiver has to pick and choose among the media messages contending for his attention.

Unless the receiver is "tuned-in," literally and figuratively, he will never receive the message, no matter how widely it has been broadcast. The choice of messages to which he will be exposed is decided on the basis of criteria that are under constant study by marketing people of all the large distributors of commercial and government information. The competition for the attention of receivers is fierce as the level of information perception reaches a saturation point. Today many people watch television morning, noon, and night, from six to twelve hours per day or more, and the time spent watching the tube is increasing each year. For certain individuals the ultimate asymptote of total immersion for twenty-four hours daily has already been reached!

The individual is forced to receive only the information that is disseminated. He is helpless in setting up the menu, as it were, but the menu is large and getting larger as ever more channels are opened up to public and commercial exploitation. As newspapers have become consolidated, so that today there is less choice among newspapers than ever before in the last one hundred years, the airwaves constantly increase the number of information streams directed toward receivers.

The community of police managers, striving to transmit messages to the community, must compete with experts. They must become experts, too. A part of this new expertise is the renewed verity that *sincerity* is one of the most valuable commodities that a pitchman can sell. Once the receiver has the slightest suspicion that he is being gulled, he can—and does—turn off manually, as well as cognitively.

The ability of receivers to "selectively perceive" specific content and ignore other aspects of a message has been studied and documented for decades. Now it is well known that a number of receivers can listen to the same transmitted message, say a political speech, and perceive entirely different messages.

This has been put to use by candidates, whose practice of speaking in "glittering generalities" is designed to exploit the selective perception of listeners. Thus the time and care spent in establishing an overwhelming "set" of positive approval of one's appearance, style, and manner by a galaxy of introductory clues may become as, or more, important in conveying a message than an actual appeal to specific arguments, even those directed to the self-interest of the receiver.

A serious student should look up the references cited to assist in the exploration of the newer, more complex communication models that might be applicable to particular problems. Receivers of information are rather intractable. They introduce their own "noise" and make their own decisions as to what the signs are or what they mean. Even when the signs are accurately perceived, they may ignore the significance, react in diverse ways, or selectively reject any or all of the signals.

The receiver is a system of response potentials, and the signals may, or may not, act to trigger responses. Ultimately, the communication process may be seen as bound more by the receivers' input than by any specific message from the sender! That is, at least as far as influence is concerned. This is not necessarily a denial of the power of operant conditioning as an influential process. Rather it notes that *influence may start long before the actual message.*

We know the signal is not merely a trigger that sets off completely independent responses. For behavior does change, under influence. To understand the dynamics we must consider the results of many communications, between many people, over longer periods of time, always remembering that there is a completely interactive relationship between senders and receivers.

There are still other considerations if one is to understand the ramifications of a useful communication model.

1. A communication once completed has a separate existence. It may be repeated by word of mouth or, if written, may be read and reread at intervals for an indefinite period of time. Each time this is done a communication event takes place once again, with perceivable consequences, which may be more important to a criminal-justice agency or to community performance than the successful accomplishment of a single program—"fallout" effects, as it were. On the other hand, the original communication may conflict with communications sent out at a later date with a different message.
2. All receivers of the communication have the potential of influencing the sender—or the "repeat sender." This influence can be active, by responding. Or it can be passive, by the nature of the receiver's image to the sender at the time the message was conceived, organized, and sent.
3. The intended receivers of a communication may not be the ones who are to be influenced. Secondary audiences or reference groups may be the ultimate target of intended influence, and, as such, this purpose should be decisive in determining the character and nature of the communication.

This points up, among other things, the importance, if one is to use the communication model effectively to change performance, of having information beforehand that clearly outlines the behavior anticipated, with as many substantial reasons as possible included in the message and the *addition* of organized face-to-face persuasion by persons with whom the receivers can identify.

Changes in values and attitudes, it appears, require a more extended "surround" of influence, in every dimension, temporal and environmental. Although more difficult to attain, successful changes in values will be more effective in the long run, for not only does such change ensure proper performance of mere actions, but it also provides the support and energy that leads to creative improvements and extension of the kinds of performance that are desired.

The development of a scientific attitude to community affairs, if it can be accomplished, can be a far more important accomplishment than a single action program. If this attitudinal change can be developed it should produce self-sustaining performance on every program and subprogram every day and everywhere that will be most productive in reaching police and community goals. Unfortunately we do not know reliable methods for changing values and attitudes. Until we have developed better methods of effecting such changes, we are forced to work with the attitude and value set in our existing environments.

The topical mix of values and attitudes existing at any given point in time appears to be a result of general familiarization by the mass media with a sequence of currently focused ideas, in which the topics of the day are assigned values. One year it may be the Vietnam war, the next, the Watergate scandals, local corruption, police heroism, or even an exciting sports event, with little observable effect on basic attitudes or values.

The modification of attitudes and values, like difficult cognitive matter, appears to demand a very high level of motivation, though not necessarily directed toward the objective of modification, per se. Methods that seem to have met with a reasonable degree of success commonly rely on a demanding person, significantly important to the receiver. If, additionally, messages of the existence of a widespread consensus among a related population can be conveyed, influence will be magnified. Undoubtedly, the key to self-sustaining goal-oriented performance is *attitude*—it is really a self-defining statement. In the last analysis, nevertheless, attitude, value, performance, and all will exist when *action* by the receiver confirms the existence of the intended influence without mental reservation. One is reminded of the Puritan dictum, "It is not enough to do good, one must also receive pleasure and happiness from doing good, else it is as naught."

Perhaps, as so much of behavioral science has proved, we are merely confirming ancient wisdoms.

The attainment of this high level of communication-oriented influence, in real-life situations, however, encounters a number of obstacles. Many of these obstacles have to do with ideals of liberty and privacy, which is the American entitlement under the Constitution. Nevertheless, the subject has been studied at great length in "total environment" situations, such as prisons, hospital wards, and prisoner-of-war camps.

The changing of attitudes via charismatic leaders with whom people can strongly identify is well known, even notorious, to such contemporary "happenings" and groups as followers of various gurus. The "Moonies" are only one example. The processes operating in political campaigns and administrations with "strong leaders" from bureaucracies to military forces are similar and appear to be effective communication vehicles when carefully applied over a period of months or years. Actually, the appearance of a unitary charismatic figure may be only the more dramatic instance of a process that is endemic. Many people remark about the attitude change a fourth-year college student manifests as compared with the person he was at his high-school commencement. This change is usually held to be the product of intensive communication experiences with schoolmates and teachers at the university, rather than the product of any physical or emotional maturation. Research findings here are inconclusive at present. On the other hand, it has frequently been noted, that the best rehabilitative treatment for juveniles is simply *aging*. The number of persons charged with violent crimes goes down dramatically when distributed along the age continuum. Age, or its concomitants, is a great peacemaker.

Diffusion of Information [18]

If Figure 5–1 is extended, that is, if the receiver becomes, in turn, a source of signals, we can expect such repetition to add "noise" to the transmission and eventually to extinguish the original message unless there are correct reinforcing signals via other transmitters and receivers from the original source.

This atomic view of diffusion of rumor and other information appears to model the actual diffusion of information as determined by research. The distortion of messages in the process of being communicated from person to person is a characteristic of special importance to police and community because of the great public excitement, disorder, and even violence that has resulted from unfounded rumors. A good deal of effort must be expended to dissipate rumors once they start, or, even better, to prevent them from arising in the first place.

The modification of message content is well illustrated by the ancient game of Pass the Word. In this game children (or adults) sit around in a circle and the "message source" whispers a phrase or a sentence into the ear of the person next to him. That person passes on the whispered phrase, as he or she understood it, and so on, until the end of the circle. The last player announces the phrase as he believes it to be. The foregone conclusion is that the phrase is quite often ridiculously different from the phrase that started the game. *Ecco rumor!*

It is a basic fact of group-human life that communication will occur. The communication will be about what interests people. They will be interested in everything that contacts, or seems to contact, their lives—and this includes, above all, police and community relations.

It behooves police and community leaders, therefore, to stay on top of every communication event, ready with correct information to allay public alarm with facts, lest rumor get the better of the situation and it run out of control.

The establishment of information bureaus, rumor-control centers, and press-information units or officers is now a regular part of police administration. To do their job efficiently a virtually continuous monitoring of media output is required. It is no longer sufficient to assign an aged or disabled officer to the task of razoring out newspaper items to be collected in a scrapbook and referred occasionally to the chief for his attention.

Not only is a visual monitoring of major news programs necessary, but a new staff service is now required in all large police departments to collect rumors from all sources and identify their origins and the paths by which they were diffused, and if the effort is warranted, to prepare plans to vitiate their effect.

Communication and Thinking Patterns [19]

There are many ways of thinking about thinking. Great scholars over the centuries have reminded us of their preoccupation with the subject of thought itself. René Descartes' comment "I think, therefore I am!" reveals that, in his opinion, thought was not only basic to existence, but without thought there could be no existence. There are many others who pursued even more intensively this subjective approach.

There is another group of philosophers, however, who try to retain the viewpoint of an outside observer. Charles Peirce, Percy W. Bridgman, and many of those who have been in the forefront of empirical science in this century hold that we can have no precise knowledge of thought itself or even of intuition. To believe that we do have is self-delusion, in their view. The reality of thinking is the reality of operationalizing a thought in one or more signs. It is our perception of the signs we use, to ourselves, that deceives us into the conclusion that we are aware of thought.

This internal soliloquy, the selection of signs, comparison of them, rearrangement and reallocation of them in the world within our cranium, is no different from the use of signs in person-to-person communication. It appears that we even use the same language signs in these inner dialogues with ourselves. It is as though we experience within ourselves, via signs, the mixing of experience signs with other experience signs, arranging and reordering, in a creative communications process within ourselves to reproduce the experience as we relate it to another or convince ourselves that, that was the way it really happened, could happen, or will happen.

Research appears to substantiate that the language we use in interpersonal communication is the same as the one we use internally in our own thinking. This language is one of signs and syntax of probable sequences of letter and syllabic frequencies, of temporal stops and starts, of visual, auditory, tactual, and other sensory symbolisms, all of which are well learned, habitual, and inevitable in their particular patterns of usage by any individual.

Nevertheless, the body of the language is not the body of the person. It is a learned adjunct to his personality, a foreign element in his brain and personality, not phylogenetically implanted but, as it were, painted on the structure of the organic human being.

Other languages can be painted over the structure to be used either in place of or in addition to a native language. We have all met people, born in one country, living for long periods in another, who gradually acquire a language mix that is neither their native tongue nor their adopted language. On occasion they will appear to have fluency in neither language. On rare occasions we encounter persons who seem completely bilingual, especially when the learning of the languages has been simultaneous, as when a child is brought up under bilingual conditions at home and at school.

In a very profound sense, however, all languages are foreign in that they are not instinctive biological reactions but depend on being acquired. This acquisition is not so ordered that anyone can say with perfect confidence that the language with which they communicate is so unequivocal in meaning and unsusceptible to different translation that the sign proffered is the correct one.

One suspects that the real reason no such guarantee can be given is because there is really no precise translation possible. Although the letters of the roman alphabet are the same in English, Spanish, French, German, Italian, Polish, and a number of other languages, the similarity is only superficial. In the first place, the sounds of each letter are different in each language. There are subtle nuances of sound and inflection that escape accurate description and are left to electronic reproduction by even the best teachers.

Except perhaps for the most simple sentences, and even there it is moot, cognitive meanings are different in each language. This is readily brought out in poetry. Translations of Schiller and Goëthe into English are poor imitations of the original in power and lyricism. The flavor of Racine, Hugo, and Anatole France is dissipated in English. The reverse is also true, of course. When translated into Spanish, *Hamlet and Macbeth* are . . . well, they are *not* Shakespeare.

As language reflects—and is—thought, the basic incongruity of ethnic and language enclaves in a large society is revealed as an almost impassable barrier to comity and agreement, except in areas that have become multi-lingual or have been preempted by the mass media.

Here, perhaps, is the unspoken motive for "representation" on police forces. Each group, certainly when language and culture are grossly at variance, but also, more invisibly, when "communities of interest" are involved, is isolated from influence on police or the larger society.

Each occupation, each technology, profession, job, position, role model, develops its own language and thought processes. A veritable Tower of Babel is being erected by the progressive increase in size and complexity of populous society.

The declaratory judgment of the Book of Genesis stands as a warning of what is to come. Can it be stayed—or repealed—by the mass media's new version of the melting pot?

Words [20]

Let us return to a more analytic review of what are the most important signs: *words*. Words have both meaning and emotional communication potential, although a given word may be held to hold more of one than of the other.

There is a difference, too, in a word as it is listed in the dictionary, and as it is uttered, as an *event*. In the dictionary, a word is defined as having a one-to-one relationship with a meaning. True, there are often many cases where a word is assigned several possible meanings, the precise one intended designated by the context of its use. The word "saw," for instance, is assigned a dozen or so meanings in the compact edition of the Oxford English Dictionary, with another dozen or so subsidiary uses, to boot. Nevertheless, a word listed in the dictionary has a definite, even if alternative, meaning, and the word is the symbol of that meaning, like a code.

As a word is uttered, as an event, or even when read in a continuous context, it becomes unique to that occasion, inextricably buried in and a part of the other words used at that time and on that occasion by that speaker or writer and perceived by that receiver.

The receiver cannot readily tear meaning out of and away from context. The attempt is often made, nevertheless, as when we hear cross-charges of ". . . but you said this, . . ." or ". . . you called me that!" Unless we have the full background and the actual context, what was called or who it was said is vitiated at later recountings. In such cases, the *"occasion* is the message."

Earlier in this chapter we considered a word as a sign of probable evidence of an entire message, in which emotion, semantics, associations, and connotations are all intertwined indissolubly and responded to without conscious thought. Of course, words come to have special meanings in themselves as words, rather than as symbols of other meanings with specific and particular emotional and associative content. For example, *freedom* and *democracy* are associated with a *good* feeling. Words such as *nigger, honkie, thief, sniveler,* and even *crybaby* convey a negative value judgment, as well as a semantic meaning.

Words have a reality as words, but they are often taken to be the reality of the meanings they are supposed to symbolize. When we apply the word *intelligence* to a person, we have placed him in a favored class of persons. However, we have not specified exactly what we mean. It may mean that we have seen him in various situations and he has reacted in a manner denoting an understanding of implications and a judicious selection of alternative responses. Or it may mean that we are familiar with the fact that on a standard intelligence test he scored within the upper two percentile of the general population, or, again, we may mean that he is a scintillating conversationalist. Whatever we may have meant, that individual is now labeled "intelligent," and we, and perhaps others acquainted with our judgment, will react to him in a certain way.

The difference between our judgment and reality is not mentioned and probably goes unnoticed, as it is with those cases where we use such labels as "nice personality," "friendly," "poised," "charming," "interesting," or "boring."

We are constantly faced with the dilemma of choosing the best words to aid our intended communication but still be brief. This choice must be from our individually limited store of remembered words, as physical embodiments of our message.

Part II

Psychosocial Contexts

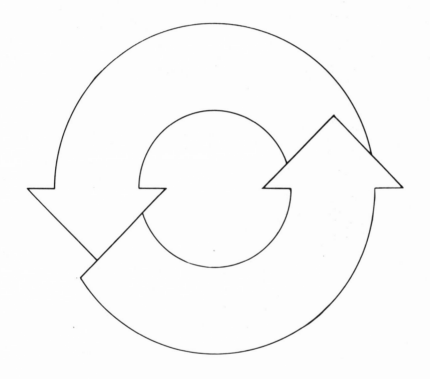

Chapter 6

INTERACTIONS

Nor let the beetle, nor the death-moth be your
mournful Psyche.
                    —John Keats, *Ode to Melancholy*

Here we reach for aid to cope with our central topic, police-
community relations, by going a bit further into applications of social
psychology.

The basic concepts are *interaction* and *personality*. We go on,
however, for the interactive relations that different personalities
have with each other and the fusion of these separate relations
and personalities in a cohering group create a new entity, a group-
personality, or ethos, that behaves like an overriding and separate
personality common to each member.

This dominant *ethos* of a people becomes as much a part of the
individual's ego-equipment in coping with life and its problems as
any other aspect of his personality and culture.

No study of police or community can ignore the overpowering
pressures of the prevailing and unquenchable thirst for liberty
permeating the American ethos.

What Is Interaction?

Interaction is the term used to denote the mutual adjustment of individual courses of action. In the ordinary course of events, individuals
do not act independently of each other; rather they act reciprocally to
influence each other's behavior even when not in each other's presence.
Individual actions are almost always performed with a view to their social
consequences, that is, what other people will do in regard to what the
individual is presently performing.

Thus, while communication as described in the previous chapter may
be involved, here communication is viewed as remembered or anticipated.
Actually, *that* is the point of *influence,* the effect of communication on
human beings that prevails *after* the fact. The concept of interaction can

be very useful in explaining and understanding human actions, which are so often based in social causation.

Interaction may involve many people at the same time, instead of only two, three, or a small number. The size of the group may be an important variable, capable of changing the number, quality, and nature of the interactions in many ways.[1] A small group—family, friends, work-unit— for instance, frequently will have immediate or long-term goals. In a large group such focus on the attainment of a single goal may be rarer, though it does happen on occasion, as in war, religious commitment, political campaigns, or even football rallies.

Researchers in this field have often assumed that the group tries to adapt to certain conditions posed by reality.[2] The actual findings of research indicate, however, that the group tries to control such factors as the behavior of its own members, its place and conditions of meeting, but tries to accommodate only to those factors it cannot control, such as the behavior of outsiders, the weather, and so on. Thus it encourages and enforces integration of the members with each other insofar as it serves the group.

A group's twin concentration on goal attainment and on internal controls to retain internal solidarity is what makes a group a social factor important to other groups and individuals. Goal-attainment efforts inevitably affect other people, and the control phenomenon keeps the group viable, able and ready to continue goal-attainment efforts.[3]

Almost every performance of a group will reveal these twin phenomena: goal attainment and internal controls. Community meetings demonstrate this in clear-cut style. First the meeting is called as a result of group integrative efforts. In fact, the calling of the meeting is an effort at forming or preserving the group. Then will come the discussion about the goal of the meeting—the group effort. During the course of the meeting there ordinarily will come comment about the pros and cons of the suggested goals—an evaluative phase. During this period emotional values will usually be displayed, positive and negative about the group and about the goal. Finally there will come increased concern with control of individuals and group. Decision, pro or con, is usually suspended at this point, with heightened feelings of well-being and contentment or unhappiness and dissatisfaction.

Of course, the same process can be observed in other group efforts during the course of its existence.[4] In almost every case it will be quite clear that the process is ongoing: a differentiation of roles, formal or informal, that apportions out the behavior and emotional reactions permissible to each role position, a division of labor, as it were.

The Role Concept

The role concept is one that has been discussed before.[5] The phrase describes the appearance of an apparent differentiation of performance and feelings that has been observed and reported for centuries by various commentators.

It is not necessary that a role be *assigned*. It may not be perceived as such either by the role player or by the other group members. It just seems to observers that it appears, like Topsy, and for identification purposes is given a name: role allocation. Once named, the concept can be verbally handled and defined as the rights and obligations of a group member. In formal groups many key roles may be explicitly given written descriptions, for example the role of a police captain or major in a police department or a job description in an industrial company. Informal groups develop roles without written notice and remain as a matter of general agreement.

There may be minor discrepancies as to how such roles are to be played by each member, but there is a large area of shared meanings in such role definitions. The actor and the other players know each other's role in intimate detail, literally thousands of information bits. They expect role compliance, and they enforce it by multiple policing measures, from wages to approval, from penalties to physical pain, from laudatory praise, even worship, to ostracism and expulsion.

The mutual expectations of role performance in all its elements or *normative anticipation*,[6] as it is called, demand obedience to norms within certain rather narrow tolerance limits. The roles, as systems of norms, order the behavior of each member, differentiating, allocating, and rationalizing individual and group efforts at goal attainment and group integration and identity. Inasmuch as this is attained, it can almost be said that the group, as an entity, has a role and a system of norms—an over-system of systems—as in the minds of insiders and outsiders that group acquires an identity, an ethos, or, as some have claimed, a soul, in recognition of the devotion to the group that can be elicited. Some examples are various organizations bound by a common religious faith and famous military units glory-bound in enemy territory.

The identity of such groups becomes as palpable as any other construct in the behavioral sciences, and it is treated as such by those who deal with such organizations as practitioners in police-community relations, as military commanders, or as charismatic religious leaders.

The Concept of Personality

The concept of personality [7] refers to the thought that each human being is a unique individual. It has philosophic, even religious, overtones and has been basic to political theories of democracy, liberty, and individual responsibility. Like most concepts of man, it can hardly be called a fact. Again, as we have repeated so many times before, regarding other concepts and models, and will again in this book, the daily reality that we observe appears to be explicable if we use the idea that each person is a specific complex of characteristics making him identifiable as a particular person.

The idea works in ordinary life: We recognize Joe and Susie, know their names, talk to them and about them, and when another person acts in a certain way we say, "That's just the way Joe would do it."

Joe is a particular entity to us. We can pick him out of a crowd, as we can Susie and hundreds of others.

The most appalling thing we can say about a person is to pick out one of his characteristics, skin color or slant of eyes, perhaps, and say, "Those people—they all look alike to me!"

Most people intuitively accept the concept that each person has a personality and that it represents the totality of who and what he is. The question remains however, just what is personality? How did it get that way?

These questions are sticky, and though it may be easy to obtain a consensus that personality exists, that does not mean that we could get agreement as to what it is. There are many theories of personality, which try to to answer some of the questions. Let us list a few of these propositions to illustrate the range of thought:

1. The Bible describes man as a working model of the Supreme Being, motivated with the desire to assert dominion over all living things (Genesis 1:26); he has free will, knowing good from evil (Genesis 3:5), and a permanent enmity toward women (Genesis 3:15) over whom he must rule (Genesis 3:16).

   Humans, as the Old Testament describes it, have always fought and killed and competed, loved and hated, though not all individuals have done so. Particular organizations of personality depend on early training, and there will, nevertheless, be differences between people, even unto those who will be violent (Genesis 6:5, 13; 9:5).

2. Other religious philosophies offer theories of personality ranging from a denial of any free will to a completely deterministic personal fate to a free-form random action and reaction chaotic psyche.

3. Behavioral science itself is comparatively young, and the theories that have sprung therefrom at irregular intervals are even younger. The fertile soil of philosophy has provided some, clinical experience others, laboratory experiments have contributed a share, and even mathematics has provided the conceptual tools for a few approaches.

We have already mentioned one of the oldest and most influential modern approaches to personality: *Psychoanalytic theory*. Taking some of the language of the ancient Greeks, and using much of their mythology as example, psychoanalysis is an intricate, comprehensive system based on the assumption that there are dynamic interactions of psychic forces that develop with maturation and environmental experiences.

Instincts are seen as a subsystem of the personality called the id. Present at birth, knowing nothing of reality, but only its own gratification, it is said to operate only on a *pleasure principle* by a *primary process* of forming mental images of the object desired, as in dreams, wishful thinking, and hallucinations.

Since these wishes cannot be satisfied merely by images, a second subsystem is called into play: the ego to deal with reality, to perceive, solve problems, organize and store knowledge, and act to achieve the real objects of desire in what is called the *secondary process*.

A third subsystem of the personality, a hierarchy of values, is acquired at first from nurturing parents, then other members of society, particularly those with close, intimate relations with the individual. This superego includes conscience and tends to place *values* of good or bad, right or wrong on everything of which it becomes aware.

As a mnemonic device, far less than a full statement of this theory, it can be said that the id represents the phylogenetic, or biologic, inheritance that is present at birth but may not appear until physical maturation; the ego represents psychological aspects of the personality; and the superego represents the social aspects.

Since its introduction by Sigmund Freud, psychoanalytic thought has been greatly modified by his disciples, who placed different emphases on various mechanisms by which the personality is seen to operate.

Anxiety, a basic concept, is a state of tension that seeks release. Freud, himself, distinguished three types of anxiety: *reality* anxiety, stemming from threats in the real world; *neurotic* anxiety, arising when id impulses break through ego controls, and *moral* anxiety, springing from feelings of guilt.

In each type, anxiety energizes the organism to deal with a perceived hazard and to eliminate it. If rational action does not suffice, the ego is forced to use irrational measures. The irrational measures, distorting or denying reality, operate on an unconscious level and are called *defense mechanisms. Everyone* uses defense mechanisms.

Freud emphasized the concepts of deveolpmental stages in the formation of personality and their crucial importance; the interplay of id, ego, and superego; and the concepts of anxiety and defenses against anxiety. Most subsequent personality theory incorporates these ideas.

Stimulus-response theories of personality grew out of Pavlov's early experiments in conditioned reflexes, which indicated that a living organism's response to stimuli could be transferred to other stimuli. Learning theory grew out of this, documented by the early work of J. B. Watson and later by many others. Although there are many different approaches based on the stimulus-response concept, all are concerned with the change in behavior patterns that occurs with planned and unplanned experiences. The stimulus-response concept commonly avoids introspection, and intuition and such mediating processes as perception, interpretation, and reasoning. As a group they are called S-R theories.

Primary drives, such as hunger, thirst, fear, and anger, are recognized. *Secondary drives* are learned in the individual's social context. *Cues* are stimuli that can be distinguished as arousing the organism and indicating direction for appropriate response. *Response* is behavior aimed at reducing drive. *Positive reinforcement* (reward) reduces drive, which strengthens the bond between stimulus and response; *negative reinforcement* (punishment) weakens the bond between stimulus and response and decreases the likelihood of the response being elicited by the next application of the stimulus.

Personality, in S-R theory, is the total pattern of all the S-R bonds that are built up with living experiences—active and dormant, inhibited or released. Which bonds are established, remain, or become extinct depend upon the organism's biological or acquired physiological attributes and previous state of S-R bonding.

It has been observed that anxiety-filled bonding experiences are often highly resistant to extinction and tend to generalize associated stimuli to other situations. Too, preverbal learning appears not to be "labeled" in a way that permits it to be recalled consciously or communicated to others. Thus it is more difficult to be identified and made the subject of relearning situations. Persuasive as the argument is, S-R theory has been criticized for ignoring such complex cognitive processes as the concept of self.

Self theories of personality, of which there are many, see the *self* as the unifying force in human behavior. The self is the experience of the awareness of being and functioning. From this, the theory reaches for a set of overlapping ideas in the various presentations, predicated on the subjective experience of which the individual is the center. Thus to the individual, his perceptual field *is* reality, and all experience is translated into terms compatible with maintenance or enhancement of his self. Behavior, then, is simply goal-directed attempts to satisfy his sensed needs. Since his perceptual field is unique to him, his behavior will exhibit unique manifestations.

Existential theories of personality spring from the ruminations of a number of philosophers reacting, in part, against contemporary changes in values and traditions. Sören Kierkegaard, Martin Heidegger, Jean-Paul Sartre, Paul Tillich, Rollo May, Erich Fromm, Gordon Allport, and Abraham Maslow are only some of the contributors to this view of the human role and condition.

The holding is that man's drive is to find the "best possible" way of life, which means to actualize all his potential and to "fulfill" himself. Because the guides for this goal today are not clear, however, man is confused and under deep strain. Two solutions are offered:

1. Surrender the quest, and submerge into the group; or
2. Strive unceasingly for that fulfillment, which is the complete sense of *Being* (as contrasted with non-Being, which has various levels, the most complete of which is death).

Thus existentialism calls on the ability of man to reflect on and question the details of his own existence. The essential freedom of man is basic to this theory of personality, with the power to choose new patterns, and the ability to translate new insights into action. Existentialists see social life as leading to anxiety. Because it emphasizes individual behavior and value schemes, existentialism has been accused of moral nihilism. Its attack on norm compliance is pervading, and it calls for a more daringly innovative approach to all problems of human existence, with all challenges to be met with courage and determination.

Trait theories of personality have become common coin in everyday speech. We call people lazy, dishonest, maladjusted. Employers ask for workers who will be punctual, industrious, courteous, and honest. Police departments constantly seek candidates who will be observant as patrol officers, meticulous in their clerical tasks, and astute as detectives. Attempts to formalize these criteria have been mainly a matter of description and classification of intuitively perceived variables. This is not to say that the gist of trait theory is a static list of attributes. It reaches for a dynamic explanation of behavior and personality as these traits interplay and overlap.

The great advantage of the trait theory to the behavioral scientist is that many tests and scales have been developed to "operationalize" these traits in forms that demonstrate different degrees of a trait. The tests identify negative versus positive valences, are replicable with a considerable degree of reliability when measuring some individuals—that is, the same results recur—demonstrate varying degrees of correlation with each other, and thus have been found useful by personnel administrators and others in charge of the selection, training, promotion, and retention of personnel in many large and important bureaucracies. Scales and tests for traits have been used in school for the classification and assignment of children to various types of schools, special classes, and training programs.

Unfortunately, there have sometimes been gross errors, and children have been sent to schools utterly inappropriate to their nature and capabilities. For example, children fully able to cope with life's problems in a mature way have sometimes been placed in schools for the retarded. The existence of these tests, and this concept of personality, is tempting to administrators faced with great problems in the management of people and the necessity of making decisions as to their fate.

In recent years there has been some tendency to call for "psychological tests" of police candidates in the natural administrative desire to avoid the cost and casualties of mistakenly hiring mentally disturbed, emotionally unstable, or potentially dishonest persons or persons with other undesirable traits.[8] This is usually met with great resistance by various groups who feel their potential employment opportunities are thereby diminished if they do not represent the most favorably situated ethnic bloc. Some of these tests and scales have been discarded by order of the highest courts in several states as being not provably valid in selecting or promoting the most meritorious candidates.

Nevertheless, the notion of personality inherent in the trait concept is current everywhere for ordinary use in understanding and predicting behavior. An intensive survey a generation ago found almost eighteen thousand terms used to describe human traits. It is essential to select from among this huge number a more manageable few that will serve the purpose of usefully describing personality.

A mathematical technique, factor analysis, has been adapted to select among all conceivable traits those fewer *primary* traits that underlie patterns of interrelated secondary traits. Assuming the validity of the basic assumptions of factor analysis, a researcher can reduce his concern to sixteen or twenty primary traits. However, the particular traits selected vary from study to study. At any given time in recent years there are a number of such factor analyses going on, attempting to resolve such questions as: primary traits necessary in probationary officers, if they are to be judged good police officers five years hence; how to select people who will work best in community settings; accident-proneness, and many other interesting and important problems.

Whether this technique is suitable for identifying basic personality variables common to all people is doubted by many. There is even doubt that there are such common dimensions to personality. Too, there is objection to the lack of weight given to the matter of *self*, of unique individuality.

Today there are a number of attempts, using computer models of human learning and problem solving, to come to a more accurate understanding and predictive ability regarding human personality.

In sum, the problem in devising theories of personality at the research level is the dilemma of choosing between significant problems, which can be handled only by somewhat subjective, immeasurable means, and trivial problems, which are amenable to rigorous methods. We can learn, it seems, a lot that we can rely on about very unimportant matters; but about matters of the human personality that are important, we are still reduced to rule of thumb and trial by error.

Research is continuing—discoveries come almost daily—but the issue, as usual, is in doubt. Nevertheless, by familiarizing one's self with theories of personality that are current, the community and the police practitioner may be given a better grasp on the stuff of human personality and be better able to deal with the human problems encountered.

Normal and Abnormal Personalities

The term abnormal implies that there is a "normal." In dictionary terms, normal refers to what is average. Mathematics, too, uses normal in an "average" sense, although it provides a number of different averages, each useful for a different objective. Thus a "normal line," is a line equidistant in angular terms from each side of a straight angle, and therefore, under our current terminology, 90 degrees from either side. Mathematics also provides what is called the arithmetic mean as an "average," but also uses other "averages," such as the median and mode of a frequency distribution.

There is a difference between the term *norm* as a sociological idea having to do with expected performance or states of being and *normal* as a psychological concept.

None of the behavioral sciences has been able to describe the normal personality in precise terms. However, most would agree that normal behavior will represent optimal development and functioning of the individual consistent with long-term well-being and progress of the group. Such words as *optimal, well-being,* and *progress* are indefinite enough to make us uneasy. Since we have seen the multiplicity of groups with which an individual is simultaneously involved, we must be just as unhappy with the word *group.* After all, to *which group* are we referring?

The problem of defining abnormal personality is even more difficult. In a statistical sense abnormal would mean any deviation from the normal, or, if there are tolerance limits for normality, from the majority of the normal. Psychologists, however, opt for a sense of *pathology* in this term, a pathology, however, that will be as valid in one culture as in another and will distinguish between desirable and undesirable deviations. This includes, in practice, sexual deviations, juvenile delinquency, drug addiction, psychoneuroses, psychoses, peptic ulcers, alcoholism, and even unethical business practices, and a wide number of other "deviations," including mental illness, mental disorders, and psychiatric disorders.

On the other hand, there are many eminent psychiatrists and psychologists who deny that there is such a thing as mental illness merely on the basis of a finding of abnormality. In this view the unrequitable urge to steal cars would not be seen as pathological but as a rational solution to the problem of obtaining the use of a car.

Nevertheless, thousands of people are hospitalized for alleged mental illness, tens of thousands more are "treated" in rehabilitation centers and reformatories. In view of the conflicting opinions, one is not surprised at the low rate of successful treatment and the high rate of recidivism. It is surprising, however, to discover that mental illness incapacitates more people that all other problems combined. Almost one-half of this country's hospital beds are occupied by mental patients, and it is estimated that one-tenth of the population is hospitalized for mental illness at some time in their lives.

The figures are even more impressive when we note that for every diagnosed mentally ill person, public-health authorities report there are some twenty more who are not hospitalized but are seriously incapacitated for emotional or mental maladjustment.

If we do the calculation: 22 million people now alive will be hospitalized for mental illness, and public-health authorities claim there are twenty times as many, that is, 440 million, seriously incapacitated; obviously, we are left with a palpable statistical absurdity. Who is left to be "average" in any sense?

The ramifications of statistical arguments and the distorted impressions that are sometimes left by uncritical acceptance of "figures without fact" will be discussed in Chapter 11. There is no doubt, however, that all of this has a serious impact on police and community affairs. The number of certifiably "unstable" people is legion, and the fact stands as a warning to PCR practitioners in all their programmatic efforts. This fact of life must be handled without exaggerating its importance and without using it overmuch as an excuse for unsatisfactory performance.

In point of fact, spectacular abnormality is not usually important. The difficult problem is the imperfectly drawn line between the normal and the abnormal, as people differ by imperceptible degrees, with most people clustering about a central point as to any identifiable characteristic. Too, individuals will change from time to time, the cause apparently associated with a variety of factors.

Though medical scientists are often able to separate physical pathology from health, there are intrinsic and extrinsic factors that render this difficult in regard to mental conditions, which apparently includes personality. As long as behavior, presumably the result of an individual's personality, does not transgress the law, police and community people must accept it at face value.

The view of lawyers and those familiar with the practices of certain other countries is that the use of alleged diagnoses of personality as a base for identification as a member of a class, a potential patient, or a "non-citizen" in any way is a tool so dangerous in the hands of government that it should be forbidden at all costs.

The idea behind "personality" is that in some ways a person's behavior is predictable if we know what kind of a person he is. If we know what his predispositions are, the presumption is that he will tend to behave in a certain way, all other things being equal. It would be interesting if we could apply the same idea to groups. This we undertake in the next section.

Application to Groups

Personality in formal behavioral science is a term always applied to individuals. However, it involves a number of presumptions, is subject to controversial opinions, and has not, to this date, been overly convincing at a rigorously scientific level to many scientists and other persons. Nevertheless, it has been a useful concept. Would it not be as useful if we were to try to apply it to groups?

The *personality* is the largest possible unit in psychology and the smallest possible unit in the study of groups. Social psychology focuses on "individuals in groups." The *role*, in this sense, is the acquiescence of the personality to the demands of the group.

Theorists have noted that every group develops a constellation of roles definable in terms of expected rights and obligations, that is, a *status system*. These rights and obligations regulate the relations between occupiers of different status systems.

Some status positions are *ascribed* in that they are the result of being born into a position, for example, family connections, age, sex, religion, nationality, ethnic background. A child is expected to obey his mother. Despite recent changes in popular conceptions of appropriate roles, the courts of domestic relations will still, all other things being equal, grant a mother preference over a father when it comes to questions of caring for a young child. Some statuses are better described as *achieved*, as the rights and obligations attending the president of a university, a religious figure, a policeman, or a community leader.

Every individual is seen as filling a set of statuses, as he or she concurrently occupies the positions of parent, child, employee, club member, little-league coach. An enumeration of all a person's concurrent statuses is called his status set. Each status set is conceived as being related to other status sets, on either a horizontal or a vertical bearing. The status set of the president of a corporation is deemed to rank higher than the janitor, because of its higher prestige and desirability.

Differences in status sets without any vertical ranking are such as the comparison between the status of a professor of physics with a professor of law. Within the university there may be no difference in rank, though there is obviously a horizontal difference in kind.

Under other circumstances, the rankings of the two professors may change. For example, within the physics department, it is very likely that the doctor of philosophy would have more prestige than a law professor who happens to be teaching a course on the legal liabilities involved in radiation hazards. As to a question of law, however, the opinion of the professor of law would be given more weight, and his position more deference, than the physics professor.

Tedious though it may be to enumerate such horizontal and vertical matrixes of prestige and the relationships of status sets, they can be instantaneously summed up in individual and group reaction to real-life perceptions.

The continuity and predictability of these group reactions give groups a patterned, even unique predisposition. As roles are assumed and become habituated to the individual, a group becomes more than the mere summation of the role positions that defined it orginally. To observers, there appears to be a spillover, or integration, of role-position patterns.

Actually, the role concept has at least three different aspects:

1. *Prescribed* roles: Expectations of the group as to a position holder;
2. *Subjective* roles: Position holders expectations of their own attitudes and performance;
3. *Overt* roles: Actual performance of the position holders, in social interaction with other position holders.

Ideally, of course, the three aspects of role are identical. In life, however, there are varying degrees of lack of correspondence between them. We need not be surprised at this when we consider the multiplicity of status sets and the interactional rules that distinguish each paired set of roles as they interact with each other.

A police lieutenant, for example, is in the middle of a set of role expectations that vary as to his sergeants, his police officers, his captain, and other officials of higher rank. When to this we add the patterns of behavior expected of him by community members of various positions, from juveniles and clergymen to political officeholders, complainants, and suspects, and compound all with literally thousands of similar set statuses in a large police department, the uniqueness of that organization's "personality" as compared with that of any other organization is unquestioned. The personality, and even—to stretch the application of another concept a bit—the *ethos* of the New York City Police Department is unmistakably different from that of the Los Angeles Police Department, and both are different from the Miami Police Department. Granted there are many similarities, as there are between individuals—but it is the *differences* that make personality identifiable.

The establishment of the *personality* (or, if preferred, the ethos or even group attitude) of the entire police department and a determination of how it will interact with communities of interest may be a productive effort to a community or police executive.

Motives and Incentives

Personality and the Social Order

Certain people, identified by psychologists as "antisocial," exhibit a marked lack of ethical or moral development. In terms of role models they do not perform as expected. Too, they may not expect the usual of others. They are frequently in trouble, profit little from experience or punishment, and maintain no real loyalties to any person, group, or code.

The American Psychiatric Association [9] uses a category called sociopathic personality disturbance, with subclasses of antisocial reaction, dyssocial reaction, sexual deviation, and addiction to alcohol or to drugs.

The number of people that can be denoted as antisocial is difficult to estimate, but practicing psychologists have included in their consideration shady performers, from lawyers, doctors, and businessmen to evangelists and politicians. The rush to such classification sometimes reaches for prostitutes, rapists, and imposters of all kinds. Because only about 1 percent of all first admissions to mental hospitals include a diagnosis such as this, and in view of the large number of such admissions, a question mark must be added to a substantial part of the mythical "average" population.

The issue, as far as police-community relations (PCR) is concerned, is pointed up because antisocial personalities are often likable, intelligent, even spontaneous. However, their life is concentrated on the "now," without real consideration for past or future and with a certain callous disregard for the rights, welfare, or happiness of others. The irresponsibility and impulsiveness they manifest have been described as emotional immaturity. The considerable intelligence they show in excuses and rationalizations for their behavior often saves them from the sanctions often administered to other norms breakers.

Pejorative descriptive phrases are often used by clinical specialists to describe their personalities—inadequate, schizoid, cyclothymic, emotionally unstable, passive-aggressive, compulsive—none of which, it appears, has offered much help to either community or police specialists in dealing with them. Descriptions as to possible causal processes involved in the development of such personalities include, once again, pejorative rather than operational descriptions: inadequate conscience development; egocentric, with low frustration tolerance developed from prior experience with others; hedonism combined with unrealistic goals as a result of never having learned to delay satisfaction; acting out of tensions and anxieties, rather than to worry about them; playing a theatrical role to impress and exploit; psychosocially developed rejection of parents' constituted authority and discipline; learning deficiency prevents acquisition of skills and profiting from mistakes. But, of course, such phrases can and have been used as invectives rather than impartial scientific comment. Whether or not they have technical, factual meaning to clinicians, the use of these diatribes does not offer much help to community or criminal justice practitioners.

The effect such persons have on the social order may be obvious to some. However, when we consider the large number of persons describable in these terms, one is tempted to feel at first bewildered and then dismayed at the impossible job of separating them—if that were legally possible—from the rest of humanity.

Problems of the social order remain. The dynamics of PCR appear to be unpiercable by recourse to study of the antisocial personality. The concept of personality, as far as antisocial types are concerned, appears to rely upon trait theories of personality and is subject to the weaknesses of such theories. It is however, a frequent recourse in clinical and evaluative situations.

The motivations of the antisocial personality, as described, would appear to rise in his jaundiced view of the world and of his desire to attain personal objectives without the hindrance of compliance with specific role expectations.

Other approaches to personality do not appear much more useful to the practitioner in police-community relations and community affairs generally than the one just described. Our traditional libertarian views of the right to privacy and of the value of individual freedom and responsibility make any planned behavior modification, except, possibly as therapy, a device not available to modern community problems.

Conscious and Unconscious Motives

There appears to be great consensus on the probability of the existence of unconscious and subconscious motives that affect the personality and, consequently, the performance of people. Several theories of personality assume the existence of such motives. On a clinical basis, there is considerable evidence that such motives can be disclosed, understood, modified, or diverted. On a wider canvas, using a sociological model, the analysis is even more complex and subject to variables either not within the knowledge or control of police-community people or forbidden to them under the constraints of law.

Oliver Wendell Holmes has said that it may not be true that people ever have a conscious or reasoned moment in their lives, but we must assume rationality in people or the whole structure of civilized intercourse falls for lack of responsibility.

Although this space does not permit a full discussion of psychosocial contexts of motivation, it can be said that motivations of behavior, in a Freudian, psychoanalytic sense, are the product of "energy structures." Layer on layer of derivative motivational structures can emerge. Again, however, the literature does not reveal that these concepts have been operationalized in ways that have been useful to community practitioners.

Many psychological theorists, however, emphasize that the motivation for directed action can arise from structural considerations—that is, an innate desire for order and coherence in the perceived universe. This urge toward a world view that is consistent may motivate a grossly distorted view of objective reality and consequent behavior, attitudes, and emotions that would otherwise be incomprehensible.[10]

Symbolic Interaction [11]

We spent quite a bit of space and time on the communication model in Chapter 5, noting that words or signs are objects in themselves, but also that by habituated association, they can become symbols of other objects or symbols of the attributes of other objects. Such psychoneurological symbolic association is not restricted to simple words or signs. The human limit of this associational ability has not been determined, but it manifests itself in countless ways during every living moment.

We proposed, in that previous chapter, that words or signs stand for what it is agreed they shall stand for. The agreement, however, in the natural development of language is not necessarily an act of conscious volition. We learn a language, unconscious of any process, by merely doing it.[12] The associations of a language have sometimes been said to be merely social conventions, but once established, they are not something that can be put off lightly. Sometimes they cannot be put off at all, no matter how energetic the effort.

Language habits, once ingrained, are extremely difficult to eradicate. The persistence of "foreign" accents, syntax, gestures, and facial expressions demonstrates how deeply ingrained symbolic associations can become and how psychologically necessary they are.

Symbolic association is not restricted to language. It appears to be immanent, to at least some degree, in every paired experience in which one event becomes associated with the other, and, in effect, there is an interactional relationship established between the two events, such that one may symbolize—or "stand for"—the other. Recall from psychoneurologic memory may be conscious or subconscious. Having occurred in the past, it is recalled to the present. Actually, the past event may have occurred only "symbolically" by reference to other past symbolic associations.

Thus symbols become identified with objects and events and as far as the individual is concerned are treated as the object and interacted with as though they are the objects or events. Any social act is essentially a meaningful communication. Through symbolic interaction with others, the tiniest infant commences to develop a personality. Such symbolic interaction with significant other people must be continued, all evidence indicates, for the babe to grow into a functioning person. Cessation of symbolic interaction is devastating to the human personality, as the experience of prisoners condemned to solitary confinement proves. Under such conditions of deprivation of face-to-face interaction, the prisoner's use of symbolic interaction—of words, books, pictures, remembered events of all kinds—becomes the only thread to follow to locate his own identity. Benvenuto Cellini in describing the retention of his sanity in his *Autobiography* recites the importance of keeping a calendar on the wall of his dungeon, inscribing a crucifix with all the sacred symbolism of that holy token, identifying scurrying rats as companions, recalling past scenes and hoped for new ones, as imagery on the screen of his memory. All this is symbolic interaction.

When words are used, for example, *pig*, the *Man, politician, PR, nigger, Watts, Chicago Seven, civil rightist, honky,* their symbolic meanings often take over, and they are reacted to from the wealth of symbolic meanings that have been annexed to these symbols. The symbolic meaning of a threatening gesture is as frightening, perhaps more so, as a physical blow and is often treated as such.

The obvious symbolism of the "V-Sign" of uplifted fingers is only a simpler version of the great, complex patterns created out of symbolism or expressed through symbolism.[13]

Thus our motivations and incentives eventuate from the *symbols,* rather than from reality elements. We spend our lives making associative symbols and then reacting to them.

Attitudes, Values, and "Sets"

Predispositions of various kinds have been given names by behavioral scientists.[14] We are familiar with some of them from ordinary life: habits, beliefs, motivations, traits, preferences, tastes. Very commonly discussed are observations of what appear to be stable tendencies to accept or reject broad *classes* of situations, such as entire groups of people, religions, political beliefs.

Such preferences are called attitudes and are a species of prejudgment, although the term is without the denigrative connotation of "prejudice." Most of us have encountered this phenomenon in reality, and a positive or negative attitude to classes of things is as commonly found as are people. They are as much a part of our personality, however we define that elusive term, as the ability to form associations of any kind and in that sense can be seen as a part of that process.

Police and community people are always interested in "attitude to the police," "attitude to the increasing (or decreasing) rate of crime."

To the extent that we have predispositions to be favorable or unfavorable to an object or event of a class, we are said to have attitudes. In any case, there are any number of instruments that have been devised to measure this predisposition, whether or not it exists in the form in which it is conceptualized. It is a useful idea, because it can lay the groundwork for measures designed to change those attitudes from unfavorable to favorable in regard to police and community efforts.

*Value*s is the term denoting a very broad and rather abstract predisposition toward ideologies and qualities, such as materialism, altruism, hedonism, ethnocentrism, honesty, chastity, neatness, work ethic, and others of this sort. There is, however, no very sharp distinction between attitudes and values as ordinarily used by behavioral scientists.

The same overlap can be noted in the concept *set,* which refers to a more temporary condition, usually involving the muscular tension of sets of muscles, as well as mental anticipation of the need for a certain response, usually physical in nature. The concept is of particular use in police-community relations because of the numerous street incidents involving what appears to be psychological and muscular sets responding violently, once the appropriate setting has been established.[15] One example of this is the response of a policeman when he receives a radio call announcing an armed robbery in progress. His entire organism will take a "set," preparing him for alert, vigorous action under dangerous conditions. Hormones flow, blood pressure goes up, muscles tense; his mind is alert, his eyes sharpen for signs of the reported offender. His reactions under such conditions are likely to be quick, with strong muscular action, and violence not too far away. His reactions to a motorist innocently blocking his way are likely not to be as calm or polite as prior to the taking of the "set."

Just as many cases coming to the attention of police-community specialists arise from a similar set affecting the reactions of ghetto youth on being ordered to move on by police authority. Of course, sets can be toward a mild, even passive reaction as well—under different circumstances.

All three, attitudes, values, and sets, are of importance in police-community matters, and all three have been the subject of considerable research. Attitudes, however, appear to have received the most attention. Tremendous amounts of work have been done in attitude measurement, in measuring the effect of attitudes of various kinds on the variables involved in police-community relations and in how to change attitudes in the endeavor to minimize the behavior that unfavorable attitudes are presumed to encourage.

Whatever the nature and dynamics of attitudes in the personality, it seems quite clear that our methods of examining them, our instruments and how we use them, will define the reality of whatever attitudes will mean to the researcher. At this point it is enough merely to state that attitudes, values, and sets are treated by behavioral researchers as though they are an objective reality affecting the performance of people involved in police and community matters.

Alienation [16]

Discrepancy between expectations and promises of life as contrasted with rewards actually attainable seems to have resulted in themes of frustration and estrangement, which have evoked sympathetic responses from many groups other than the individuals directly affected.[17]

Roles and values that attain prominence almost overnight often come up against the consent of significant numbers of the population. Life-styles and manners, from community control of schools and Black Power to Gay

Power and Equal Rights for Women, are seen as offensive or even in contravention of biblical injunction. While urbanism, itself, may not breed alienation,[18] the lack of structural relationships between the slum-area people and the other parts of the city make it unlikely that the slum dweller can really learn the norms and roles that would mean full integration into a single society of common interests. Failing that commonalty, alienation, the identification of strangers as enemies, seems the only natural consequence to be expected.

Thus the concept of alienation has not only subjective but also objective components, having to do with the individual's objective situation in a social structure.[19]

It appears that increased reward can reduce the attitude of alienation,[20] thus affecting long-term value systems more toward the direction of materialism in a regenerative cycle. The effect of this on police-community relations has not been determined as yet, although it is the subject of much ongoing research. There are a number of community programs in which juveniles have been put on allowances for their continued avoidance of being caught up in the criminal-justice system. There are others in which former juvenile delinquents are put on salary and directed to maintain their contacts with youth gangs to convey the message that cooperation with the greater community is not all that bad and to aid some of the youngsters on a more personal, intimate basis than would be possible to a social worker who would not have the background of common experience that allows communication with potential delinquents.

In his early writings, Karl Marx offered his theory that alienation is caused by the impact of technology on human relations.[21] The machine system, he held, tended to become paramount to the employee's freedom, turning him into a mere instrument, engendering a feeling of powerlessness. The division of labor, which reduced the area of responsibility and understanding of the employee, was seen as having the same effect, compounded by a loss of meaningfulness to the employees' main concern in life, his occupation.[22]

Alienation has been the term of choice to describe the attitude of those swarms of people who turn to wholesale looting when favorable opportunities arise, such as police strikes, electrical failures resulting in blackouts, or major disasters from floods, fires, and hurricanes, in which the established order tends to become disestablished by more "primitive" instincts.

It is difficult to find studies that are not contaminated by bias and prejudgments. Often the purported moral superiority of researchers interferes with any effort at impartial investigation. One recent example of this, a case of looting during a blackout, was the target of agonized cries against "savages who would take advantage of a disaster."

This high preachment was met with an appeal to an even higher moral law: "We must not blame poor people who take what they need to eat, or take what they've been taught are good to have, but will never be able to afford."

Following this was the discovery that a majority of those arrested for looting had jobs and could at least afford more than welfare recipients. This was taken up by the first faction as justification for demanding long penal servitude for the arrestees.

After this evaluation it was necessary to face the reality that the cost of supporting large numbers of people in jail could not be equated with the value of what they had stolen or could possibly steal in the foreseeable future.

But the next move in the scenario was to remind all concerned that it was "necessary to make an example, whatever the cost, otherwise no one and no one's property would ever be safe in the city again."

The implications of all this for police and community may be profound, but it is unfortunately quite undecipherable.

From our previous discussions about community, norms, and compliance, it might be commented that looting was seen as an opportunity to improve without violating any firmly established norms against it—particularly since the store owners were seen as strangers, if not enemies. Perhaps there is not much difference between the attitudes of alienation felt by those who were without a job and those who were employed. The feeling of estrangement—a pervasive attitude—is manifested frequently in our multi-cultural society, with competitive stances rather than cooperative positions being common.

Chapter 7

CONFRONTATIONS AND CONFLICTS

What is a minority? The chosen heroes of this earth
have been in a minority. There is not a social, political, or religious privilege that you enjoy today
that was not bought for you by the blood and tears
and patient suffering of the minority. It is the
minority that have stood in the van of every moral
conflict, and achieved all that is noble in the history
of the world.
—John Bartholomew Gough, *What Is a Minority?*

In this chapter we turn to one of the most exasperating aspects of police-community relations. All of criminal justice is involved in nothing more than conflict and confrontation—and the police are in the front line.

Tension is the lot of all members of every community. For the community is pervasively erosive always, especially in the ghettos of central cities, where life is savage, at best, nor does habitude ease its pain or penury. Community life, it seems, is tensioned life.

The very foundations of government in this country have trembled at issues that commenced with low-level perceptions of conflict and confrontations, which then escalated to shake two Presidents loose from their high office.

The qualities of life that are injured by the state of tension in the community are the very qualities that communal life cherishes most. Thus, the expression and suppression of internal conflict is what police-community relations is all about.

The Benefits of Conflict

Confrontation and conflict, contrary to the conclusions of many people and even some behavioral scientists, are not necessarily dysfunctional, either for individuals or communities.[1] The survival value of aggression and conflict is well documented.

Confrontation, which contains the seeds of violence against perceived potential enemies, serves to identify such foes to members of the community who might not otherwise be aware of the enemy's role. This is an educational experience and is exhibited among birds, dogs, insects, and men.[2]

This phenomenon appears to be quite common where group survival has been important to survival of the species. The intensity of a confrontation against outsiders is increased as its locale approaches the insiders' demographic center. Vigorous defense inside home territory is frequent and highly visible in many species, including man.

Still another function of confrontation and conflict is its ability to extend a community's turf, as well as to more clearly differentiate it from other communities, in affirmation of a proud identity.

Yet another frequently noted consequence of conflict is the identification and selection of future community leaders, developing a ranking order among them and among the other members of the community as a necessary preliminary to successful organization for common purposes.

The training of leaders by confrontation and conflict and the tempering effect such training has on their abilities appear to have paramount community survival value. Behavioral scientists have discovered considerable evidence to indicate that conflict is the consequence of specific frustrating situations. However, just as much evidence tends toward the conclusion that conflict and aggression are not merely reactive to such outside stimuli but, on the contrary, will arise spontaneously from inborn phylogenetic urges. Insofar as the latter is true, as to the natural history and phylogeny of conflict, it is unrealistic to expect that removing all frustration—were that possible—would eliminate community conflict. Conflicts will appear notwithstanding the most strenuous efforts to eliminate cause, to suppress, or to confine participants. The simple fact is that conflict appears because we are built that way; and thus conflict will exist in any community devised.

It is not a question of whether conflict and aggression satisfy any basic human need—it is merely that the efforts of those desiring to ameliorate police-community relations are not economically directed if excessive attention is given to the elimination of outside stimuli to conflict. It would appear to be more efficient in a cost/benefit sense to try to *redirect* the spontaneous or induced aggression into channels that offer hope of more productive end results than bloody noses, burned-out stores, not to say dead police officers and citizens.

Perhaps that is one of the subliminal rationales for the frequent occurrence of police athletic leagues all over the United States, despite their costs, lack of identifiable benefits, and much negative criticism, particularly by those who yearn for "professionalism" in police work.

The value to the community of conflict and confrontation can be listed, as discovered, to date:

1. Dispersing of enemies
2. Defense of community and individuals
3. Selection and training of future leaders
4. Distribution of members

If confrontation could be eliminated in a community, at least the above four items of community life would be discouraged. Police and community members must consider, then, not only the probable impossibility of eliminating of conflict and confrontation under American political conditions, but also that definite losses would be entailed.

There have been attempts in past history to eliminate both conflicts and confrontations in communities. The effort to confine communities—to ghettoize them—has a long and dishonorable history, although when effectuated with sufficient harshness and rigidity, the method was effective in isolating that community's internal conflicts from the larger society. Aside from any moral or humanist compunctions, that method has not been able to survive the American political system's open character. It has been tried for more than one hundred years without success.

Suppression of all conflict, effectuated by the most severe punishments and remorseless enforcement, too, has worked at various times and places in history: in maximum-security prisons and in highly structured societies with religion and magic supportive of norm enforcement. Among slaves, especially when they are greatly outnumbered by the master class, a considerable degree of success has been achieved in suppression of conflict in a community. However, this, too, has not been successful under the American system. Curfews have not worked here; attack dogs have not been successful; nor has easy identification of a community by its branding or by its skin color been sufficient to permit suppression of conflict in this country.

Elimination of the causes of conflict as a method has been found to be a fruitless, will-o'-the-wisp task. Conflicts arising from blatantly illegal brutality have not been reduced substantially, in numbers, when police are deprived of their night sticks. There is statistical evidence that there are more citizen-police confrontations today than when police punishment was a regular part of a tour of duty.

It appears that our genetic implantation to seek conflict and confrontation is not amenable to resolutions variously called suppression, confinement, or elimination of cause. We must seek elsewhere for new methodologies or become resigned, as practitioners, to a continuing high level of conflict and confrontation between community and government. Perhaps this is the price of democracy and most would consider it to be cheaply bought, granted we retain our personal freedoms. There is, however, even among respected academics, researchers, practitioners, and eminent commentators a feeling that eternal conflict is too high a price for democracy as we know it. They are willing to go "Beyond Freedom and Dignity" to attain the kind of orderly society many of us want. That may be so, but there are a number of other resources available that have not been given a fair trial. In justice to our own intellectual—if not moral—integrity, perhaps they should be given a chance.

The importance of appropriately courteous manners in public interaction is often talked about in police-community circles but with little force or attention given to its effectuation.[3] There is little organization or persistent visible effort toward this most important technique for reduction of conflict in interpersonal contacts.

Polite manners, as prescriptive behavior, go much further than the mere avoidance of "trigger words," such as pig, chink, whitey, jungle bunny, guinea, pot-walloper, wetback, P.R., grease-ball, and so on.

Polite manners reach for symbolic peace offerings and are frequently observed in animal behavior but with much more punctilio than in human society.

Actually, polite manners involve a distinguishable process in which "displacement activity" substitutes for potentially aggressive behavior and thus inhibits aggression.

The fact that polite ceremony reduces or eliminates the frustrating aspects of the personal encounter is obvious to the careful observer. When exploited to the fullest, however, politeness includes not only cognizance of another person's presence, but also recognition of his identity as a human being of importance to the performer and constitutes a *ritual of appeasement.*

This ritual of appeasement, to be effective, must be endlessly repeated if it is to be an unambiguous communication of appeal for friendship.

Really polite behavior proclaims its purpose to all observers, and that is the characteristic that establishes the recipient of the courtesies as the starred center of many communication channels along which messages of aggression and conflict would be inappropriate.

The channels established are consonant only with messages of friendship, granted the other necessary ingredients become available.

Such reversals—from being cocked for conflict to a relaxed basking in warmly supportive admiration—take a little while to appear, for mobilized energy takes some time to dissipate, but the communication, verbal and nonverbal, thus established serves to lower tension even further. Under low-valenced energy levels, continued communication of supportive messages opens the door to close personal relationships.

The cultural arrogance that forbids the ceremony of politeness to certain individuals or groups can be reduced by insisting on a ritual of appeasement behavior. That performance may take considerable effort but is well worth it. Of course, appeasement behavior goes much further than merely formal behavior; it reaches fullest flower when it becomes the very substance of the communication on a continuing basis.

The Community Confronts Itself

America lacks the long history of social evolution in close contiguity that has permitted many European, Asian, and African peoples to develop a unified set of norms, values, attitudes, role perceptions, customs, and traditions. Each influx of immigration has brought people with quite different social colorations and complexes. Not even the climatic environment has been suitable to developing similar occupations, styles of living, or even dress. The damp but mild Northeast, with minimal snowfall, is contrasted with the heavy snowfall and bitter cold of the North Central States. The arid Southwest has fostered ways of living and even thinking quite a bit different from other areas, and the coast of the Far West varies from the salubrious southern California oceanfront to the rainy, tumultuous seacoast of Oregon and Washington. In between, ways of living have had to adapt to mountain and plain, forest and wheat field, great lakes and great rivers.

Our basic values, insofar as they are relatively common to all Americans, reflect many different components of our national experience. Some of these basic values are in irreconcilable conflict. We value individual success, "getting ahead," in contrast to submission to a group average. We want equality of opportunity, but we treasure material goods and prerogatives, which we insist are inheritable and so, inevitably, the children of the rich begin on a higher step on the ladder of opportunity.

We extol independence and freedom of action but practice ever more specialization and division of labor, which increases functional dependency of one occupational group on another in unhappy competition for separate goals. We verbally deny the influence of class, yet all our actions emphasize class and other distinctions. Religious freedom and disunity have weakened cultural integration and have often served more as focuses of division than of harmony; and the tenets of all religions are ignored in business or other worldly affairs. Recurrently we raise up national figures and just as frequently remorselessly tear down their reputations in what have been called "public burnings," sadistically enjoyed by some groups and hated by others. Polarization becomes the routine situation.

The mass media give much of their content to portraying urban battles and contentions, listing the contestants, to sharpen and keen the interest: federal versus state governments; liberals versus conservatives; manufacturers versus consumers, enclaves of blacks versus whites; Latins versus Anglos and blacks; suburbanites versus ghetto denizens; labor versus management—the list is endless. Medical analysts see anxiety, depression, conflict, and tension burdening every human relationship, chilling sentiment and affection.

Gone is the faith that sociological insight could or would lead to social harmony. We enforce laws that have been judicially declared to be hypocritical and harmful in that they label as criminal otherwise normal law-abiding people and divert rational priorities of time, money, and effort in law enforcement. Ghetto life is still brutal. Could we have expected anything different? Unresolved charges of mass corruption, from Watergate to Koreagate, from Washington to state capitols and city halls, fill our news columns.

Even within religions, schisms arise on heated issues, from disputed changes in liturgy to abortion, from sex equality in the priesthood to gay power.

Voters know more about the candidates than they ever did, as do community people and police. As a result, neither parochial politics nor traditional admonition work with the silky ease they once did.

Our political system today is geared to conflict. The warning of the Founding Fathers has not been heeded. On the contrary, factions, now called vested interests, are the operating units of our government, with a congeries of functions of dubious morality: lobbies, organized write-ins, purchased media influence, and government regulatory agencies captured by those they were designed to supervise.

Periodic election campaigns exacerbate conflicting positions and personalities without resolving political position or providing any consensus on legitimized heroes or fallen idols. Pervading discord between communities and religions, between ethnic, occupational, economic, and social classes is not healed by any of the many changes that are perennially heralded. Students are not now demonstrating—but the generation gap has not been closed. Blacks have made much progress in education since the Brown vs. the Board of Education of Kansas case of 1954, but the general educational level of our schoolchildren is probably lower.

This is the backdrop to the police-community relations scene. The question is whether the study of local relations of any kind makes any sense under these conditions. We are all on a national stage, reacting to national and even international events. The state of war in the Middle East is reflected within twenty-four hours in the prices posted at the corner gasoline station. But there need not be war; merely a hint of a suspected expectation of tension is enough to set off a sequence of inflationary events that are as meaningful to the individual as his job. Will he continue in his employment or be forced to seek unemployment insurance next week?

Tensions

Conflict has been said to be the father of all behavior. That is, opposing forces in the social group lend firmness and repetitive identity to behavior patterns.

Tension-carrying situations can be studied by *motivation analysis:*

1. Examination of the situation to determine the content of different stimuli, for example, is fear involved? How much? Is anger involved? How much? Is hate, anxiety, love, disgust, respect involved? How much?
2. Determination of the relative values or intensities of the stimuli involved. Quantitative determination may be difficult but it aids enormously both the effort toward objectivity and communication among all concerned.
3. Evaluation of the correlation of the behavior patterns with each set of motor patterns analyzed.

Motivation analysis is an attempt to make reasonably objective, research into the inner motivations of the organisms studied. Substantially, it starts by determining gross behavior patterns, such as fight, flight, talk or walk, or whatever, and analyzing the smaller motor patterns that accompany the larger movements.

The behavior patterns of animals and children have been analyzed to determine that such a behavior pattern as flight, in a dog, is usually prefaced by a laying back of the ears; or that the behavior of crying in a baby is very frequently prefaced by a squeezing together or pursing of the lips. These are simple situations and relatively simple organisms. The motor patterns so identified are considered to be illustrative of inner motivations. In the case of the dog, the gross motor pattern of flight, prefaced by the smaller motor pattern of the laying back of ears, is the motor-pattern picture of fear. The pursing of the baby's lips and the crying that shortly follows is the picture of the infant's subjective feeling of anguish. Konrad Lorenz and others have analyzed various combinations of two or more emotions, or motivations, such as fear and anger, noting the sequential motor patterns exhibited by organisms.

When we examine more complicated organisms and more complicated situations, such as police officer and citizen confrontations, the job becomes a bit more difficult, but one that has been studied at length, though there is still much work to be done.

Even more difficult, however, is the study of macrosituations involving an entire community in a state of anxiety, tension, and frustration. Scientists have tried to approach this problem by conceptualizing indices of these attributes of the community as a whole, such as: numbers of arrests of community residents, unemployment figures, or even answers on a questionnaire drawn up to elicit the kind of individual responses that can be summarized to give a reading on the entire community. This difficult problem is far beyond our present ability to solve to any satisfactory degree. Discussion is reserved for Part VI of this book.

At a psychological level, tension is sensation felt by the individual when there is a disturbance in his equilibrium to the extent that larger amounts of energy are mobilized. The sensation itself appears to be that of increased muscle tonus, plus cognitive and hormonal dissonance between exciter and inhibitory processes in the central nervous system. It is often felt as being unpleasant, but not necessarily so.

The entire physiologic set apparently calls for release by activity. The particular level and pattern of neural, glandular, and other components involved in hostility, fear, anger, pain, and other tension-connected syndromes differ from each other.

It may be that the pattern of reaction is specified by the relative levels of the components. However, there appear to be levels of intensity that a given reaction can attain, which may be a function of "more of the same" components in a stable relationship to each other or possibly a change in the proportionate intensities of each component involved.

Perception of increased danger often will result in an increased intensity of a pattern of fear, anger, hostility, and aggression, but there are wide variations. Sometimes increased danger will not have the result of a more intense reaction pattern. Whether this is due to the inhibition of perception, the overloading of perceptive faculties, or some unknown complex physiological reaction is not known at present.

Metabolic states, permanent or temporary, that is, whether high or low, temporary fatigue, or previous overstimulation, can influence the intensity and kind of tension-induced reaction. Learning and experience, too, affect the individual's pattern and intensity of reaction.

The similarity to psychological "set" is clear to the layman. There is, too, a direct analogy to *motivation* to reduce tension, or to attain distant goals, which are perceived as likely to lead to such tension reduction.

The numbers of tension-ridden people appear to be much higher in this country today than in past years. Another contemporary phenomenon is that action to relieve this tension seems to be more toward resistance and revulsion against government and authority than before. Perhaps this second factor is of even more importance than the first. Especially, since police, called to perform many services not heretofore provided, are more constantly in the public eye—not only face to face but by reason of media coverage and TV dramas. In 1977 there were more than three hundred separate programs in this country each week dealing with police and crime.

With tension a dominant theme, and police/crime a synoptic object, the attempt to release tension through channels related to police, crime, violence, community action, or other method would seem to explain the constantly increasing interest in police-community relations.

Community Impact on Policing Systems

In previous years, police departments responded to local political leaders, the power brokers of the nineteenth century and the first decades of the twentieth. Police departments became more independent under the strong police chief system, learning to avoid knuckling under to precinct captains and reaching for more impartial enforcement policies. The large metropolitan police departments reached a peak in this regard, covering so much territory and so many inhabitants that the contending forces tended to cancel each other out, while technologically improved communication and supervisory systems retained information and control in the hands of the central police administration, thus avoiding overinfluence by local pressures.

This was so as long as community attention was riveted elsewhere than on the police. Starting with the civil violence and demonstrations of the

1960s, communities began to look more critically at their police. Civil disorder has mostly passed, but an even more widespread critical examination of all government, including police, continues. Sparked by investigative reporting, mass-media presentations of incredible allegations, which turned out to be not so incredible, after all, and ending with the confirmed public opinion that everyone in government is guilty—"it's only a matter of who is to be investigated this week"—the end result has been to make all citizens and all police excruciatingly sensitive to official behavior of all kinds, including their own.

Almost without exception, police departments yearn to keep every unfavorable news item out of the public eye and seek to restructure every reference to reflect credit or at least to mitigate the negative aspects. Press agents, public-relations counsel, information officers, media-relations experts, all have jobs with police agencies today. One is tempted to comment that the major community impact on police has been to sensitize them to public opinion and arouse their desire to control it.

Levels of Conflict

The increase in violence directed against the police, attested to by the abrupt leap in injuries and deaths of policemen in the line of duty in the past fifteen years, has resulted in a number of changes in laws and procedures designed to ameliorate this condition.

Organized combat-style approach tactics have been developed, which in many areas are used for all citizen-police contacts. Not too many years ago, a patrolman on duty in New York City did not carry handcuffs, nor in the course of ordinary events would he see a pair in use in his entire career as a policeman. Now cuffs are a part of every rookie's equipment and remain with him for the rest of his professional life as a patrol officer. In those days, the officer's sidearm was concealed under his tunic, to be revealed only for the rare occurrence of a combat situation. It consisted of a small revolver firing a .38 caliber "short" cartridge, required comparatively little skill to handle, and was small enough to be put in his trouser pocket. Today, many officers are equipped with armor-piercing or dum-dum .357 or .44 magnum firing revolvers, pounds heavier, an impressively visible presence on the officer's hip. To many a citizen, this is an obnoxious personal affront. This is aggressive behavior by the police.

It may tend to reduce citizen resistance to police commands and directions, but it does so by explicit power rather than by persuasion or partnership. It is the opposite of "emission of appeasement signals" that has been suggested by behavioral scientists as a method of encouraging cooperation and compliance.

Granted that it might be suicidal for an officer to expose himself as unable to retaliate in a combat situation, the obtrusive visibility of the sidearm, if anything, makes the officer more vulnerable to a determined opponent, who can thus determine the source of his most immediate danger and take measures to nullify it. Its effect on a less resolute foe, at best, probably adds to rancor and accentuates the foe's bitter sensitivity to every nuance of harshness or impatience in the tone or manner of the officer. Whether or not this is a factor in the high incidence of civilian complaints of police *brutality*, which on investigation are discovered to be merely loud talking or impoliteness, has not been determined, but it seems worthy of inquiry.

To one trained in negotiating in ordinary civilian life—not to mention a citizen seeking friendly, supportive counsel—it would appear that the presence of the gun is as oppressive a factor as it would be at a poker table or at a birthday party.

Aggression is manifested, communicated, and received by *signs of threats.* Such threatening signs indicate hostility, and while they may serve surface peace in the community, much of that peace may be due to the uniting of those who do not possess the gun against those who do. The greater the strain put on supportive social interaction by such hostile signs, the greater the burden placed on other conditions—ecological, psychological, and sociological—to maintain peace.

Many researchers believe that under the tension-ridden conditions of the ghetto the visible gun is a constant irritant and begetter of traumatic incidents. This is not to say that the presence of the gun in a tense situation is as provocative as berserk hostility. It is passive enough, but it vitiates the ritualized formality directed to exhibition of nonaggression that military and social etiquette have demanded for centuries. Redundant repetition of assurances of nonhostility is the symbolic meaning of formal rules of etiquette. Visible, intrusive possession of a deadly weapon, plus instruments of physical restraint, is hardly redundant repetition of assurances of nonhostility.

Compliance with formal rules of etiquette, with all due ceremony, can and does become enjoyable for its own sake, creating ever warmer, affectionate, and supportive qualities.

When our servants and masters deal with us because they love us,

police-community relations will be in good hands, for cooperative interaction will have become pleasurable for all. It is simply that if "good"
police-community relations are not the product of behavior that springs
from natural inclination, it just will not happen.

Of course, conflicts are not restricted to police-citizen contacts. There
are police-police and citizen-citizen situations of an adversary nature. It
might be useful to summarize the genetic evolution of hostile behavior
as described by scientists: [4]

1. Hostile behavior proves to have survival value, thus it is retained in
   subsequent generations.
2. Hostility addressed to defending one's group norms against those of
   another group likewise proves to have survival value and persists in
   subsequent generations.
3. Hostility to members of one's own group, expressed in cruel taunting
   and ridicule of those who violate group norms, proves to have survival value for the group.
4. Friendship, in this view, is merely the inhibition of hostility and aggression and arises from an appreciation of common norms, that is to
   say, customs, manners, and style.

In consideration of the dynamics of communication, the absolute necessity for almost unending redundancy in sending messages of nonhostility
becomes quite apparent. It is not as if no message equals friendship. On
the contrary, the state of our biology translates "No message" as pure
and absolute hostility!

The facility with which the activity of humans can be redirected toward
displaced objectives is well noted in the literature. Anger aroused by one
person can be shifted to another.[5] The anger and frustration that is the
hourly harvest of crowded sleeping quarters and packed transportation
facilities, inadequate vital services, and the sheer meanness of living in
squalor produce an energy, an aggressive urge that is easily displaced
toward the easily available target: the stranger, the police officer, the hostile one.[6]

Aggressive feelings are no strangers to police officers either.[7] The culture shock to them on first being assigned to ghetto zones is well known.
From neatly mowed lawns to festering garbage piles at the end of an hour's
drive on the expressway is more of a "trip" than many can stand without
reaction. Tension-energized hostility in police is easily shifted to convenient hostility objectives with equally irrational actions ensuing.

It may be impossible under today's conditions to suppress hostility
reactions. Many scientists believe it is impossible under any circumstances.

It may, however, be quite feasible to redirect them in a ritualized way: formally redundant policies, procedures, words, gestures, stances, that is, all sign objects affirming nonhostility.

There have been endless lists made of Complaints of Citizens Against Police [8] and balancing lists of Complaints of Police Against Citizens,[9] all to no point, probably. Even if all their respective complaints could be fully resolved, entirely new lists of complaints will quickly develop. Granted our pervasive, bubbling hostility, genetically implanted, ecologically fed, we can find new items for the list as old complaints are removed—if they can be removed.

The Importance of Being Black

We weren't so important when we were colored, but now that we're Black, it's a whole different thing. Being colored was being like nobody—almost but not quite a person. Now, being Black, that's something else. I'm beautiful, now, with something good to live for. We're *power*, Black Power, and that's really something. If you can excuse a play on words, I am now a member of a class of distinction!
—Fred Carter, sociology student

The models and schema scholars make to help them understand reality are often spoken of as reality itself. For many decades American society has been spoken of as if divided into three "classes," rich, poor, and middle class.[10] It is only a half century since each of these classes was, in turn, divided into three separations. But, of course, the really big division in American society for a hundred years has been that between white and colored skins.[11] The various colored races were distinctly of a different class in every real meaning of the word. They lived differently under different laws, with different opportunities, different diets, different occupations, hopes, dreams, cultures, and even, in a great measure, a different language.

The coming of black consciousness brought that separation out into the open. By accentuating the unlikeness from white, by calling themselves black, about 15 percent of our population have accepted the position thrust upon them: that they are different. However, by grasping the fact of difference, they have assumed the same cultural fictions of all ingroups everywhere: "Not only are blacks different, but in some spiritual way they are better than the rest of the population." They have discovered their "soul." The still abundant residuum of discrimination against being black is no longer so painful. As the Jews have borne up for millenia against persecution, *because* they were Jewish and a Chosen People, as opposed to *goyim*, the strangers; as the Catholic Irish have retained their identity against a stranger in their land for hundreds of years and in this country remain "more Irish than the Irish," so now the blacks, too, have an identity.

As religious groups of all kinds have persisted, convinced that they were somehow *better* than their tormentors, group survival has always been the result of intensifying the differences between ingroup members and the outgroup, socially perceived as inhuman strangers. As an integrated group called "black" they retain survival value for group and for member. They have learned the rules of today's game: Morality consists of commitment to the good of one's group or oneself.

To call this "racism" would be incorrect, it appears. White scholars have disapproved of the notion of race as being the assertion of the preeminence of trivial physical characteristics, arbitrarily chosen after the fact, to find a false rationalization in a pseudoscience. If one defines "ethnicity" as the perception of physical or cultural traits that results in a consciousness of kind on the part of members of a group or in differential treatment by persons outside the group, blacks are on both counts an ethnic group.

It is interesting that at the height of the Black Power movement, certain Americans were called on to step down from positions as leaders of the black movement because their skin pigment was not black enough. What had been a term of opprobrium, now became the badge of merit. It makes very good practical sense. The term *Negro*, meaning black in Spanish, did not make the point clear enough, being diluted in translation. They are no longer on the fringes of an ingroup, longing to enter, but forever forbidden by the color of their skin. Rh factors were admitted, religious dissidents and even atheists were admitted to the white power structure and to the benefits, material and spiritual, thereafter available to them. People with short noses, long noses, even the pug-nosed Irish were admitted, with easily identifiable labels on them, red hair, freckles, a liking for whiskey. Only the Negro was kept out.

The answer, a stroke of genius: We are now black, and we have our own group! All we have to do now is to rigidly exclude those who do not fit our orthodox requirements and "Keep the faith!"

It is important to be black, because if your skin is dark and you are not black, who are you? As a black, now, respect and jobs can be demanded; and the demands, enforced by the power of the vote and of the dollar, will be met.

That is the route gone by other "ethnics." It has worked before, and it will probably work again, as long as we have our present political system. There appears to be no gainsaying it, however emotional the backlash. The police and all the communities of interest are bound by this historical reality. There can be no police-community relations that do not take into consideration the demands, as well as the bare needs, of the community of interest we call black.

As a significant minority in our political infrastructure, they are making steady progress in amassing appointive and elective political offices; and also in the economic sphere, in education, in industry, and in even that bastion of financial power, banking.

The black community of interest is not a localized ghetto neighborhood any more. They cannot be walled off and treated to a parochial diet of "services." The black community is nationwide, with international ramifications, and, supported by "affirmative action," must be considered with even more care than other communities of interest with objectives more in keeping with the status quo. Whereas business people, as a community of interest, homeowners, parents, professionals, and many other groups all want to continue the way things are, the black community of interest is trying to build a new place for itself. This calls for new adjustments—some of them very difficult for other individuals and groups to accept.

The problems of adjustment are not solely those of the non-black community. Many black individuals are finding it difficult to adjust to the new roles that are demanded of them. Many mourn—quietly—for "the good old days," offensive as that may seem to young, militant blacks just making their way financially, educationally, and professionally. There appears to be in the black community a rising incidence of physical and mental illnesses more characteristic of the patterns of the white majority, as blacks enter into the competitive race.

This is not the America de Crèvecœur exulted. We must remember, however, that he arrived, worked, and wrote about an America of boundless forests and free homesteads, where New Americans were an obvious asset and benefit to the existing establishment. The New Americans provided cheap labor in the cities and on the farms, and in tilling their own holdings they provided cheap food for the rest of the population.

The New Americans of today, the blacks, say they have paid their dues; they are now ready for a "piece of the action."

Of course, not everyone agrees with this evaluation. The facts stare us in the face, however: 25 million black Americans, with all the political, economic, and moral force inherent in a group that will become more potent the more it is forced to identify itself as separate.

Whether in arrogance or with quiet pride or simply as Americans, blacks are demanding the service and respect owed every citizen. All community and government agencies are being called on for higher and different levels of performance. In a great measure that is why there are now courses in police-community relations and books such as this one. For the demand for new dimensions in government accountability, sparked by the black revolution, is spreading to all sectors of the American community.

Latin Power is an expanding coalition of Chicano, Puerto Rican, and Cuban-Americans, loosely united—in part by a common language but tied together even more by a realization that in unity there is political power— is starting to make itself heard in the land.

Claiming some 20 million members, and as such the second-largest minority in the country, their urban villages have become localized strongholds of political and economic power in the largest population centers. Following the lead of the blacks, they plan a political and economic future for themselves.

Of course, that route has been well traveled by now. Alexis de Tocqueville,[12] the noted French traveler and writer, described its workings in 1835 as simply an attempt at rationalizing and making effective lawful means for lawful ends, legitimized by our political process and by tradition. The vying for power and leverage by special interests *is* the American scene.

The "importance of being black," however, is that this leverage is now being exercised at a grass-roots level, involving a huge, self-interested community. Accepting the identity thrust upon it by the larger society, the black community is now using its easy identification as a factor in its own unification and bid for material benefits.

Colored was a term of derision, even contempt, creating division and confusion among a large segment of the population. *Black,* on the other hand, is a rallying cry and an example to other ethnic minorities and subcultures in American society. The full significance of this movement has not, perhaps, revealed itself. Subcultural appeals at one time were only the subjects of sentimental songs, from "Rose of Washington Square" and

"Avenue C" to "Abie's Irish Rose," "Sorrento," and "Green Pastures." "Ethnic" jokes were the reserve standby material of stand-up comics. Today the ethnic appeal is a rallying cry from New York to San Francisco, and all subcultures are responding.

The words *class consciousness* have attained dimensions never dreamed of by Karl Marx, the Populists, and other theorists of the nineteenth century. If a "social fact" is a *belief* that is acted on, we are witnessing the birth of myriads of "social facts" as homosexuals act on their belief that they are a disadvantaged group; those who hate homosexuals discover the same qualities about their group, loosely allied with another group defending their mores against pornographers; and those who consider freedom of the press equivalent to the "freedom of consenting adults" join the rush for group identification.

Leading them all, at the present time, in mounting skill and success are the blacks. It is exciting to be involved in police and community in the midst of this transition. There is every promise that the working out of the black revolution will be a fascinating and inspiring reenactment of the American Dream.

The Quality of Life [13]

The "quality of life" is not usually treated in works in behavioral science. Nor is there any easy definition of the phrase. It becomes even more difficult to set down the parameters of a "good" quality of life for a large number of people.

The temptation to surrender the task is great, for is it not true that what would be considered a good quality of life is something unique to the individual? Each person desires his own pattern of conditions, which will include not only physical and social environmental features, but also health, perhaps wealth, and ever greater—perhaps even exclusive—opportunities for "self-realization," however that may be defined.

When one tries to visualize an operationalized version of this Utopia, one is faced with insuperable barriers. Plato and other philosophers, secular and religious, have reached for expression of the ideal for a few thousand years, without much consensus on specific items.

If we restrict the focus to only matters of direct relevance to police and community affairs, perhaps there is a better hope of success. It appears there is abundant evidence from natural history that conflict provides many otherwise unavailable benefits, and, in any case, it is inherent in the human constitution. Further, the evidence is that conflict can be modified in its expression so as to reduce or eliminate all injury to participants.

The ways in which this can be done have been minutely analyzed and found in many cases to have become genetically patterned, after having been autonomously developed, their survival value proved for individual and for species. This same behavior, with the effect of being unambiguously inhibitory of aggression and conflict, can be reproduced consciously, voluntarily, and habitually as the result of learning.

The elements of this behavior on a communication level are: first, redundant messages of appeasement; second, the messages will be especially clear and influential if they single out the recipient as special and unique, as playing a role not easily played by another; and third, appreciation of his role as one of value and significance.

These three elements appear to set the stage for the establishment of personal bonds. When the performance goes beyond these three simple elements to the point where actual aid, support, and care is offered *and accepted,* the bonds can reach high levels of intensity toward the level we call personal friendship.

Some philosophers have held that a society that is not founded on personal friendship and love is hardly worth bothering about. It has been noted by social scientists that when a community has solidly founded its values and meaning on the members, *as persons of individual worth, each with a precious contribution to the group,* the devotion of the individual to the group reaches a height such that it is greater than the value of one's own life. The readiness with which people are willing to sacrifice their lives in defense of the other members of a close-knit community is a common observation in both animal and human natural history.

Such devotion is rarely, if ever, the consequence of a dry demand for dedication. It is the result, it appears, of the group members having earned that dedication by their own proved, fervent sodality in many specific instances of redundant communication of inhibited aggression, that is, *appeasing* behavior, as a background to actual assistance and support. In such cases, the dedication that appears is mutual, not an act of submission to authority. One might think that the society worth dying for is the only one worth living for.

Where there is no inhibition of aggression, where appeasement behavior is not *constantly* manifested, the quality of life is reduced, at best, to an arm's length, quid pro quo contractual relationship. At worst, it is one where every man's hand is raised against his fellow; where neighbor and police are equally unsafe, where aggression and conflict are the only communication.

Konrad Lorenz has theorized that where ritualization of aggression-appeasement occurs, it identifies friends as well as enemies. It provides the ceremonial matrix that fertilizes friendship and common bonds of cooperation. One knows who is friend and enemy by his behavior long before the presence of an actual break, and appropriate measures can be weighed and fair judgment of future action taken.

This is not merely a descent into banal sentimentality. It points the way to operationalizing a quality of life that is directly in line with the objectives of successful, facilitated community relations with police.

In the first place, it provides a guideline to all police-citizen contacts: appeasement! This does not mean that either police officer or citizen must become vulnerable to attack, either symbolic or real. On the other hand, it does *not* mean the retention of offensive postures that send out messages of probable attack.

The ferocious wolf—so loving in his domestic relations with his mate —does not present his throat to the fangs of a strange female wolf.[14] That could be fatal. He does not, however, present his bared fangs to her. He does present—and this has been carefully observed—a nonthreatening stance, half sideways, with the side of his neck and shoulder within biting distance but with his own teeth turned away until friendly communication is established. If he does not care to continue the communication, he turns away unthreateningly.

This complex behavior is noted so consistently in the wolf that the unavoidable impression is that it is genetically implanted, as a result of its proved survival value.

One could say on this basis that the quality of life, insofar as police-community relations are concerned, depends upon the reduction of aggressive messages and the increase of messages of non-aggression and actual appeasement, verbal and nonverbal, between community and police.

Chapter 8

SOCIOPOLITICAL PROCESSES

Man is by nature a political animal.
  —Aristotle *Politics,* Book III

Here we discuss the relationship of political processes and social realities, with an implicit orientation to the American scene.

The political mechanisms of each country control the levers of power that start or stop many of the social forces within its boundaries. Often political action in one country will have a major, even devastating effect on people residing in distant foreign lands.

The United States is, perhaps, the most powerful force in the world today, and as such, its sociopolitical complexion and process are of importance all over the globe. In this country, the impact of government is ever visible in the daily lives of the residents. It would be impossible to evaluate police-community relations without considering the political dimension.

Having come this far in this book, you may wonder why, if so much is known, is there any problem with such a relatively simple thing as police-community relations—a subject that has been around for a very long time? Why don't we just stick together the pieces that will make up a good set of relations and set it up in City Hall, or wherever it belongs, and let it work while we take our attention to other matters?

It is not that simple, because we don't really know that much about human beings. We know about sociology and psychology, but those are only complex constructs by which we try to reason and forecast by analogy. We know about the technology of communication—and try to use it for analogy, too. But even technology is only a brute-force solution to a problem. If we, humans, can't fly through the air—let's make a machine that will do it for us. We want to stay underwater for a long time? Make an aqualung or a submarine that will carry us and maintain us in a life-sustaining envelope.

Going to the moon is solved technologically in the same way: We build a machine that takes us, with all our human frailties tenderly wrapped within a self-contained atmosphere, with heat and ventilation, familiar foods, excretory facilities, and a wheeled vehicle to perambulate about the moonscape.

Human beings have not been changed by any of these technologies. Actually, we know hardly anything at all about changing humans that wasn't known centuries ago. Human relations is really mostly unknown territory. Whenever we intervene in human relations it seems to turn on us, and we are invariably surprised at the consequences. We have not discovered what social machinery works best and under what circumstances that might be.

Which of our social institutions are worth keeping? Which worth relegating to the junk heap? We truly do not know! Most of our important activities, from policing and education to managing cities—including, to our surprise, public transport, social services, and medical services—do not rely on advanced technology. It seems we do not know how to improve them to any significant degree.

It is easy to sympathize with the despair of the social scientists and to forgive them when they offer such pseudo-technical solutions as Skinnerian boxes to infiltrate our nervous systems with behavior modification plans that admittedly go "beyond freedom and dignity" and approach the terror of the holocaust of World War II and the imaginative devilishness of *Clockwork Orange*.[1]

The American Dream of our Founding Fathers of a humanely effective, liberty-loving land is not dead. There are many concerned people out there pointing out the errors of our ways. But they do not seem to have created the insistent, effective demand that will stimulate supreme creative innovation in the social sphere and the high productivity that consumerism has created in the technological world.

There are some signs that this revolution in social engineering is about to start. There are mounting instances of privately run "public services" that offer better services at lower cost.[2] Competitively aggressive, they furnish security and mail services without tax support and even show a profit.

Americans are not as violent in the streets as they were in the 1960s when they marched by thousands, objecting to government policies. The level of criticism, it appears, has reached a different plane. It is more sophisticated at a higher level and is expressed in ways that are not as easily contained as a street demonstration. It takes the form of massive civil suits against the government and its agents, with tremendous awards being given by juries. There is a strong movement to restrict the activities of government by groups who previously sought ever greater extension of government services. Too, there is a hunger for righteousness about the land that calls for honesty, fair dealing, and an openness that has not been seen for many a long year in either Washington or City Hall. Not only are there outcries of disapproval at the slightest peccadilloes or irregularities, but now entire administrations come into power without political credos but evangelically affirming almost inexpressible virtue. Further, these administrations are being held to the virtue they preached.

The bona fides of every individual and organization are subject to challenge. The public is in a "show-me" attitude as never before about the motives as well as the competence of government. Skepticism, lauded as a prime virtue in scientific research, appears to have penetrated every social force and movement in the country, attaining some of the qualities of a social movement itself.

Social Movements

In a sociological sense, social movements are collective behavior that reflect underlying changes. In responding to these changes, however, new *perspectives* are created, which culminate in new lines of action and eventuate in new institutions. On a psychological and communication level, however, the same phenomenon can be described as information and perspectives fed into the public domain by "gatekeepers" of public information, whose personal standing with their communicants is such as to be influential in creating such new perspectives.

Perspectives, as used here, are complex sets of attitudes, values, and perceptions that are patterned into an ordered view of the world. Those who share the same perspective tend to make the same assessments of good and bad, of what is possible and what is impossible; the broad outlines of an ideology emerge at the same time that various sporadic individual and small-group actions take place, forming and being formed by the developing ideology. As the actions and beliefs spread, they take on the character of a full social movement. That is, it becomes coherent, cohesive, and lasting.

Some of the characteristics that help to identify a social movement have been said to be:

1. A distinct perspective
2. A strong sense of solidarity

3. A sense of dedication to the exclusion of other concerns
4. A conviction that certain ultimate actions should be taken
5. A move to act in the direction of such ultimate actions.

Examples from recent history that fit the above typology are the civil-rights movement, the Black Power movement, and the Gay Power movement. Some people have felt that the reaction to the events and revelations of Watergate were on the way to becoming a social movement.

The fact that there is opposition to a social movement does not deny the movement's identity. If anything, it may strengthen and energize it. The community of people involved in the social movement, threatened by outsiders, feel even closer together.

As social movements change and evolve, there are internal problems as to the rate of change desired by different members: Some want immediate results and are willing to go to extremes of violence, while other members draw a line at the amount of violence they will support or condone and are willing to settle for more gradual change.

Basic strategic objectives of social movements appear to be:

1. Inform the public of the nature and advantages of the movement
2. Convince as many nonparticipants as possible to consent to the changes desired
3. Persuade, finally, a power structure to effect the changes.

The prime concern of police agencies in a free society is the method used by the movement to attain these three objectives. The mission of the police is enforcement of existing laws and the maintenance of order. Thus, if public information and awareness is sought by provocation of public disorder, the police come on the scene in an active role. In that case, the tactic taken by the leaders of the social movement is to try to nullify police effectiveness. Specific tactics used may vary from increased violence against the police themselves to obtaining the de facto consent of the police to the acts of violence that are contemplated. Some of the methods that have been observed in recent years are: obtaining the consent of the police to restrict themselves to the perimeter of the violence; distracting and disorganizing police operations; obtaining top-level cooperation in the redeployment of police forces.

On the other hand, if public awareness is to be achieved by peaceful means, the police function is to protect the rights of the members to communicate with the public, subject only to minor regulatory ordinances reasonably designed to protect public safety.

The other two objectives of the leaders of a social movement must be conducted by lawful means and for lawful subgoals if the leaders are not to be subjected to charges of criminal conspiracy. It is in the investigation of allegations of such criminal conspiracies that charges and cross-charges are often made of police overzealousness, which often result in, or cause, a deterioration of relations with segments of the public.

When fact situations can be unequivocally spelled out either as peaceful, lawful actions or as clearly criminal, the police mission in each case is clear: protect and support all lawful endeavors and suppress all unlawful ones.

It is in the gray areas—where there is reasonable cause for suspicion that unlawful activities are being performed or contemplated—that the police task becomes difficult. How much surveillance is to be permitted in a free society? If the police are to be not merely reactive but active in the prevention of crime, just how energetic should this function be?

This is a question that has not been answered as yet.

Associations, Organizations, and Institutions

We have discussed groups before as being people together. We have also indicated that groups need not necessarily be together in space. We have also used the term *communities of interest* to identify a group of special interest. Let us try to take an even broader look at the idea of groups.

First, there is no reason to believe that any analysis or classification of groups will be satisfactory for all purposes. Even if we have a single purpose in mind, different classifications, from time to time, might become more advantageous or relevant than others.

Second, consider the enormous numbers of groups that any society contains. Counting all, there are probably more groups in a society than there are people.

Some groups include other groups: The teacher group includes all college professors, all high-school teachers, and all adjunct teachers, who teach as part of other jobs. Too, it includes brunette teachers, redheads, blondes; tall, short; male and female, each as subgroups, alone or in combinations—all without end.

The teacher group is itself part of larger groups, such as all professionals, sedentary workers, taxpayers, Americans, or simply living creatures. There are groups of groups, such as the National Association of Manufacturers, the Association of American Colleges, the United Nations, the Organization of Petroleum Exporting Countries (OPEC), the Union of Soviet Socialist Republics, and the United States. We can even speak of groups we have probably never seen and may not exist (such is the power of language!)—the Martians who live among us, as one example.

Thus groups include other groups and are themselves included in still other groups, cutting across categorical lines in every imaginable way. We shall, therefore, use a classification of groups that helps us in our purpose in this book.

Statistical Groups. These are groups that have no interaction among themselves and have this identification thrust upon them by students and scholars. The group of people receiving welfare payments is important to the study of relations of people with government, though they do not, and may not ever, interact as a group with one another. The group that has attained a college degree has significance to community study, as has the group that is illiterate, and the proportions between them may be quite important. Statistical groups are identifiable by a class description, as has just been done. They are also describable by enumeration, one by one, named, or with other item labels, such as social-security numbers.

Societal Groups. These groups are identifiable by a consciousness the members have of being of the same kind. It has been observed that people everywhere tend to group themselves into patterns that appear to be a recognition of others like themselves, as *they* define such likeness. The reason, whether it be genetic implantment, cultural modification, or the result of political propaganda, for its existence is important and merits description.

Examples are: ethnic groups, religious groups, males, females, youth, senior citizens, secretaries, lawyers, baseball fans, tourists, and countless others, depending on situations and circumstance.

Social Groups. This is an ambiguous phrase and is presented here only because a large number of behavioral scientists have used it to denote a group that interacts on a regular basis. Examples are families, friends, neighbors, clubs, and so on.

Associational Groups. This term labels people who have banded together for common purposes. They tend toward structuring their relationship about position statuses, with designated rights, obligations, and expectations for those who fill these positions. The role players may change from time to time, but the formal statuses, the positions, tend to remain, to be filled by new designees.

Bureaucracies. This is a term of many meanings, indeed, often used pejoratively to symbolize distasteful complexity, impersonality, rigidity, and red tape. Here the term is used descriptively in a nonderogatory sense to identify a formal association with a complex administrative

Types of Groups

	Statistical Group	Societal Group	Social Group	Associational Group	Bureaucratic Group
Consciousness of kind?	No	Yes	Yes	Yes	Yes
Social interaction?	No	No	Yes	Yes	Yes
Social organization?	No	No	No	Yes	Yes
Organizational goals externally determined?	No	No	No	No	Yes

Figure 8–1

hierarchy and specialization of skills and tasks. Bureaucracies often have quite specific organizational goals. These goals, specific or in general terms, are externally determined. Thus a corporation is owned by shareholders who determine, ultimately, the goals of the corporation. A public agency, too, has its goals externally determined by legislative enactment (usually in very general terms) or by executive order (sometimes quite specific).

Insofar as a bureaucracy tends to determine its own goals by internal processes, it reverts back to being an association. Probably no association has all its goals so completely externally controlled and determined as to be a "pure" bureaucracy.

An analysis of the five types of groups along four different dimensions [3] appears in Figure 8–1.

Of course, the five categories of groups, statistical, societal, social, associational, and bureaucratic, are in some degree rather arbitrary divisions. Is the television audience watching newscaster Walter Cronkite a social group because there is communication? Note, however, that it is only one-way communication, at least at the moment, until telephone calls start coming into the station or a letter or telegram is sent. Is instant mutuality of communication necessary to denote the difference between a social rather than a societal group? Note, too, there is no cross-communication between viewers. Does that mean there is really only a huge number of dyads, newscaster and each viewer? Perhaps the easiest solution is to accept the fact that there may be numerous subclasses within each of the categories.

The student might reasonably ask, "Why classify in the first place?" Fundamentally, because that is the way to reduce data units into manageable pieces. Life presents its manifold variety often without discernible order, each a unique product, and chaos in the mass. It is our task, as scholars, to shift abstraction levels and look for patterns that will be useful in comprehending the whole.

Each group is undoubtedly different in its living detail from any other in certain respects but similar to others in other ways. The job of the scientist is to focus on similarities and correlations even though that may blot out some of the particulars.

The particular four dimensions of analysis used in the typology previously diagramed—consciousness of kind, social interaction, social organization, and organizational goal—were chosen because of their relevance to our study of groups with community impact. An additional comment should be noted: Associations and bureaucracies are distinguished by the existence of a formal organization of norms and statuses, together with a reach for objectivity and impartiality, at least as an ideal, in evaluation of performance and motivation. There arises inevitably, however, an informal set of interactional norms, particularly those in face-to-face contacts, which affect the specific role performances and expectations, the esteem with which each person is held, and the impartiality of evaluations of performance and motivation.

This informal organization arises within every formal organization and is of varying degrees of influence. It is important to note that whether or not the association or bureaucracy will perform as expected will depend to a great measure on the support provided by the informal norm-enforcement machinery.

Efficiency does not lie in the rationality and order of a table of organization but *in the way it works.*[4] Thus a specialized police-community-relations unit, however stable in formal structure and internal organization, will not ordinarily be able to produce much effective output if the informal normative structure of the entire police department is not supportive of the existence, aims, and methods of the unit. Cooperative goodwill, even enthusiasm, is only the barest necessity for successful performance.

This is not to deny the correlative necessity for clarity and directness in formal lines of communication and control, for example, avoidance of division of responsibility. The problems of coordinating authority and influence are just as important as the informal structure.

Much of what the police-community student is concerned about is community groups with strong informal connections, overlapped in an indiscriminate way with formal structures, legal, economic, governmental and private. The practitioner's task becomes one of coordinating this confusing maze of associations and bureaucracies.

Institutions. In order to avoid further ambiguity in terms, let us define *institution* as an "organized procedure." It is not a group at all. *An institution is, in essence, a complex norm.* It is a way of doing things that has developed over time and has become widespread and expected. Thus modern nations have an institution of *policing* by paid employees.

Some of the employees are paid by private persons or groups, but we generally think of the police as paid by the government. Each police department will be an association, probably a bureaucracy in intent, but not quite so externally controlled as to goals as to be a pure bureaucracy, as the word has been defined here. But even primitive peoples will have an institution of policing their people; it is, however, without paid employees. Each society institutionalizes the activities it needs, according to the conditions it faces. Although we have institutionalized the practice of medicine, an Eskimo tribe in Greenland may have no such institution; instead, the rare incidence of illness or injury may be treated by ad hoc measures that may appear useful to tribal leaders at the time of occurrence.

Another point to note is that institutions are different from other norms in that specifically organized associations and bureaucracies are required to sustain them. We comply with the norm to say "Good morning!" but no association exists to maintain compliance.

The institution of banking requires the existence of organizations we call banks. Our institutional system of entertainment is supported by such organizations as theaters, nightclubs, bowling alleys, and massage parlors. The *family* is an institution, but your particular family is a social group, perhaps verging on an association. Government is an institution; the United States is an association.

Social Force, Power, and Authority [5]

In Chapter 4 we discussed these terms cursorily. Here we will apply them in a socio-political context.

Thankfully, in the interest of flexible and creative expression by poets laureate and teenagers, there is no authoritative body that has the power to decree the meaning of a word nor to decide which words shall be accepted or rejected by our English language. To balance the matter, the loss of stability in the language becomes a liability in the search for neat definitions.

Social force is one of those expressions that has been used in divers ways for many different purposes. In this book, let us define it as the absolute reduction of the social choices of an individual. It has been so used by a number of behavioral scientists, and the definition has demonstrated its utility. Placing a person in jail has definitely limited his social choice as to the people with whom he will interact, where he will be, and what he will do. All of these social choices have been curtailed by imprisonment. Actual imprisonment, then, is the application of social force. All social choices are thereafter limited. A fine or other monetary penalty or charge will limit the ways the subject can spend his money— limiting his social choices insofar as he could have used the money to purchase various goods and services: His social choices have been limited. Execution, of course, is the ultimate social force. All social choices are thereafter eliminated. Our definition intuitively makes sense: social force—or *force,* for short—is the reduction or limitation of alternatives otherwise available to a human being.

Power is not the same as force. It is the *potential* for the use of force and constitutes a source, therefore, of influence over the choices made by the subject of the force. Once power is used, however, it has lost its potential and loses its influence. For example, the threat of prison, held over a person unless he performs a certain act, does limit his social choices *if* he complies by performing the demanded act. As soon as he does, however, the power is discharged. It exists no longer. Or if he is put in jail because he has not performed, the power to limit choice is equally extinguished. There is no longer any power to limit choice.

The police officer who commands the youth group on the corner, "Get off this corner, or I'll lock you all up!" is exerting power, and his influence is made visible if they do move off.

If they refuse to move away, and he arrests them, the youths' social choice to stay, move off, go into the corner candy store, or whatever, is removed, but the power of the officer is now exhausted. He can no longer arrest them any further; the power to arrest has been used up.

The threat of force is power, made manifest only if it produces the fact of reducing or closing off alternatives by the individual threatened. Power often resides in the mere belief of the subject that the person with power can limit his social choices, and under such threat, he permits himself to be influenced—a perfect example in which belief in a social fact makes it a reality.

The Elements of Power

It is perplexing to examine power in society, because we see its effects but cannot observe the phenomenon itself. Isn't that similar to electric power? We cannot see it, but we can see its effects. It is no wonder that we know so little about power. In the preceding section we tried to define it and came to the conclusion that power is the *potential* for the use of force to restrict the choices of an individual. We will try to elaborate.

Power relations exist everywhere in society—starting with parents over children, teachers over pupils, it continues through life, ceaselessly: Holdup man over victim; wardens over inmates; judge over jury, lawyers, court staff, and even over the spectators. The police officer, who exerts power over citizens, is subject to the power of his sergeant, who is, in turn, subject to the power of the lieutenant, and so on up the line to the mayor, over all city departments, and if the mayor is like most people, he or she is subject in a great measure to the power exerted by an electorate and a spouse. It is endemic in every society, ubiquitous in pubs, pews, and all other places where people group together, or communicate, even at a distance.

Please note that *power* is not prestige, competence, talent, or ability. *Power* implies the potential to coerce against the will, or to coerce will, that is, forced consent, as the lesser of two evils. Power is not even synonymous with influence. The chap who writes the nation's songs may have influenced the course of that nation's history, but we cannot say that he has exerted power. The songs, as ideas or expressions of emotion, exerted influence that may affect all eternity, for who can tell where it stops? But the songwriter did not limit anyone's choices. He personally had no power to coerce wills; his influence is persuasive, it cajoles, it seduces.

What about the person who by his shrewd use of persuasion and cajolery obtains great influence. Would we not then say that this person has "power"? To be consistent, the answer must be: If the influence has grown to the point where any individual's choices can be limited against his will—despite his will—then the influence has been turned into power as far as that individual is concerned. The path the power takes may be invisible to its subject; he may be unaware of its source, its implications, or how it has been exerted. An example taken from a French novel illustrates the point: A famous detective of the Sûreté is discharged for reasons that are incomprehensible to him. Finally, he traces the source of the exertion of this power by the police chief back through the politician to the politician's secretary and to her lover who is a notorious member of the underworld.

In this case, power was exerted by the criminal over the detective through concealed channels. It was never exhibited as a threat to the police officer but had remained as an invisible potential, ultimately revealed only by its effect, which limited the choices of the police officer. In doing so, it was dissipated into raw force.

Sheer physical strength can be a form of power in a given situation. In feudal times, when armor, shield, lance, and sword were tools of power, often weighing more than one hundred pounds, physical strength was an important resource of power. Even in those days, however, in a larger sense, the power of any one fighting man was limited. A puny farmer boy armed with a light crossbow was able to disable or kill the most heavily armed knight. Technology has made a "difference" from the days of young David with his slingshot to the Western badman's six-shooter to the laser-sighted submachine gun and the neutron bomb.

In a social sense, it is *numbers* of people that have the weight of power, all other things being equal. Particularly is this so when the preponderance of numbers is great. The Talmud admonishes, "If ten men say you are drunk—lie down!" Mao Tse-tung's work repeatedly affirms the importance of relying on people, many people. Though, as Bismark and many others have remarked, majorities can be matched by other resources. This is why slender majorities should not initiate large innovations. Of these other resources that can support the social power potential in large groups, perhaps the most important is organized lines of communication that permit coordination of masses of people toward the development of increased influence and power.

The individuals and groups encountered by police and community workers are familiar with all of the above not merely in a dry academic sense but in a dynamic and practical way, using them in the field to reach and control the powers of society. Unless police and community people come to understand all the techniques of power that are in daily use, they will become spectators rather than practitioners in the field of their alleged expertise. There is much to learn about the use and abuse of power, though this work has little space for this important subject.

An organized group is quintessentially social power, for *organization* means limiting individual choices by means of norms, among other things. The larger the group the greater the power, especially in contention against a lesser group. The factor of difference here is far greater than the proportionate difference in numbers. In military combat it has been called the N^2-Factor, and it is discussed in Chapter 11.

Organization, in regard to social power, becomes influential communications that coordinate people toward specific goals and appears to be one of the fundamental assets on the balance sheet of power. Any one of the sources of power may be insufficient in itself, but the most important today seem to be: people, organization, and money. To some degree they are interchangeable, in that people can be hired for money, as can organizational know-how. Other assets include intelligence, knowledge, skill, natural supplies, and resources.

In a particular situation, other resources may become critical: creative insight, weapons of a particular kind, specialized information, control of space or ground, and so on.

To make a more general analysis, in evaluating a power group in a community, we can state that power is based on *people, organization,* and *assets* of various kinds. A group bereft of all three will tend to have little power. All three must exist, but one element can be exchanged for another.

In order to husband their relatively weak resources in weaponry and supplies of war, for example, the Russians in World War II were able to expend great quantities of personnel in the earliest days of the war and great areas of geographical space. Replenishing their assets from new factories beyond the Urals and from American shipments of vast quantities of military stores, they were able to reduce personnel attrition and recover space. In Vietnam the constant infiltration of soldiers and supplies from the north added to recruitment of people and the cooperation of others in the south sustained them, despite American superiority in technical assets. At the present time the Arab states have exchanged some of their enormous funds in part for armament and organization and to demonstrate that more power is available, in their potential use of force.

A community group that is financed generously will acquire power, as it hires, coopts, and influences people to coordinate their efforts toward the specific goals of that community group. In a similar way, a large group of people will become more powerful as they come to control assets and organize toward goals.

Social Power in the United States

The Search for Methods for Social Power

We have been examining the elements of social power. We now come to the subject of how these elements operate in the living scene in this country. It would be possible to describe this in either figurative or literal terms, and it would be quite possible to include quantitative measures of various aspects—how many persons are arrested per year, for what crimes, and such. The incidence of civil disturbance or hostage taking is statistically enumerated, case by case, on a local and regional basis. Sheer description, however much the amount of statistical information included, would not give much understanding. It is the comparison of patterns that calls for and inspires insight. Let us then try to trace the patterns of social power that have had historical significance and appear to have left traces in human conduct that can be seen to this day.

The earliest recorded descriptions [6] of the exercise of power called for submission to an authoritative figure, kingly or divine. In some cases, in ancient times, as in the Egypt of the pharaohs, both secular and sacred authority were concentrated in a single monarch. The definition of justice was simply: the decision of the king. The power of the king to enforce his decision by limiting the social choices of his subjects was absolute. Suballocations of power were apportioned to each in his rank, over all inferiors down to the lowest-ranking members, family heads, who had the same absolute power over the members of their families. At each level, authority was equivalently co-equal, but all were subject to the next higher level. Ultimately, all power resided in the king. This form of organization was known as a hierarchy, and that it exists to this day is testament to its survival value as an organizational type.

Since survival value is not the residuum of theoretical argumentation, but rather the resultant of empirical conditions that affected reality, there may be something intrinsically *useful* to people in the hierarchical idea. It is purely speculative, of course, but one imagines that the successful creation of a social organization in which the decision as to social choices was deferred to those next up the line in the hierarchy enables the concentration of human effort that results in success of the organization's objective, which is, primarily, to survive as an organization.

While hierarchies are small in a migratory, pastoral people, the development of agriculture and the domiciling of population in one place permitted a vastly more stable communication of power messages and the increase in size of hierarchical groups. The invention of writing, permitting the inscription of the divine kings' words as spoken, as the *law,* increased the body of communicated power messages and the uniformity and stability of the organization, though it changed and grew with each day's divine contribution.

The Judaic contribution put a stop to the continual change of fundamental law—now inscribed in stone as the veritable words of the one God, divine and unchangeable. Expanded by Moses in the Pentateuch, written on flexible papyrus or parchment scroll, light and portable, the Law was well adapted to the pastoral life adopted by the Jews who left Egypt. Power then lay in those designated by the Law, each in his station, high priests and rabbis, who interpreted cases of difficulty that were not clearly spelled out in the Pentateuch.

In ancient Greece, citizens tried to develop social power out of public opinion formed in discussion in the *agora.* Discovery of the elements of rational order, presumed to be persuasive because of natural appeal to persons of proven good sense, was the focus. It was assumed that women, the young, and students of lesser wisdom would obey the examples set by the wise men. On the contrary, scholars now feel that the opening of the subject of norms to discussion tended to extend itself, in the nature of an open inquiry, without the group attaining any consensus as to norms or any natural flowering of norm-enforcement social machinery, and in defiance of philosophers' adumbrations of democracy and morality. On the contrary, various persons of wealth hired their own police to enforce their private desires, losing the power base of citywide consent on common goals and ideals, and of ways of encouraging compliance with actions contributing toward reaching common ends by common means.

The Romans—to condense the history of a thousand years to a few phrases—developed formal enforcement systems of officers assigned to exercise power. Such power, institutionalized as *authority* in agents of central power, was found at all levels of their complex civilization. Vigiles patrolled the streets to enforce traffic laws, criminal laws, and laws against disorder. Tribunes were given authority, that is, institutionalized power, to defend the lawful rights of citizens against vigiles and other government officers. The application of power over persons was everywhere manifested by a formal interactional system, with individuals designated to wield power in each instance. Each power system was expected to produce the social product intended: The vigiles were expected to produce freedom from street disorder and to expedite traffic in the crowded streets of congested Rome and were rigidly disciplined toward that end. Roman ideals of discipline and devotion to the law were not treated casually but with extreme rigor in the day of the Republic and early Empire.

After the Crucifixion, the early Christian church soon abandoned the co-equal organization they had enjoyed as Disciples and then Apostles to set up various hierarchical systems and provide a priestly interpretation of the Bible to worshippers. The later Reformation, starting with Martin Luther, enjoined communicants to read the Bible themselves, developed many separate sects and denominations, with a large degree of control of individual churches by the members themselves.

The Founding Fathers of the United States were inheritors of these traditions about authority together with their own personal experience in the exercise of power as leaders in the several colonies. They were further fortified with extended readings of the works of David Hume, Jean Jacques Rousseau, and Montesquieu, distilled from even earlier utterings of John Locke, Michel de Montaigne, and others, who had grasped the deepest implications of the struggle between liberty and authority.[7]

Liberty [8]

The combination of utter philosophical rationality and supreme realism, which found expression in the basic documents of this country, categorically admits the apposition of authority and liberty and tries to provide the political means to attain the common goal effectiveness of one with maximum realization of the other. One can seek widely in the libraries of ancients or moderns and not find documents to match the coordination of authority and liberty expounded in the Declaration of Independence and our Constitution of 1789.

When one tries to capsule the meaning of America to the people who have inhabited it since 1789, one is tempted to say that the most important theme is the one called by the Founding Fathers, *Liberty*.

This leitmotiv ran through all the debates in Philadelphia in that hot summer in 1787: Liberty—how to best obtain, ensure, and retain it. The Declaration calls for the liberty to have life itself, to have the liberty to extend life's benefits in the pursuit of happiness, and to have, simply, liberty. The word runs through all public and private discussion of politics and morals in this country for the entire two centuries of its existence and is as contemporary an issue today as it ever was.

Liberty in freedom of movement, in being able to seek one's opportunity freely; liberty in becoming who and what one can make of oneself. That is the American hypothesis: If everyone is free, then it will be better for everyone. It has been accepted by the oppressed everywhere and by the rich and privileged: "Only in America." The "streets of gold" that turn-of-the-century immigrants dreamed and laughed about were known not to be paved with golden cobblestones to be ripped up and sold piece by piece. It was a metaphor to them, a phrase descriptive of the boundless opportunity that existed in America for those lucky enough to be permitted to enter the land of liberty to become rich, liberty to be free of government tyranny, liberty to keep what one could earn, liberty to grow without let or hindrance from king's agents or pitiless laws. From de Crèvecœur [9] to Sam Adams and Jefferson; [10] from Daniel Webster and Jackson to Walt Whitman, to the Four Freedoms of Franklin D. Roosevelt, to the recent national revulsion against the crimes of Watergate, we see an ever recurrent return to concepts of freedom and liberty, which are the real meaning of the United States.[11] The senators of the investigating committee, who shed tears of sorrow and shame on television screens all over the country at the belated revelation of the desecration of ideals of American liberty and the presidency, were living symbols of our national commitment. Hardened politicians and ordinary people in the rest of the world are no different, each wants liberty for himself, and enshrines liberty's dream in his heart. As for the realization of it: Social service and care may be greater elsewhere than in America, friendliness and cooperation are often in greater abundance in other lands, but nowhere is there more love for liberty, or as much willingness to run its risks.

The existence of the Constitution is founded on the belief that restraints on government are necessary if citizens are to have liberty.[12] The parts of the Constitution that have worked best are those that were borrowed from older constitutions of the several states and had proven their worth in living government. Experience was preferred to a priori theory.

No part of the government devised by the Founding Fathers is sovereign of its own right, not the President, the Congress, or the Judiciary. Cooperation is mandated in the document, else there can be no functioning of government. This has not changed, and however we may bewail the creaking of the machinery, we have found it better to oil it rather than to change it.

Above all, the Constitution stands as a substantial barrier to government's potential for interference with liberty of the individual. It is almost pointless for a police officer to bemoan the difficulties put in the path of agents of government in apprehending, convicting, and imprisoning those charged with crime. That is the way Americans want it. That is the simple fact.

The fractioning of the power of government necessitates cooperation and goodwill between the various branches for government to work at all. The separate branches have little power by themselves and all are subject to the Constitution. The reasons for this arrangement are found in the grain of the people who came here: fear lest one power should absorb the rest. Not even the national legislature, with all its qualities of representativeness, has the power to change the Constitution one whit. The British Parliament has had no such limitation since the 1600s, for it is supreme; it was then and remains today a sovereign and constituent assembly. It can make and unmake any and every law, change the form of government or the succession to the crown, interfere with the course of justice, extinguish the most sacred private rights of the citizen.[13]

This is not possible in the United States. Centralization of power to limit social choices went against the pith of the first Americans—and it still does.[14] No town, village, or county wants to be ruled from Washington, nor even from a state capitol. If we are to be ruled at all in our social choices, we bow only to those to whom we have voluntarily consented, and then, for only a short time.

The search for liberty is in our blood, and we have never stopped seeking more of it. Behavioral scientists seek to describe an originating life-energy or drive. To the political scientist, on freedom-bent, what other drive than what has been called "self-realization"? What other than reprisal against an offending social climate? The never-ending search for freedom of choice, of access to alternatives, unhampered by the personal intervention of other human beings, starts with life itself, in parturition —the *parting*. Behavioral scientists have given so many names to it: sexual energy (Freud); libido (Jung); psycho-life (Adler); self (Rogers); self-actualization (Maslow); drive (S-R theory); actualization of potentialities (existentialism).

To accomplish one's own objectives there must be relief from restrictions on choice. What—other than the search for relief from restrictions on one's options—is liberty? Alfred Adler's comment, "Liberty alone breeds giants," makes the point, and Americans have been encouraged to become a race of giants.

The great American search has been for ever more *liberty*. In the failure to recognize this, we may discover why successive criminal-justice orientations have not been persuasive.

When we turn back to the concept of the human organism, filled with life-force, seeking satisfying options from its environment and resisting frustrations and obstacles to its search, we have an approach that may provide a readier guide to police and community performance. This analysis places freedom's ferment in the very biological makeup of the organism and confirms it by every event contributing to psychic development and growing interactional awareness. It is intellectually appealing on the micro- as well as the macro-level, provides easy working plans for practitioners, and supplies the communication content necessary for analysis of specific situations in terms of simplified communication models.

None of this denies the validity or possible usefulness, in a proper case, of any of the biological, psychological, or sociological models. Being of the practical world, we must accept economic models of reality, lest we become financially bankrupt, as well as intellectually chauvinist. All of these are useful.

The sociopolitical model of man and of man's groups as being liberty-loving is accepting of all other disciplinary models. It merely provides a subject matter that is within the consciousness of people and capable of ready comprehension and use. This demarche in academic approaches has substantial historical basis, as shown by all the previous discussion.

Factions

James Madison in *The Federalist* warns us against "factions" among the people as a hazard to liberty. Most political scientists in discussing this conceive of "factions" as being groups united in common interests but in opposition to the common good of the public. In the tenth paper Madison comments on this "dangerous vice" because it introduces confusion, instability, and injustice into public councils and provides ammunition for adversaries to liberty. That the conflicts of rival parties tend to disregard the public good is common knowledge and that the rights of lesser factions are decided not according to the rules of justice and right but by the superior force of an interested and overbearing majority are Madison's themes.

Madison does not leave it there. He goes on to point out ways that factions could be eliminated: first is the destruction of liberty, for it is liberty that gives rise to factions. That, of course, would be worse than the disease. It is liberty that is sought, and the fact that liberty is the occasion and opportunity for the grouping of people to force their will on others does not signify that liberty is evil, but rather that the benefits of liberty provide the freedom that permits people to organize together.

Madison offers another way to eliminate evil factions: indoctrination of every citizen with the same opinions, the same passions, and the same interests. This solution, too, is unworthy of consideration. Diversity of interests, he saw as natural and desirable and latent in the very nature of human beings, not to be constrained.

The cause of faction cannot be removed, it appears to most scholars. Relief is to be found only in means to control its effects. This control is suggested to lie in the voluntary selection of wise people to represent each group of interests, and the setting off of one such representative against a sufficient number of representatives of many other diverse interests so as to balance and temper the actions of all.

Madison feels that in this way undue power over individual choice is vitiated by leaving that power among many diverse, yet balanced, interests, rather than lodging it in the hands of a coordinated group of interests, whether public or private, nationwide or local. Great and aggregate concerns, he suggests, would be referred to national or regional control, and local particular interests to neighborhood jurisdictions. At all times, however, reaching for a fair representation of all diverse interests in favor of, or in opposition to, specific issues being decided.

It is important to note that as partisanship plunges headlong into conflicts, the rights of the smallest minorities must be bruised unless there are outer limits set that cannot be invaded by ordinary processes. There we have need of constitutional barriers at local, regional, and national levels, which set limits beyond which the individual's choices may not be restricted, even by majorities.

Police-community relations, too, seem in need of such considerations —to maintain an eye on great, common goals, while minimizing choice limitations on individuals to only those absolutely necessary. Together with the above, there could well be—following the example presented in procedures for amendment of the Constitution—regular provisions for obtaining general consent of a much greater consensus for any sweeping changes.

Police and community experience of the last two decades indicates that the political wisdom so painfully and bloodily acquired two centuries ago can be used on the local level. The social process of choice limitation exercised by police on community, if not mitigated by the controls and restraints found necessary on statewide and national scale, are bound to erupt into painful confrontations.

Pluralism

The diversity that inevitably results in factions in the political sphere results in a cultural pluralist society of widely different beliefs and practices.[15]

Under our system, cultural differences do not limit a group's right and obligation to participate in all the functions of the community. There are many characteristics that may deny full membership to Americans, but they can be subsumed under three main criteria: age, criminality, and insanity. The young do not vote for those who shape and mold their futures. The choices of the young are severely restricted, without their consent. Too, although the laws are being changed, the old may be forced to retire from a career, despite competence and skill. Persons adjudged criminal are imprisoned, put at forced labor, kept in solitary confinement, and even executed—the ultimate loss of choice. Persons voluntarily or involuntarily committed to mental hospitals are confined to receive painful and disabling treatments, without their consent.

There are other pluralistic aspects that result in involuntary limitations of choice: poverty, educational deficiencies, mental retardation, and, despite laws to the contrary, certain ethnic and racial groups. The complex problems of affirmative action versus reverse discrimination have not been resolved, and both sides are at odds: disadvantaged minorities, which have received some benefit from legislation and administrative rulings in their favor, and "non-disadvantaged" groups that have found fault with the practices of public and private institutions in this regard.

In the welter of such pluralism, the police-community interface inevitably participates in the trials and testing going on in the country at large.

Evolution and Revolution

It is obvious that sociopolitical patterns can be changed by the elements discussed in the preceding sections. When power is exerted to restrict choice, so that change moves relatively slowly, it is called evolution.

It is indeed a mistake to consider that evolution, either biological or social, is a progressive development toward ever higher forms. Aside from the dubious relevance of a biological model for social processes, survival value, in the first place, does not have any reference to "higher" or "lower." Survival, or the probability of survival, ignores pejoration.

It is easy to imagine "lower" forms surviving and "higher" forms becoming extinct. Natural history provides numerous examples, however one decides to define "higher" or "lower."

It is pleasant to think of the human form and mind as being higher than the anthropoid forms that may have preceded them. It is not a fact, but merely an egoistical wish. The changes in social forms and processes that can be observed in human society indicate changes in terms of survival characteristics, but the cyclic return to older forms indicates a complete inability to reach any higher plane from which there is no returning.

Unless, that is, we assume an eternal value, to which we can refer, and convert the implications of all observations into terms of coming closer to, or moving away from, that parameter. In that case, it might be possible to determine which social structures are better adapted to attain that value, though it might still be a difficult chore. That, however, is a task for an idealogue. Policing methods arise from social needs, and certainly none of the forms tried over the centuries have any "eternal value." We do not know the shape of the future. Our policing methods will almost certainly evolve.

Part III

Measurements

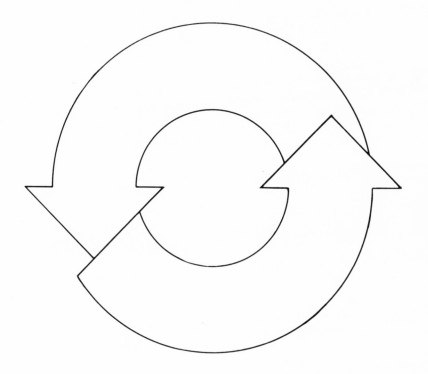

Chapter 9

PLANNING, IMPLEMENTING, AND MONITORING

. . . nobly planned to warn, to comfort and command.
—William Wordsworth, . . . a Phantom of Delight

This chapter discusses the problems involved in planning, implementing, and monitoring. The particular emphasis is on the necessity of making plans in measurable terms. Without some kind of measurement, plans are really not in operational form. Without operationalization, a plan tends to be more of a policy—or even a diffused philosophy. Philosophy, no doubt, is valuable, and of course policy is essential to guide a program over rough spots. Nevertheless, program plans are designs for *doing,* and as such, certain identifiable persons are going to have to go somewhere at a specific time and do very specific things in itemizable and exact ways. The more precision with which these matters are described in advance, the more nearly it can be determined if events occur as anticipated, that is, if the plan worked.

If police-community relations is to become an applied science, it must, at some point, face the problem of measurement. Planning, implementing, and monitoring all call for measurement. The simplest decision involves a plan; in fact, the decision itself constitutes a mini-plan: to do *this* rather than that. Any plan, however rough or detailed, without measurements at least on a minimal basis is inconceivable.

Even planning to go from *here* to *there* distinguishes two places by some comparison, as to fixed locations, and such comparison is the beginning of measurement.

Implementing—putting planned actions into operation—also calls for measurements as valid and as precise as monitoring demands. Monitoring, "watching over," a program to assure that it is being performed under the strictures laid out in the plan, according to specifications, calls for maintaining performance within tolerable, measurable limits, otherwise performance tends to slide into a-lick-and-a-promise on bad days and overperformance on other occasions.

The whole question of measurement is a technical subject, which, at its fundamental level, is based on a set of concepts abstracted from the empirical world of our experience.

What Can Be Measured?

There are many matters of interest to police administrators and community leaders and they are talked about all the time. There comes a time, however, when talking in general terms is not precise enough for either of the parties to the communication. Measurement is demanded if either party is to know exactly what the other is talking about. For example:

"There are *many* residents of this city that need better police protection. It is up to you to provide it," says the president of the local Parents-Teachers Association to the local captain of police.

"Fine," says the police commander. "The question now is, 'How many residents are involved, what is meant by *better* police protection, and how much of it?' " A number of other questions come to his mind that are too complex to put into nontechnical jargon.

Now, even if we grant that the community leader is in a position to give an actual *count* of the number of residents of his concern—which isn't likely, in the ordinary case—it is almost certain that he has no idea of that kind of "better police protection" he wants. Actually, what he probably wants is a lesser incidence of muggings, burglaries, or other crime.[1]

Now, a change in the pattern of crime, or other events calling for the interest of the police and the public, may or may not be within the power of the precinct commander. It is not merely a question of having the police *agree* that there should be a change. It is a matter of what should they do to aid or instigate such a change? How should they do it? Who is going to pay for it? And, is what is being proposed likely to cause results hoped for, without other unanticipated consequences that would be undesirable?

It might be useful to start by discussing what can be measured.[2] That is, how much change of exactly what is wanted, how much will it cost, and how many other things will have to be changed? All of these questions call for measurement.

What can be measured? The only thing that can be measured is difference. There is no such thing as measurement in an absolute sense. As mere humans we have no sense of the absolute but only the ability to perceive some of the differences that may exist when we compare one thing with another. If we hold up two sticks next to each other we can note a difference in length between them if there is a difference large enough to be perceptible to our imperfect senses. We can note differences in color, in texture, and we may even judge, by bending the sticks across our knee one at a time, their difference in flexibility, and if we make this comparison to breaking point, their difference in ultimate strength. It is worthy of note that in comparing the strengths of the two sticks we can destroy that which we measure. This is a common occurrence. *The act of measurement often changes that which is measured.*

Our ability to note differences is quite coarse and limited. We have not discovered ways to measure, for example, community attitudes without, in the process of measurement, changing the very attitude that is being measured!

The ubiquity of error in measurement is surprising to one who first undertakes to measure the qualities of humans, their abilities or performances, or their natures and values. Error is everywhere endemic. The necessity for considering the probability of error is as necessary as discovering what and how to measure.

Since measurement is at bottom simply a comparison, our first task is to discover standards with which to compare. A standard must be relevant to that which is to be measured. Not only must it be from the same universe of things—a test designed to discover community attitudes to the police is out of the universe of tests of human attributes—but it should measure only what it has been designed to measure, for groups similar to the one on which the standard itself has been calibrated.

A test of community attitudes standardized on a rather well-to-do community like Palm Beach, Florida, or Palm Springs, California, would be of doubtful value if used to test residents of Watts or Harlem.

In any case, there may be a large number of equally qualified researchers in the field of community studies who would disagree on the relative value and usefulness of any battery or series of tests of human traits or qualities. Attitude to police is quite judgmental, as are all other attitudes, values, and character traits. All of these are really "constructs"—that is, they are concepts in the minds of humans trying to measure other humans. Actually, nature itself may view things quite differently! It is not merely a matter of affirming or denying the physical existence and measurability of human attributes as an article of faith. On a philosophical level there is much that cannot be rigorously proved, that, nevertheless, has been found helpful in explaining, understanding, ameliorating, and even predicting. We use these constructs as we use electricity, by pushing buttons and enjoying the illumination even though we know next to nothing about wiring or switches; even scientists are ignorant of the nature of electricity itself.

We do not deny the evidence of our senses. We can see people, we can count their numbers, we can note differences between them, and count those who display such differences and note approximately in what degree. Counting seems a very trustworthy method of measurement—it fits in with our traditional ideas and intuition. It is there and we count it, at first on our fingers, and later, with the sequence of numbers as the standard of comparison, by allotting one number to each item.

Perhaps that is why so much of the knowledge that has accrued about communities and criminal justice consists of numbers—massed statistics. People are counted, crimes are counted, complainants are counted, as well as miles of patrol traveled, gallons of gasoline used, numbers of delinquencies, rates of crime clearance. So many cases of citizen complaints against police, so many cases of police officers assaulted by civilians, and so on are all listed interminably.

The costs of obtaining, collating, and retaining these figures are enormous. Their value for useful work in criminal justice or in police-community relations has not been proved. True, they provide a façade of knowledge when they are included in a report. However, one must be careful to be sure that the figures are accurate, that they really measure what they purport to measure, and that they are truly relevant to the purpose for which they are being used in the instant case.

Why Measure?

We have had formal police organizations in this country for more than one hundred years. Organized scientific research has undergone a great revolution during this period, and community and police relations are only beginning to participate. We are just commencing to understand that impressionistic, descriptive studies have not been able to produce either acceptable or rejectable hypotheses. Too many questions are still open, too many generalizations remain unresolvable because of a vagueness of terms and magnitudes.

This does not mean that measurement is the answer. If the concepts we have been working on are very wrong, if the elements, samples, and populations have been injudiciously chosen, measuring will not help much—it may add to the confusion.[3] It is rather that measurement is a necessary step in the operationalization of research, and the rigor required to justify the measures proposed to the sophisticated research community places the entire research, its generating concepts as well as its methodological design, under a focused criticism that insists upon identifying suspicious data, inadequate design, erroneous assumptions, and value-laden conclusions.

We have concentrated on the symptomatology of social behavior—violence, crime, disorder—rather than reaching for more insightful, critical probes into the nature of humanity, causal relationships, and impelling conditions. There is no reason to believe that a mere increase in the number of factors assessed in multiple-factor analysis should lead to particularly important selections of factors that will solve problems if the entire factor concept that we have been looking at it is in error.

Thus we should measure, not because measuring incorrect objects will turn them into correct objects, but because, in the act of measuring, the fact that they are incorrect may become obvious, and we can go on to seek more correct objects.

The Limits of Measurement

There is good cause for the reluctance of social scientists to use measurements.[4] The awareness that a human being is an intensely complex and changeable thing, withdrawing from a cold stare, warming to a sympathetic eye, has been the deterrent. Can one measure a wisp of smoke? At one time the comment was valid—but now we do measure wisps of smoke! Another objection was that zeroing in on a specific measurement necessarily ignores countless other relevant, dynamic elements that should also be taken into account, as is attempted in case studies and even in depth interviews, where the unique aspects of personality are encouraged to display themselves to the observer, sans calipers, sans scales, but with an understanding heart and mind. But we have found that even complex matters can be measured, counted, calibrated, and evaluated. We have new technical resources, from computers to electron microscopes and brain-scanning machines, to assist. An intercontinental ballistic missile or a space shuttle vehicle will involve counting and coordinating five million or more distinct elements. Granting that the human being is more complex by a factor of at least ten, and perhaps twenty, should that discourage us? Is not the gain to be obtained by the study of man even greater than that to be had by the study of war or space?

A final objection to the measurement of human beings and their relations to other human beings appears to be a certain reluctance to tread on areas reserved strictly for theology. It is as though a concordat has been reached between scientists and theologians to divide the world of knowledge between them. Theologians and ethical philosophers to preempt all that is sin and virtue, good and bad, the origin of life, and all eternity. Scientists, then, to restrict their endeavors to the immediately useful in a materialistic sense.

Perhaps, in the days of Galileo Galilei there was such an unwritten concordat by implicit agreement. Nevertheless, such a contract would not be binding on those who were not a party to it. Today, we see no bar to reaching for new ideas, whether or not they transgress the fashions of another day or overflow into the channels of thought of previous toilers in the worked-dry vineyards of scientific inquiry. *Criminal justice,* as a university discipline, must transgress in this fashion if it is to do its work. As to the reluctance to discover too much of the truth of man, we are already ankle-deep in the mystery of life, as evidenced by the recent revelations about the functioning of genetic chains as sequenced decisions about the kind and quality of life-to-be.

Measurement, as an empirical rather than a theoretical concept, is faced with the open-endedness of reality rather than the closed system surety of deductive logic. It is based on the assumptions inherent in all our perceptions of reality. The lack of this general knowledge, it seems, has resulted in restricting measurements to only those efforts that were so much a part of intuitive wisdom that there was little or no objection to the kinds of measures used and to their applications.

Now that we know that *all* measurement starts in midair, as it were, and from that point tries to pull itself up by its own bootstraps, we are relieved of embarrassment when we are caught with our assumptions down. We can say, we knew it all the time, we just wanted to see where this new set of assumptions would carry us.

It should be noted that different kinds of measurements intrinsically contain different kinds or levels of information. This is something that is often ignored by practitioners and academics alike. It is quite customary to see intelligence quotients correlated with other attributes such as "good looks," "orderliness," "pleasing personality," and other such constructs. Interesting! However, the commonly used Pearson correlation index is predicated on variables that change linearly and continuously, two conditions that no research scientist seriously believes exists in the constructs mentioned.

Nominal measurement is the mere naming of elements, to differentiate them from other elements: Say, naming oranges to separate them from apples. The entire class of the objects we call oranges is distinguished from the class we call apples. The class of *round* objects could include both apples and oranges, as well as gold balls and all other similarly shaped objects of whatever size, weight, or substance, from buckshot to planets.

Naming does identify; it compares one element with another element along a particular dimension, in short, it fits our definition of measurement: comparison. Let us give a more detailed definition: comparison of elements according to rules that permit assignment of symbols to indicate the nature of the comparison. The symbol, or name, *orange,* indicated a class of objects. It could just as easily have designated a specific object, which we called orange to differentiate it from any other object present, apple or anything else. Usually, however, to indicate a singly named object we would add another auxiliary symbol, such as *this* orange or *the* orange or *that* orange. If it was a particular person you wanted to indicate you could say this man or that woman, but you probably would say his name: John Jones, here, picking him, as an individual, out of all other objects, people, and even from all others named John Jones.

Note, we could have said "round orange," giving that object two names, both correct, but each referring to a different dimension.

Ordinal measurement is the comparison of elements as to their relative rank along a single dimension. We say, this object is *longer* than that *other* one, which is *shorter.* We can put an entire series of elements in such a ranking order without too much trouble, merely by paired comparisons, moving them about until all of them are in "size place," or rank order, along the dimension of length. Further, we could indicate their rank order by a set of symbols that would indicate the nature of the comparison, say, "longest," "next longest," "second next longest," and so on. Probably you would find it easier to call the longest number "1," the next, "2," the one after, "3," and so on.

Of course you could reverse the sequence and make number "1" the shortest, "2" the next shortest, and so on. In each case you might indicate the direction the sequence took.

Rank ordering comes to us intuitively, right out of the world of our experience, just as did "counting" and "naming." It seems, somehow, natural to put things in size place. We do it all the time. There is, however, one little trap that we fall into sometimes: When a sequence of numbers is used to indicate the rank order, for example, 1, 2, 3, 4, 5 . . .

and so on, we sometimes overlook the fact that those numbers are nothing more than *ordinal*. They show the places in the ordered sequence, but they have not acquired the right to be added or subtracted. The number 2 object is *not* one half as long as the number 4 object. Nor is it one-half as long as, nor does it have any determinable relationship with, any other element in the series, other than rank order.

In the confusion of collecting information about programs in criminal justice and community affairs, this important fact is sometimes overlooked. "Better than" does not necessarily mean worth $100,000 more than!

An example might be I.Q. scores. Even if one consents to the possibility that intelligence scores are a valid differentiation between groups of people along a real dimension we denote as "intelligence," there certainly is no logical reason to believe that an I.Q. of 1.30 has picked out an intelligence that is 30 percent higher than one of 1.00. The numbers just do not mean that. If the numbers mean anything at all—and there is much contemporary doubt—they might mean a rank order along a specialized dimension best described as "whatever that particular test measures, if anything.

Differences in rank do not denote any difference measurable in any specific units, only that one is more or less than the other, a relational difference we call rank order or size place in colloquial parlance. There is, however, something implicit in this: Each rank denotes at least one element, and, therefore, if we count the number of ranks, we shall know the number of elements in the series, or the *count*, as we have called it before. We maintain that level of information in rank order, that is, we include the "count." In the event two or more elements are the same size, we add up the numbers indicating the rank for each and divide by the number of elements involved. Example: If the second and third sticks are the same length, and the fourth is the longest of the series of four sticks, we add 2 and 3 and divide by 2, giving us 2.5, which is assigned as ranks to the second and third sticks, as having equal but separate ranks of that order. It is merely a convention and does not change the fact that ordinarily one cannot validly add, subtract, multiply, or divide the symbolic numbers indicating rank.

Intuitively, we feel most human attributes and performances are comparable along such a rank-order dimension, nor is there any mathematical, statistical, or logical reason to believe that devising more complex measuring methods will somehow instill more information than rank order, if that is all the information we have. Measurement cannot improve on what is.

Equal-interval measurement is called the next level of measurement because it contains all the information of the previous ones with a little bit more. In this level of measurement the intervals between each named and ordered element are expressible in equal intervals, and we thus have a comparison that conveys this information. The area of a neighborhood may be expressed in square miles or in acres or in the metric system in hectares. Each square mile is the same as any other square mile as to area, as is each acre and each hectare. A neighborhood covering 12 square miles is twice as large as one of 6 square miles and four times as large as one of only 3 square miles.

The equal-interval units of square miles permit comparison, in effect, by counting the number of such equal intervals that fit into each element-neighborhood.

Number of miles of streets that require patrol in a neighborhood is another example of measurement by an equal interval, in this case, linear miles instead of square miles. In the prior example of the set of four sticks, if each one had been described as being so many inches long or so many feet long, the number symbols indicating the quantities of the equal-in-length inches or feet contained in each stick could be used to compare each stick by specifically stating how many inches or feet it is longer than the others.

Let us say the two sticks in the middle of the series of four previously described are found to be exactly 5 inches longer than the shortest stick and 30 inches shorter than the longest stick in that series.

Now that we know the difference between the sticks in inches we can say that the longest stick is 35 inches longer than the shortest, by adding 5 inches to 30 inches, as the total difference between those two sticks. The same could be done as to the heights of the boys in a street gang: If we had a foot-long ruler we could measure the differences between their heights in inches. After recording the measurements we would know how the boys ranked in size-place and the differences in height among them. For instance, there may be a difference of ten inches between the tallest and the shortest, with most of the heights clustered around the tall end of the scale. But we would not know the total height of each. To discover this, we would have to use another scale, for an equal-interval scale is not sufficient.

Ratio-level measurement involves discovering where the natural zero is in the empirical world and measuring in equal-interval units from that point. Thus the boys in the previous example could have their respective heights measured from the ground up by standing them in their stocking feet against a wall and measuring up to the crowns of their heads. The tallest would still be ten inches taller than the shortest, but we would also discover that the tallest boy is, say, 68 inches, and the shortest one, 58 inches. Further we could say that the tallest boy is exactly 10/68 taller than the shortest.

In the case of the four sticks, if we measured them on a ratio-level measurement scale, we would measure from one end to the other. Say we discovered that the shortest was 36 inches, the two of equal length were 40 inches, and the longest stick was 72 inches. Now, we could say that the longest stick is two times the length of the shortest (or, conversely, that the shortest is one-half the length of the longest) and the two of equal length are exactly 4/36, or 1/9, longer than the shortest stick. Further, we could say that the longest stick is 32/72 longer than the two of equal length.

Unless there is a *natural zero,* the ratios between the scores cannot be said to mean anything about reality. In the example of the intelligence scores, we would have had to find in the empirical world a zero intelligence to consider even the attempt to make intelligence test scores ratio-level measurement. Zero intelligence has no meaning in the reality of human capacity, thus ratio-level intelligence scores are not available.

This is an important point because simple as it may be to find a natural zero in physical attributes, such as linear, volumetric, or weight measurement, the psychic and other internal characteristics of human beings show no natural zero. Could you recognize and measure zero personality? Since we cannot find in the real world zero intelligence, or for that matter zero magnitude of any human characteristic, we cannot scale those attributes on a ratio-level scale.

Actually, the measurement of individual, and group characteristics often meets with this difficulty, sometimes without being realized by the parties to the measuring process. To guard against the possibility of error from this cause, experts familiar with problems of measurement should be consulted.

Planning As a Continuous Process

Planning in police-community relations (PCR) to this date has tended to be something of an intermittent concern. In typical crisis-oriented fashion, it is as though PCR is an occasional batch, to be cooked up, served hot, and consumed to the last morsel before we find out what's been cooking! Most people in the field today, however, know there are better ways. This does not presume that there is any end to effort. On the contrary, PCR is a continuous labor, requiring constant planning, implementing, and monitoring.

Planning, implementing, and monitoring lead not to final solutions or Holy Grails. They lead but to more planning, implementing, monitoring, a never-ending sequence as part of the programmatic process itself. There are as many ways to describe the planning process as there are plans. Here is one way to look at the matter:

1. A plan is a design to change an existing state of affairs. It is the measure of what is to be done, and the units of this measure must be familiar without translation to those to whom it is to be addressed.

2. It may start with a random thought out of the blue—a chance idea. Or it may have been first conceived as the result of a concerted effort for a new approach. In either case the idea must have come from a mind prepared to recognize at least the possibility of change. What is the environment that encourages the development of such a state of mind? There appears to be no way to describe the conditions that permit original thinking, except to say it is an environment that allows for the discovery of *something*. The social and physical milieu must not forbid the new. Of course there is a probabilistic notion here, in that some environments tend to discourage innovation more than others. There have been many devices contrived to increase the probability of a new idea emerging.

3. Some of these ways are seminars and "idea sessions," or seeking out alleged experts, or taking the opposite tack, seeking out people previously unacquainted with the subject. We have tried organized and unorganized formal research, brain-storming, contests for ideas, conferences, and even "sleeping on it." All of these methods and many others have been used to prepare minds to receive, invent, or stumble onto new ideas. The only evaluation of these methods that makes any sense is: Did it work?

4. In this search, if we commence by assuming that the basic elements of new ideas will be the matrix of culture and constructs in the minds of the planners, we can agree that it is important to choose with great care the minds that are to be involved in the plan. The problem is that the tendency of almost every selection process is to choose minds that are similar to each other and compatible with the constraints of the selection process, thus losing the diversity of intellect that a more random effort might provide. The loss of diversity is balanced by the fact that if a contributor produces ideas that are too new to be tolerated by the group, the ideas would very likely be rejected out of hand.

5. In any case, however new the minds, the ideas will be the product of previous personal experiences of the participants in the planning process. Consciously or unconsciously there will be pervading attitudes, predispositions, having to do with submission or rebellion, of being

concerned with things or with people, with feelings or with more objective realities, each in a unique pattern that will affect the way ideas will be conceived and received.

6. Very often the deadlock between the planners of the new and the defenders of the old will be resolved in favor of retention of the old either in substance or in form. This is not meant as reproof—often the old is truly better than the new. Too often new solutions bring in new problems—even disasters.

7. From examination of the record, the only way the new plan can attain acceptance is by obtaining the support of those powerful individuals who can constrain choice or, in the alternative, persuade individuals who control an information flow that influences others.

Georges Clemenceau once said that war is too important to be left to the generals. Are police and community relations in the same class? Does this mean that though the decision to implement or to abide must be made by specific police and community individuals, the really innovative ideas must arise from "outside"—from new minds?

The events of life batter the status quo constantly. Change is inevitable and occurs every instant to some degree. Thus, merely to retain the status quo requires organized planning. To channel change along predetermined lines, then, requires constant planning.

Planning Police-Community Relations

Urban areas today are the scene of an ongoing process between society and a formal organization dedicated to policing norms. Neither side is very much interested in change. They have been surviving reasonably well, up to this point, as entities, as groups, as individuals. Any change requires diversion of attention and energy from what has become satisfying and effective. The mass of society and the core of the police departments envisage no radical changes. Those who seek change appear to be in the minority.

This minority appears to be of different shades, however. Some few of them are of an insurgent spirit, "rebels." For them the act of revolt is satisfaction itself. It appears these individuals identify elements in the old merely to resist those elements. They may appear to adapt to the new in society and organization much more easily than the rest. In some cases their mutinous attitudes subside, and they will thereafter fight for the-new-that-has-become-the-old as stoutly any other reactionary. Still others remain forever rebels. It may be helpful in planning for police-community relations to seek out those restless personalities to assist in planning, keeping in mind their characteristics and the possible effect their performance might have not only in the present, but also in the future. The decision as to what personnel to involve in planning is a basic problem in developing any change strategy. With what do the people who are chosen identify? is a very important question. Are they interested in the objectives as already set forth in a plan? Or are they really more involved with different objectives? Do they identify with the *ways* things have been done, rather than ultimate goals? What specific elements are dear to their hearts, spring from their very nature?

People cannot be expected to change much, though there are flexible types, more representative of a new, more adaptive society, toward which we seem to be evolving. Police organizations tend to engender close internal mutually supportive relations, affection for its style and all its ways. The members will not easily change their patterns of thought and action. The methods and goals of any community of interest are often equally dear to the community member.

The mode in which these two opposing forces will adapt to each other and to any plan for change in previous accommodations has been described by long-term observers such as Robert K. Merton. Typical patterns have been noted and given names.

Conformity as a mode of adaptation implies that individuals and groups that are satisfied with expected goals and the available means for reaching those goals are not likely to respond to any appeal that calls for change. Instead, they will tend to resist both the form and substance of planned change. If under considerable pressure, they tend to accept the form of the change, to avoid negative feedback, but in core performance there remains prolonged resistance. It has been noted that some changes take one or more generations to be accomplished.

Innovation, as a mode of adaptation, is rarely found as a typical response, except in some small organizations designed expressly to discover and apply novel concepts. Think tanks are one example, as are a few self-contained revolutionary organizations dedicated to overthrow of national or international power establishments. Even these organizations, however, inevitably become repetitively structured in their approach to innovation. It appears that a great truth about humanity is operating: We quickly become "set" in our ways. This is most curiously illustrated by the never-failing effectiveness of the modus operandi file in criminal investigation. Even though just about every criminal knows about it, he cannot avoid being who and what he is, and that controls to an amazing degree, what he does. Innovation can be more easily introduced, however, if the planned change can be directed either to the means or to the goals, rather than to both. It appears to be easier to install new means to attain familiar goals than to modify a method for the achievement of strange goals.

In similar vein, if an individual or group is permitted to go about its accustomed work, in patterned, habitual ways, the fact that the goal has been changed is often cognitively suppressed, and massive, substantive change is effected without resistance.

Ritualism, as a mode of adaptation, as discerned by Merton, is one wherein realistic goals are by-passed compared to an insistent clinging to means. This is not the variation cited as "Innovation," as described above. Rather, it is a rigid adherence to patterns of behavior that have come to have meaning and values in themselves. In fact, what had originally been devised as means have themselves become goals, consciously or unconsciously. This is bureaucracy's vice everywhere. Insistence on forms rather than content has frustrated clients of bureaucracies since the dawn of history. Police departments are no exception. Ritualism is a common sight: Professionals and experts of all kinds—those eminently qualified in any specialty—become addicted to their technique and use the thought and behavior patterns unique to that speciality in preference to all others.

It is no special quirk of the professional's mind that makes him overly susceptible to ritualism. All of us fall victim to it—or, from another point of view, we are the beneficiaries of it. As the poet said, a wall should not be removed until we're sure why it was put there in the first place. Maybe the reason still exists!

Retreatism, a fourth mode of adaptation, is the rejection of both goals and institutional means. In the 1960s it was called "turning-off," a state of being *in* society but not *of* it.

Rebellion as a mode of adaptation considers the system as the barrier to the attainment of goals, and the stage is set for efforts to destroy the system.

To take the measure of all these methods by whatever means possible, but basically by referring as much as possible to hard, objective data rather than subjective impressions that are related at second or third hand, seems to be the most reasonable approach to police-community problems. Groups or individuals in police and communities can be assessed in regard to the above matters. Standard tests are available to scale attitudinal aspects of individuals. Probably the most valuable measures, however, will be the readiness to recognize the above patterns, that is, by the nominal measure of measurement, identifying the above typical patterns in the groups to be involved in the planned change. If a further specificity is sought, the counting of sheer numbers of members seen to be characterized by a readiness to these modes of adaptation to change can be undertaken. The results would provide a very useful data base that would be of incalculable value in clarifying the situation to the planners as well as to the people who are about to be involved.

The "rebels" are ready recruits to the plan but may be uncontrollable in a continued program. Those who are "retreatist," or "turned-off," are well-nigh unreachable, although there are degrees of both rebellion and retreatism.

"Ritualists," placed in a new situation where their rituals are blatantly dissonant, uncomfortable, or impossible, can be eventually changed, with, however, great internal strain, dissension, and resistance. With time and patience, nonetheless, the overt resistance will be reduced to merely sighs of nostalgia, and the "new" will become the regimen. The same juggernaut method via dissonance, discomfort, or impossibility of avoidance will work with even greater results on those who are conformist.

Innovation in well-patterned relations is easier to accomplish in both police and community if the initiating moves are first made by the very top echelons of both societies. In great measure, prescribed norms are set by and continually reinforced by the most prestigious ranks of a group, who, because of both their positions and their personalities, together with their greater access to command and control of communications channels, have considerable influence.

The planner of innovation in police-community relations, however, must consider that the upper levels of both groups may have a vested interest in some aspects of the existing situation. If that is the case, any hint of a proposed change that will injure that vestment in privilege will be fought to a finish. To rationalize these two contrary generalizations, it is important to identify the particular norms and cultural *means-goals* continua. As scientific observers read it, understanding the intimate and immediate dynamics is helpful in setting up and implementing major changes in community relations.

Plans for Action

Plans for action necessarily must be designed to cope with the conditions presented with a view to the nature and extent of the proposed action.

Small action planned, small plans required! However, if the community situation is such that an extensive change in deeply ingrained socio-political currents seems to be called for, not only will special measures need to be taken, but also the time-dimension must be extended considerably.

A widely held view is that no cultural form that requires behavioral or attitudinal change that is uncongenial to personality structure or widely held community attitudes can be successfully introduced within the space of one generation. The models of adaptation discussed in the preceding section have been noted by behavioral scientists and historians as sometimes requiring several generations to evolve. Another observation, which may have great relevance to the police-community relations manager, is that sociopolitical changes appear to go through three sequential phases:

The first step, *compliance*, involves the acceptance of new attitudes or types of behavior that are the subject of massive communication and influence. *Compliance* accepts behavior and attitudes not because of belief, but because there is credible expectation of specific reward for obedience and punishment for captious capers.

The second stage, *identification*, includes the new attitudes and behavior within an ambience of a satisfying relationship with a desired individual or group, as new interactional associations are formed.

The third and last phase, *internalization*, occurs when the content of the attitudes and the behavior becomes satisfying, gratifying, even rewarding, in itself.

Some researchers have interpreted the three-step sequence of sociopolitical change as occurring relatively quickly, certainly within one generation. However, great changes, perhaps covering large numbers of people, distantly separated, with obstacles to diffusion of influence being a factor, may require more than three generations.

It has been hypothesized that what has been firmly learned at an early age is more resistant to change than attitudes and behavior learned later in life. This persuasively explains the gradual rate that some changes demonstrate.

The psychoanalytic theories that lean toward a tri-level development of personality interpret these three levels to be symptomatic of three levels of intensity of persistence of personality characteristics. The perennial appearance of tripartite models is almost enough for one to suspect that tripartism is a model of modeling! Communications researchers have presented, however, a two-stage model of influence (Chapter 5).

Sociocultural studies have produced communications versions that theorize as follows:

First, there is the body of characteristics, attitudes, and behavior that is consciously and forcefully taught and learned: "Everyone always does it this way," ". . . a runny nose is *disgusting,* wipe it!" There often are emotional overtones in the learning situation, and violation arouses strong anxiety. Such things are regarded as simple common sense, human nature, and all the learning that is acquired as a result of child rearing. These matters change very slowly in a group.

Second, there is a surrounding core of informal, low-intensity attitudes and behaviors. Although these, too, are learned, they are not the subject of a formal effort but are acquired by informal observation and imitation. Many of these items become subconscious and automatic; but if breached, a certain lesser level of anxiety is created. Such matters as these can be changed by presenting new models for observation and imitation, though the change is quite slow.

The third and last class of attitudes and behaviors is called technical, which is taught explicitly and cognitively. Often for these there is support by logical argument, such as education in classes at school. Changes of attitudes and behaviors of this group are easily effected. Apparently cognitive dissonance is aroused least when alternative logical analysis is presented to displace "technical" items. The subconscious levels of cognitive dissonance appear to generate more energy and higher levels of anxiety than conscious dissonances that can be examined in the open. Often the conscious cognitive dissonance developed when alternative attitudes and behaviors are presented to displace those existing can be dissipated by displays of logical support for the new modes.

Actually, what is observed are differing levels of *resistance to change,* and statements as to different levels of consciousness are *inferred* by keen observers of human behavior.

The planner in community relations who aims to produce action in human beings would do well to consider some of the matters discussed in this section. Both Merton's five modes of adaptation to attempts at planned change and the two-step flow of influence of Chapter 5 are identifiable in the real programs in effect today. The "three levels of difficulty" concept for changing the attitudes and behavior of human beings is invaluable in setting forth on a planning session and can help avoid much unnecessary trouble and effort. What can be expected from plans for action may depend in great measure on how well the above matters are considered in the planning stages.

Engineering Implementation

Police and community plans for the foreseeable future will be at what Edward T. Hall has called the "technical" level. That is, they will be rational and will be presented with logical substantiation. Today it is difficult, if not impossible, to present any plan in the admonitory, super-ego-involvement way that might have been possible at one time. Appeals to conscience do not work today. In feudal times, the king's policing measures had the sanctity and moral authority of divine right. It is doubtful, indeed, if a police or community program today can attain that level of social validity, except for comparatively small, isolated, and well-indoctrinated groups.

We can view police-community relations and the planning for it as a circular process, in which the technical plans of today are implemented to operate over time:

At first unaccustomed plans and procedures are burdensome, but eventually they become internalized imperatives, highly valued, with powerfully energized attitudes and performances ensured by high anxiety levels for deviance. The machinery of performance then becomes spontaneously reinforcing and regenerative, until it is "only natural."

Ideally, implementation should be self-fulfilling. If this ideal is not attainable under modern strictures against forced behavior modification, we must use less powerful but more socially acceptable methods of preparing plans in clear, unambiguous, internally consistent, and quantified designs for living and doing. This appeal is "technical," that is to say, as rational and logical as an engineering drawing of the normative structure that is being planned. The norms should be so candidly and pointedly stated as to leave no doubt in anyone's mind. The means and ends must then be equally clear in all respects. Devoted to an intellectual appeal, the plan must not fail in any detail of conceptual symmetry. But even that is not enough. There must be a constant *monitoring* of every performance called for in the plan. The appeal to the intellect is, as we have seen, a comparatively weak one. The only alternative to internalizing controls is omnipresent external monitoring. This cannot be overemphasized. There is one self-generating process that assists; a saving grace, as it were, the act of monitoring, if rigorously adhered to, tends to generate its own internalization on the part of the monitor and those monitored. It has frequently been observed that the prescribed roles attain a momentum greater than the degree bought and paid for. We obey more readily than we expect, or than we know.

The compliance attained by monitoring is often sufficient implementation for a given project—and that is the immediate objective.

To Make an Omelet—Break Eggs!

The title of this section simply refers to the fact that, much as it may be desirable, it is practically impossible to obtain the concurrence of all on any given plan for extended action. It is often impolitic to forbid participation to any concerned group, for that creates an unforgiving enemy that can possibly undo all the good offices of a thousand friends. For any individual to discover that he has been excluded throws him into the camp of all future opponents. Nevertheless, it would be fruitless to bring into a planning group an individual or group whose efforts will be directed toward scuttling all plans and all programs resulting from the plans. Such adversaries must be diverted or neutralized.

Client groups—the people who are the subject of the planned programs, the neighborhood, the community of interest—*must* be notified of the desire you have for their participation. Their effective "gatekeepers" of information and influence must be contacted and involved in the initial stages of the planning procedures. Their cooperation is as essential as anything else can be, especially in the initial stages of any plan when the ultimate objectives are set forth, sometimes in very general terms. At this stage it is not too difficult to obtain consensus—almost everyone is for fundamental benefits: safer streets, more protection, reduced costs, faster response time, more courtesy, reduced burglaries, aid for children, protection of the elderly. Even third-party power groups, that is, groups that are not directly involved with the planned program's objectives except in an institutionalized way, are concerned with the public's general welfare. There groups include banks, public utilities, large corporations, women's groups, fraternal associations, Rotary Clubs, Lions, Elks, and Better Business Bureaus. All can be notified at the very earliest stages, establishing them as "receivers" for subsequent transmitted information even if they do not respond immediately.

There are, however, a number of selfishly interested people who, eager to find or to create springboards for their own, leap into prominence and influence. They will be only too glad to accept invitations to participate and thereupon will endeavor to take over the planning and programming for their own purposes.

To accept them and to assent to their maneuvers is disaster. Here is where the breaking of eggs comes in: They must be excluded at all costs. If the plan is to be a police-community–relations project beneficial to police and community objectives, no "bull" should be permitted into the shop to "toss around the china." Enough legitimate opposition and natural difficulties will come to the fore; there is no need to look for more trouble. In some instances it is better to forget temporarily the plans and the programs until a threatened opposition can be shunted away toward other interests. There may be charges of "shabby treatment" or rudeness or "refusing to acknowledge our right to speak," which will have to be borne, if they cannot be avoided. If this must be—then it must be. Bad as that is, it is easier, and more likely to lead to eventual success, than taking into the parley an irreconcilable opponent. Better to brush them off and go it alone, immediately, if time is of the essence, than to try to carry these burdens on the journey.

True, this decision should not be made out of hand. There should be considered forethought. Possible consequences must be weighed, and if the costs are less than the benefits, make the hard decision and keep the plan moving forward.

The same is true about parts of the plan or program that might ensue. It is good to include every useful element and faction, but there is never enough money, time, personnel, or talent available to waste on internal bickering. Cut them out, and move on! Chapter 12 discusses some ways to try to reconcile dissidents. It is a difficult and exacting enigma at best, and if the problem is insurmountable in the time allotted, it may be better to avoid the issues entirely.

Chapter 10

EVALUATION

Not to oversee workmen is to leave your purse open.
—Benjamin Franklin, *Poor Richard's Almanac*

After completing a planned effort in police-community relations, the next step is to evaluate, to determine whether the planned goals of the program have been reached.

Without evaluation as to a program's attainment of goals, there can be no increase in our state of knowledge as to useful programs or details of programs.

There is no guarantee that a given evaluation is correct—but without evaluation, there is no possibility of improvement.

After-the-Fact Measurement

Although the term *evaluation* can be applied to a number of different types of judgments, we use it here to refer to the estimation of the consequences of a program of any kind.

The local community does not ordinarily initiate these evaluations and may not even be involved in some of them, except in a minimal way. Nor does the police department initiate all of such evaluations, but inevitably the police become a part of them, or at least an element in many aspects, if only in a passive sense.

Some of the evaluations are not full-scale efforts; rather they are situations or a series of situations that occur often without intention. Other evaluations are full-scale programs in themselves.

Programs of any kind that are funded by the federal government or its agencies will almost invariably call for the scheduling of an evaluation as part of the initial proposal for the grant. It appears the day is past when funding will be proffered without a demand to know what is being obtained for the expenditures. For the goal of all evaluation is to make life better, more economical and rewarding for all concerned.

There is only one thing that is invariable about evaluations of all kinds: They occur after the fact. An evaluation of an event is a judgment made after the event has occurred. There can be no evaluation of a prospective event. Evaluation is not the monitoring of ongoing circumstances, nor is it done before the fact.

That evaluation is done subsequent to the matters it judges does not mean that nothing toward evaluation is done beforehand.[2] Very often, evaluative criteria will be set up in the earliest planning stages. After all, if one is planning for something to happen, should not specific measures be cited that will indicate successful attainment of the objective?

However, this is not always done. In the plan or the enabling statute or somewhere along the line, there may be a claim that certain objectives are the reason for a program of action, but there may be no way of exactly determining when that objective is reached because of the vague terminology used in describing the objective. In such a case the evaluator is forced to design his own measures and apply them. This can result in very unhappy consequences to the project's promoters, and a bitter colloquy ensues with charges and countercharges of the inadequacy of measures and performances. The remedy is really so simple: set up criteria for evaluation before the project ever gets off the ground, in the planning stage, if possible, but certainly before actual implementation.

If such evaluative criteria have not been set up, the evaluator must proceed as best he can. It then becomes essential for him to examine all documents that mention the purpose or objective in relation to the project under discussion and to interview the chief administrators of the department and the project to determine the fairest and most representattive measures to be assigned.

The problem becomes quite difficult when no stated objectives or goals can be discovered or when only the vaguest statements, such as "to make life better and safer for the elderly" or "increasing responsibility," are available. When confronted with vague objectives, which are subject to as many different interpretations as there are people making the judgment, the evaluator should delay the evaluation process until all persons concerned are consulted to decide on what evaluative criteria are to be accepted in the evaluation report, together with all the justification such assumptions require.

To be fair, all decisions as to evaluative criteria should be presented to the program's proposers and practitioners for their comment. They can hardly be held accountable for goals and criteria that at no time were in their contemplation.

In any case, the after-the-fact judgment process will involve the collection of evidence in systematic fashion, with all the requirements of a scientific investigation adhered to at all times. Samples, if taken, will be as representative as is possible under the conditions existing, and there should be quantitative units set forth at all appropriate points in the inquiry. All data should be in before the *findings* section of the evaluative report is prepared—and the findings should be carefully reviewed before any final conclusions are drawn as to the merit, effectiveness, or success of the subject of evaluation are made.

The *conclusions* and *recommendations* section of the report, in the interest of impartiality, should be presented not as findings of fact, but as the personal judgment of the evaluator, with admissions of all bias and assumptions within the knowledge of the evaluator. Conclusions and recommendations should be founded on specific facts, either in original data or as summarized in the findings. Ordinarily, too, the report will be submitted to the planners and practitioners involved for their comment and rebuttal. Not to do so could be decidedly unfair, as all ex parte decisions must be. The confrontation of both sides on every questioned fact or conclusion, with a reasonable right to inquire given to both sides, is basic not only to fairness but also to realistic evaluation.

All of this takes time and money. Naturally, the money and effort allocated must be proportional to the money, effort, and purposes, as well as the consequences, of the phenomena being evaluated. It would be pointless for a program costing $100,000 to be evaluated at an expense of $250,000. The consequences and future value of the evaluation would have to be rather momentous to justify such disparity. All things in good measure is an old saying, but in evaluation it is difficult to know how much is good measure in estimating the appropriate cost of an evaluation. Considered judgment on this matter seems to hover between 2 and 10 percent of the cost of the program, with a preference toward the lower end of that scale.

Of course, in many cases the main purpose of a program was simply to have the program in operation. The generic term *action programs* covers many of this type. Some are pure speculation, with no well-thought-out goals or real anticipation of any major successes. In the social sciences we often hear the remark: *"Anything* is better than what we're doing now. Let's do *something!"*

It is hardly worth the bother to evaluate such programs. They were never meant to be evaluated, because nobody ever really expected any specific results. The whole thing was just a hope and a promise—until the next time. The evaluation of such programs by any objective criteria meets with intense objections from vested interests to after-the-fact assessment. There is no denying that not all things in this world can be made objective. Undoubtedly, much that is important and good on earth is so intensely personal and subjective as to be beyond our heavy-handed fumbles for objectivity. Some matters must remain articles of faith and, as such, are beyond mundane measurement. It may be that faith can move mountains, as they say, but such things are, to say the least, difficult to plan and impossible to evaluate.

We should say something about the importance of obtaining evaluative results in what computer people call real-time, that is, in time to be of some real value to those who are responsible for administering programs. We all know of one-year projects that did not produce an evaluative report until more than two years after the end of the project. What utter waste—the time and money and effort expended on such evaluations! That, however, brings us to the next section.

Real-Time Measurement

If evaluation is to accomplish any useful purpose, it must arrive on the scene in time to assist in improving performance. Good evaluation is expensive. Resources of all kinds are scarce. Off hand evaluations, self-serving estimates, and uncoordinated opinion have been used in the past and presented as purported evaluations. The time seems to have come when government and public must be more critical, and with good reason. "No one should be judge in his own cause" was first said two thousand years ago, but we continue to post millions of dollars for projects that are evaluated solely by those whose personal careers and fortunes hinge upon the alleged "success" of these projects.

Granting good intentions—for lack of proof to the contrary—intuition and opinion gathering are feeble, nevertheless, in ability to uncover factual truth. Harder times call for harder reasoning. It is rigor that is demanded in all programs related to police and to the people they serve. Today the decisions in regard to government and community are important and costly, and the numerous and complex factors involved are difficult to observe. A new level of sophistication is required, along with swift delivery of accurate judgments that can be of value to administrators who have to make the decisions as to effectiveness. If these decisions are made after it is too late to improve service to the community because the program is being phased out, the path is open to repeat bad programs indefinitely. If there is no culprit in the dock on the day of judgment, there can be no calling to account. Bad performance will have gone unremarked—to be revived in duplicate programs again and again. There can be no cumulative increase in knowledge if we do not discover equally what is bad as well as what is good and useful.

Thus the evaluative process must be considered at the very inception of the police-community effort. The plan for evaluation should be included in the project plan, and it should be scheduled for completion at a definite date, which coordinates with the time schedule for the project proper. Too, it should be commensurate with the purpose, size, and characteristics of the program of police-community relations itself.[3]

If this is properly done, the evaluation can be articulated with the monitoring effort that is necessary to maintain procedures during the course of the program to make sure they are performed in the manner planned. Evaluation, however, is quite a bit different from monitoring. There is an implicit role played by the evaluator, and not by the monitor, of devil's advocate.

Let us look at it this way: A program of police-community relations is the "baby" of the sponsors, and those who become members of the team almost inevitably identify with the sponsors and the program. All of these persons become protagonists of the theories, values, policies, and even the procedures of the program.

Such vitally interested persons monitor reasonably well the ongoing practices of the program, because very often these procedures and their rationale are within the set of matters that has become valuable to the practitioners. The success of the program is the overriding concern of the program's promoters at the inception, their worry being that their people will not follow prescribed procedures. Their interests are all in favor of good training of supervisors and exact precision in performance by all personnel. Therefore, they assure themselves that monitors will accept only approved procedures and papers on a day-to-day basis.

Evaluation, however, is a cool-eyed review of the entire program, from its originating concept right through every jot and item thereafter. It is often seen as fault finding on an organized scale, and there are often possibilities of grave repercussions to the reputations and futures of the program people. The interests are adverse, at least in the sense that the evaluator's reputation does not depend on the success of the program. On the contrary, his reputation may depend on his detection of program failures and deficiencies and his notification of the administrator before the public and the press beat him to it.

In such situations, the planning stage must allow for all these collateral problems to be resolved in time for the evaluation report to appear early enough to be of real use to all concerned.

Research Aspects of Measurement

An evaluation is an organized effort to discover a certain kind of new information: Whether a given program did or did not do what it was supposed to do. It is a specialized type of research.

As such, all the safeguards to avoid error that are customary in scientific research should be taken to assure reasonably valid results within the degree of precision and reliability required.

Above all, the evaluation when finally completed should exemplify the qualities of standardization and unambiguity. If the prime effort that is being evaluated is only semistructured and indistinct as to results, the preparation of an evaluation that shows the same faults compounds the vice. An evaluation that denounces ambiguity in ambiguous terms reaches the height of absurdity.

The evaluation report should be carefully drawn to eliminate every reasonable possibility of drawing indeterminate, unanchored summary statements that will provide ammunition for both proponents and opponents of the subject project.

Great misgivings may arise in the breast of the evaluator at the time of preparing his report because of a desire not to downgrade what may be potentially a very valuable project; but, on the other hand, he may not want to exaggerate benefits that are not objectively determinable. It is a thankless task, sometimes, to be an evaluator, but as President Harry Truman said so succinctly, "If you can't stand the heat, get out of the kitchen."

Organizing Evaluation Efforts

The realities of competitive life being what they are, there are few administrators that care to be evaluated—at least there are few that care to be evaluated under circumstances that run the risk that an unfavorable evaluation may result. Even more resistance will be encountered if, in fact, an evaluation does turn out to be unfavorable. Even the slightest hint of negative criticism will bring forth floods of rhetoric in defense.

Perhaps the most important contribution the evaluator can make to the entire police-community scenario is the importation of his own frame of reference. Focusing on the entire proposition from different points of view could bring out new slants and highlights that might have been previously unnoticed. This is not to say that such new views will be negatively critical. On the contrary, the emphasis should be on impartiality, with any conclusions only as reasonable judgments based on data and findings.

The practice in the behavioral sciences of including speculative conclusions in reports is in contrast with the physical sciences where even research reports end with their data and findings. Conclusions, being considered mere conjecture, are left to the reader and consumer of the research.

In an evaluation report on, say, an action project, to draw far-ranging conclusions is merely to substitute the evaluator's guesses for those of the action-project director.

Purpose of Evaluation

It is not possible to intelligently organize an evaluation unless the purposes of the proposed evaluation are clearly in the mind of the organizer. Because the evaluator is usually brought in as an afterthought or, at most, as an adjunct to the main project that is to be evaluated, it behooves him to try to discover the intentions—both the acknowledged and unacknowledged intentions—of the persons who have appointed him to the task. If the intentions can be made clear, they can serve as the objectives of his evaluative effort.

Some experienced evaluators have stated that evaluation should not be performed under the following circumstances:

1. When there is insufficient time, money, or personnel available
2. When the evaluation is not going to affect decision making
3. When the program intended to be evaluated has no clear continuing objectives but rather tends to shift its goals and methods at irregular intervals with little continuity
4. When there are no discernible purposes.

That is not a unanimous judgment, however, for it would appear that to withhold evaluation from such programs would perpetuate the very projects that should be terminated. The drawing of any conclusions such as the four cited above indicates that an evaluation has, in fact, already been made. Failure to substantiate such matters with the collection of hard facts can be a serious relinquishment of responsibility. None of the listed "difficult" cases completely forecloses evaluation to a conscientious evaluator. Because all police-community proposals involve public funds and public weal, there is a heavy ethical burden on the evaluator. As rationally, scientifically organized projects and evaluations become more frequent, one would expect the ethical dimension to receive more consideration than it has in the past.

Of course, a lack of resources would be a serious handicap to any evaluation. Even here, however, closer examination may reveal a poverty of funding that is more apparent than real. A Baconian sense of thrift would view alleged insufficiency as never absolute. It really is a matter of how much or how little of the resources can and will be assigned. In a truly desperate case, an evaluation report can be self-sustaining, as:

> We have examined the project as thoroughly as available funding permits, and find that because of the lack of any support whatever for the evaluative effort, the actual progress and accomplishments of this program are unknown to this evaluator and unknown to anyone who has been discovered to this date.

Such a "no-cost" evaluation, if it states the facts, can be of great importance to decision makers. The call for more light on the subject is itself a valuable evaluation, and the ethical stance of the evaluator, and even the project manager, is measurably supported.

There are legitimate and illegitimate reasons for evaluation. In this connection, too, there are rarely absolutes. Legitimacy, as a matter of fair consent of the concerned, is always faced by at least two opposing protagonists. Calling for an extensive evaluation may appear to one side to be an illegitimate procrastination to delay decision. To the other side, however, an evaluation may appear to be entirely proper, an opportunity for a program to be "de-bugged" and more properly articulated or to satisfy some other deficiency.

Factions sometimes try to use the evaluator to provide substantiation for decisions that are already contemplated—and this may be disturbing to the evaluator or provide material for political potshots for an organized group. Not to worry! Such search for objective support is a normal part of the adversary process in our entire governmental and criminal-justice system. It becomes corrupt and goal displacing in its effect only when one of the adversaries is unfairly treated or is kept in ignorance of the facts.

In every case, however, the evaluator should endeavor to discover the purposes, overt and covert, admitted and unadmitted, that are involved, so that he can make reasonable decisions not only as to the organizational structure and procedure of the proposed evaluation, but whether or not he wants to be a part of the situation at all.

Difference From Basic Research

The methods of basic research and of evaluation should be the same. Both are interested in discovering new and useful knowledge in the most efficient way possible. The purposes, however, are different. Where basic research stops with the production of knowledge, without a prior design directed to a specific application, evaluation is an applied art directed toward the motives of a client system, which usually has alternatives regarding an ongoing program and seeks in the evaluation aids to decision making among options.

Basic research is generally published, or should be published, for wide dissemination of its findings. Evaluation is not generally published, it is more in the nature of private information, refers to a unique situation or project, and on occasion publication not only would serve no wide purpose, but also may even be contraindicated.

Evaluation is different from program-intervention, too. While the evaluation accents the concerns and issues of the program, it applies a series of judgmental criteria, founded on values and assumptions of the outside world, to the program's elements and to the program as a whole. Thus the evaluation's orientation is to view the set of all things programmatic from a point outside that provincial universe. The imperative of, say, an action-program, is "service." The imperative of the evaluation is: "Does it matter?"

How to Lie With Evaluations

Another basic difference between research and evaluation is founded on the incubus of the multiple allegiances that burden evaluations. The evaluator toils in the public sphere. He has personal, ethical obligations as a professional under circumstances in which the consequences to the public and to subject-clients of the criminal-justice system are momentous. Many of the disasters of life are influenced mightily by criminal-justice systems and by the decisions made by evaluators of programs in the systems. This is not an obligation to be taken lightly.

When the time comes—as it must—to draw up a formula or code of ethics for criminal-justice evaluators, it will undoubtedly stringently mandate all ethical doubts to be resolved in favor of the welfare of the public at large.

The evaluator, too, has an obligation to his employer-client. The funding organization, the project manager, other sponsors, or sometimes all three may be involved in choosing and employing him to perform the evaluation. His obligation here is solely to impartiality and objectivity—and utility in support of the service ideals of the action-program being evaluated.

The evaluator, as a social scientist, may sense an obligation to extend the frontiers of knowledge in his field, though this may violate a requirement for confidentiality called for by his client-professional relationship.

There are many pressures to compromise the evaluator's integrity and impartiality: He may feel the program is fundamentally a good one, but the evidence to sustain his judgment may not be forthcoming. He is tempted by the necessity of earning a living to produce a favorable evaluation so that other clients will be referred to him. In a world awash with corrupt influences, it would be strange indeed if the evaluator in his central position was exempt.

His fall into bias is facilitated by the fact that however earnest the search for objectivity, it is impossible to avoid the personal equation at every level in his evaluative effort. He may routinize, even mechanize his data-collection methods in the endeavor to avoid bias, but the very choices as to what data to select and where and when it is collected involve many subjective choices. The evaluation of data, too, is brimming with opportunities for the imposition of personal value judgments. The question "What can be measured?" (Chapter 9) ultimately is answered by a subjective level of choice as to what is measured and what it is compared with. Too, judgment as to what weight shall be given to various elements of data is not easily objectified.

Analytic methods of whatever kind, even the most rigorously statistical, imply conditions that are often not met with in the real world. The use of analytic methods when the necessary assumptions do not in fact exist brings in a bias that varies with the method chosen—and selection among chosen methods of analysis provides a wide flexibility in findings that can and often is presented as objective, without intrinsic bias.

With all these methods of "lying" with evaluation, not only at hand, but not to be avoided, the question of whether to lie or not to lie is ultimately a function of the knowledge and expertise of the evaluator in intimate relation with his ethical values.

Morosely, one is tempted to comment: The question is not how to lie, but can one live with it. Evaluation has, as one of its ultimate end products decisions as to human beings, a most heavy responsibility.

Evaluation Design

The theory of evaluation design is no different from the theory of any well-thought-out research design. Research design has been called a metaphor for a *tactical plan.* Let it be so. All proposed actions and procedures should be set down in writing in summary form so that the entire picture can be seen at a glance, as well as in a separate step-by-step schedule, with day-to-day entries in detail. To succeed in reaching its objectives, the program must receive careful attention as to the balance and appropriateness of the design. Such tactical plans are discussed in many standard works on research design and on scientific research. Many of these references are listed in the notes to this book for this chapter and for Chapter 11.

Since each program presents an original problem, its evaluation is equally exceptional. After determining the purposes of the evaluation, the next item is to define the kind and types of valid information that would be germane to *this* evaluation. That resolved, the design is to be shaped to obtain this information in the most direct, efficient way at the least cost in time and money.

Ideally, the experimental model is the guide to reach for in research of all kinds. Although only rarely will this model be adapted to evaluation of a police-community program, it is, nevertheless, the model of choice. The experimental model calls for study of a group that is subjected to the program and compared with another "control group" that does not receive the benefits of the program. If the "experimental group" is different from the control group after it has received the "treatment," there are varying degrees of inferences that the change was induced by the treatment.

How valid this inference is, of course, depends upon the magnitude of other variables, known as "errors," that might have affected the results observed.

To control these other possible errors, there are various combinations of control and experimental groups that are devised to prevent or detect such errors. Typologies of errors likely to occur in evaluation are available. Some of these are very extensive—but of course the elusiveness of errors is such that no full typology can ever be presented, in all probability. A reduced classification scheme of the major types of errors is offered here:

Measurement. Improper tools, scales, or units of measurement are a common error source. Sometimes they change during the course of the evaluation. Too, human observers assigned to report measurement become more expert during the course of the evaluation, or more fatigued, and the quality of the reporting changes in either case. Also the subjects, people or things as they may be, often are changed by the act of measurement.

Time. Samples, living or dead, material or immaterial, may and usually do change with time: They age, mature, become ill, decay, rust, or break down.

Biased Samples. It is a rare sample that is truly representative of the larger population it was designed to represent. Differential selection processes, self-selection, dropouts from the program, all affect the bias of the samples.

Reaction and Interaction. Subjects may react to the experimental situation rather than to the treatment. The famous Hawthorne experiments were classic examples of this phenomenon. In this notable series of inquiries the effort to obtain higher performance from assembly-line workers by "more illumination" was found to be "contaminated" by the "error" of emotional reactions of the personnel to being placed in an elite experimental group.

Statistical Regression. It has frequently been noted that small samples, on occasion, contain extreme values that widely diverge from the central thrust of the data when larger samples are drawn. Often the average deviation will be much less in larger samples—a statistical regression toward a presumed true value.

What Is Significant?

The decision as to what is significant—that is, important—is always a value judgment. The assumption that a level of significance in analysis is sufficient cannot be checked in any known objective way. It is simply an assumption that results consisting of so many "successes" out of a given number of "attempts" is important.

What is important to one evaluator's judgment may reasonably seem unimportant—insignificant—to another. The only key is *reasonableness*. The rationale for the decision as to the level of significance should be set forth in persuasive detail.

Whether or not clients will accept the significance level chosen is their own decision, unless they decide to defer to the judgment of the evaluator. They cannot come to any rational conclusion, however, unless the reasons for the decision as to what is considered important are set forth in proper context with all relevant facts and figures.

Some specific examples are in point:

The Midville Police Department, our imaginary law-enforcement agency, has undertaken to set up a Neighborhood Watch Project. The concept is to enlist people in their own neighborhoods to watch and report all suspicious occurrences that come into their purview. Most people, today, are reluctant to report to the police things that might not be serious and do not impact directly on them. The reluctance may come from unfamiliarity with police-reporting procedures, a desire "not to get involved," habitual shyness, or other reasons. In any case, it is a frequent occurrence for burglars to walk off with the entire contents of homes under the gaze of passersby without any report to the police until the resident returns home. There are many other instances of less blatantly suspicious persons loitering around banks, schools, in backyards and other locations that are not reported in time for the police to conduct a quiet investigation and perhaps prevent a serious crime. The Midville Police Department's Neighborhood Watch Project is designed to reduce the incidence of such failures to report suspicious occurrences to the police. The hope is that there will be a reduction in crime and an improved interrelation between the police department and the public. There may be other, unvoiced goals, such as a lessening of civilian complaints against the police, a reduction of public resistance to a pay raise, or other matters.

The project, as set up by the Midville P.D., was put under the assistant chief in charge of operations. As he organized it, one sergeant and five police officers were assigned full time to recruit applicants, train them in police-reporting techniques and in observational techniques, and to organize a "high-spirited" cadre of citizens. The officers were provided with a small budget for advertising circulars, identification cards for the recruits, an office, and use of one car from the motor pool on a "when needed" basis.

At the end of the year they reported to the chief of police that they had recruited 3,000 citizen Neighborhood Watchers, had received an average of twenty calls per day from them reporting "suspicious occurrences," which were checked out by the regular patrol force. The identity of the Neighborhood Watcher was not revealed to the subject of the investigation nor to anyone else, except the sergeant in charge of the project. There were ten "graduation exercises" conducted for the ten classes that had received the course of instruction. The police had also received more than one hundred letters of appreciation from various individuals and organizations.

On the "debit" side, as reported by the assistant chief to the chief of police, fewer than one thousand of the enrolled Neighborhood Watchers had completed the course of instruction; the other enlistees had received varying amounts of instruction—some as little as a thirty-minute "induction talk" at the time they were put on the roll and given an "identification card."

The reports from the field, as recorded by the sergeant and the assistant chief, were "favorable." Complaints of overly enthusiastic investigations were minimal, that is, fewer than twenty letters of complaint were received from persons who felt they had been unfairly subjected to investigation while going about their lawful business, and only five appeared at the local district station house with complaints. There were no charges of unlawful use of force.

Some fifty arrests were made as a direct result of the field investigations sparked by telephone calls from the Neighborhood Watchers, five of them for felonies that resulted in conviction. Ten other arrests for felonies resulted in the dismissal of charges. The other thirty-five arrests were for various misdemeanors and offenses.

The assistant chief recommended that the project be continued for another year at least and, in fact, that the Neighborhood Watch Bureau be made a permanent part of the Midville Police Department. The police chief suggested an evaluation by an "outside" person, and after some resistance from the assistant chief and a few city officials, an evaluator has been hired and is about to start his evaluation.

The first thing the evaluator might notice is that Midville has a population of 50,000, with a police department of some 90 sworn officers. This might—or might not—cause him to have some instant reservations: almost 7 percent of the force is tied up in what he may have prejudged as a collateral, minor program, compared with all the tasks facing the entire police department. Whether he does or does not come to that conclusion may be a reflection on his capacity, ability, or experience as an evaluator.

Certainly the chief of police and everyone else do not need an evaluator to tell them what inspection of the annual reports of every city of 50,000 in the country would tell them: That this is an unusual situation. What they want him to do is to evaluate this heavy concentration on one project in terms of the unique situation in Midville. His awareness of this would lead him to gather much more additional information.

Like a good many evaluators, he would first concentrate on preparing himself for his interviews with key people. This preparation includes obtaining a copy of everything that has been printed on the project and enough of other published matter to understand at least the general situation of this police department. This preparation before key interviews is an elementary precaution against wasting valuable time of both parties to each interview. As much about the factual situation as possible should be absorbed beforehand, not only to learn the questions to ask, but also to understand the answers. The interviews should be designed to reach an understanding of the rationale behind the project, the purposes and policies involved, and to obtain a clearer picture of how things interrelate.

Although at this time some tentative conclusions about unvoiced agenda items might be tempting, they are ordinarily resisted by experienced evaluators: First impressions often are erroneous ones. The time to make conclusions is after all the facts are in.

One of the calculations that the evaluator might make could be:

Annual Costs

Salaries and fringe costs, totals	
Sergeant	$ 25,000.00
Police Officer × 5	83,000.00
Clerk-typist	10,300.00
File Clerk	9,000.00
Mailings	
Publications & Postage	5,000.00
Auto use @ $20.00/day	7,300.00
Rent	??
Miscellaneous	??
Total Annual Costs	$139,600.00 plus ??

He has a basic equation to balance: The *inputs* on one side and the *outputs* on the other. At this point he can be sure of only one thing: Inputs include monetary costs of at least $139,600 and possibly quite a bit more.

It is more difficult to translate outputs into monetary terms: for example, the benefit sustained, the arrests made, the cooperative attitudes of the citizens directly involved, and the "throw-off" benefits in community attitude to the police. Other benefits that are difficult to quantify in any tangible unit are the "feelings of greater safety," "of better community spirit," and so on.

Other inputs and outputs include the cost of patrol officers who investigate complaints, court costs, and the possible overbearing, or even criminal, use of the positions of power taken by a few Neighborhood Watchers vis-à-vis their neighbors. A few cases of actual "protection" and extortion schemes concocted by such semiofficials have been discovered.

Which of these matters is "significant," as can be seen, is going to be a matter of personal judgment. Whether it will be the judgment of the pro-gram evaluator, the Chief of Police, the sponsors of the program, or a combination is going to be vital to the evaluation. Thus, the evaluator, to earn his keep, will go into the specific processes and means used to keep the program in operation, noting efficiencies and inefficiencies in subroutines, from paper handling, to obtaining public funding from local businessmen to sponsor at least some of the costs involved. All of this is a matter of comparing the program with similar subroutines used in other places. It is well known that large corporations will often contribute to such a project. The number of letters that a good typist can put out is known, as is the amount of filing that can reasonably be expected from a filing clerk. Whether the assignment of five officers is not enough or too much will be a decision founded on an examination of a number of "typical" workdays.

Ultimately, however, the evaluator will return to the first thought that crossed his mind: Is the project worth it? Does it belong in this police department at all? Should it be this size? What is the maximum potential in size and development of the project, what would be its value at that level, and what would be its cost in terms of money and in terms of displacing some of the other legitimate goals of *this* police department, faced with the conditions as they exist in Midville?

Obviously there is a wide range for opinion as to what is "significant." Thus the choice of the people who are to do the evaluation is of great importance. If human beings were not affected by their knowledge, emotions, hopes, dreams, values, and illusions, the problems of evaluation would be different than they are. As it is, the difficulty of obtaining people who will accurately observe, truthfully report, and conscientiously admit unavoidable errors is a prime worry for those who choose the evaluator and for the evaluator who must choose assistants. All research is vulnerable at innumerable points. One careless, negligent, or untrustworthy employee can vitiate all the most careful procedure.

With that in mind, the evaluator must be careful to select those people as assistants whose loyalties are to the goals of the evaluator, as he ultimately finalizes them, rather than as antagonists or proponents of the program. A clinical detachment is the attitude desired in all personnel, as a necessary preliminary to setting up procedures that will become routinized and mechanical, as is necessary for accurate data collection. If there is to be discretion at any point in the evaluation, let it be as completely under the eye and thumb of the evaluator as possible. It serves no good purpose to let discretion seep down to the evaluation-worker level, in the vain hope that errors will cancel each other out, leaving accuracy as a residue. It does not happen that way. In fact, it cannot.

Guarded procedure, the careful selection of employees, careful training, and the constant monitoring of the performance of personnel are essential in evaluation. There is no other practical way.

Reporting on Evaluation

An evaluation report is a law unto itself. There are no fixed rules, only recognition that the report should serve the purposes the evaluator has decided are most important. The report is his creative act, and imagination is devising the format, style, and layout most appropriate to his theme is his responsibility and opportunity.

As guidelines: All important matters should be thoroughly discussed; the reader should not be asked to accept the evaluator's own interpretation of even "hard facts" without knowing all possible alternative interpretations. All details necessary for the reader of the report to replicate the evaluation, if possible, should be included.

Since the evaluator has just completed his evaluation, he is the person in the best position to know what should be included in the report, so as to permit replication. However, if he is wise, he will share this aspect with some knowledgeable people to assure that he has not, because of his own intense familiarity, omitted an essential detail because it seemed too obvious to him to require repeating.

It is important to remember that in a short while the final report will be all that remains of even the most elaborate evaluation. Working documents, notes, data, figures, even analyses and computations, if not included in the report, will probably be irretrievably lost, misplaced, or destroyed. If the evaluation is not included in the report itself, it very likely will never be seen again. If the evaluation report is to serve any permanent purpose, maximum care should be made to embody everything that is proper and useful.

To that end, checklists have been found to be valuable: List all information that should be in the report. Compare this list with other lists referring to evaluations of a similar nature to try to detect omissions or unnecessary or inappropriate inclusions. If all the information is in the report, the evaluator can receive his proper recognition; if it is not there, he will not. It is as simple as that. Too, if the report is to be made part of an ever-widening body of knowledge in criminal justice, why not make it complete?

Chapter 11

RESEARCH

Attempt the end, and never stand to doubt;
Nothing's so hard, but search will
    find it out.
            —Robert Herrick, *Seek and Find*

It cannot be expected that either the community leader or the police administrator can be fully trained in any of the refined techniques of research. Nevertheless, they should participate in all research into police-community relations from its very inception, because to do otherwise would be to abdicate from effective decision making about the matters that concern each the most.

Research involves technical decisions that often irretrievably affect the research product. If the findings and conclusions of research are to be implemented, the potential effect on basic community interactional patterns and values must be estimated, lest minor performance objectives be emphasized at the expense of major concerns of overriding importance to all citizens, community members, and police alike.

If research is to add to the fund of human knowledge, it must be preserved in context with the situations in which it has been obtained. Thus continuing truths about reality will become part of the equipment of administrators and community leaders.

Research into PCR

The past few years American police have received more research attention than in the previous two centuries.[1] We have had research funded for organizational issues, such as centralized versus decentralized control; the separation of crime-control functions from service functions; police tactics, such as field interrogation, preventive patrol, and response time; personnel questions such as the effectiveness of women on patrol, the selection of candidates and promotion tests, and the relative effectiveness of tall versus shorter officers; and oceans of funding for the research of police matériel, from bulletproof vests to shoes, from automobiles to computers.

But of good research into community relations with government, there is a sad dearth. Although several disciplines are concerned with the subject, from psychology, sociology, political science, in fact, all the behavioral sciences to the public-policy-oriented studies of social work and criminal justice, basic research in police and community relations has been neglected by the social sciences, except for surveys of local public opinion and attitudinal studies of specific departments. There are many "action programs," each designed to produce certain beneficial effects. In only a minute portion, however, is there any real effort to discover, impartially and objectively, whether those effects are actually attained, whether they are as beneficial as presumed, or whether the unexpected negative consequences cancel out the benefits.

The reasons for this are many. Most urgent is the acute need sensed locally for specific services, which arouses political forces to provide those services, often at any cost. The segment of the public receiving those services rarely pays directly for them. It has been said that government is a machinery for taking money from one group of people and giving it to another. Whatever the cynicism of that comment, it certainly is true that there is practically no cost accounting of services, no real cost/effectiveness measures available as yardsticks to determine whether a given service should be instituted or withheld. It is, rather, the simple availability of funds that determines whether the services will be provided. If the funds are there, inevitably their use is assured.

Thus, in a realistic sense, research into whether or not police-community relations is doing what it is supposed to do is an after-the-fact *decision* rather than an inquiry. Further, the decision will be favorable as long as the political verities remain the same, and will be negative when the money runs out or the administration changes.

Sometimes it seems the only thing that matters is *who* wants the program or service, not whether it will, or if it is even likely to, provide the benefits promised. This is not a paranoid view of public governance. It is not a matter of the "good guys against the bad guys." It is simply a political reality, foreseen by James Madison as long ago as 1787: ". . . the association of claimants for government benefits, to wield as factions the powers of groups on the levers of government."

As ever, apportionment of services is designed to maximize political support at each concerned level. Granted the biological and cultural heritage of Americans, it could hardly be otherwise.

From time to time, as a larger or a different community of interest realizes that it is concerned, additional input is provided. At this time, its political representatives will demand that its influence be felt in the decision regarding those services. Various communications have been devised, from public appeals for aid, slogans, and catchphrases to organized political campaigns. At key points police representatives are in the thick of this political process, which ranges from the boycotting of buses to mothers with baby carriages picketing for a traffic signal at a busy intersection.

One can agree with the proposition that research into police and community is not to be found in secluded laboratories, wherein serene, white-coated researchers toil in calm objectivity, applying measured stimuli and recording responses in logarithmic-scaled notebooks.

The main laboratory for police and community is the entire vital urban scene, with all the roiling struggle to make a living, to survive, and to grasp power that is the very reason for urbanism. Our research then, must participate in all of the rough and tumble, reflect it, and be a part of it.

Completely value-free research is a myth of course, but this dilemma goes further than the attempt to limit the intrusion of personal values. PCR is research into values, per se. Humans use their values as containers for objective facts. They cannot pitch facts at each other's minds without being bruised by the containers. Research into PCR that does not consider the overriding importance of various value systems, as they affect and are affected by facts, is missing the point of human-relations effort.

The Idea of Research

Research is simply a search for new knowledge. In its applied form, it is search for new knowledge that can be usefully applied to current problems.[2]

Of course, there are many ways, in addition to research, to acquire knowledge. Some of these include divine revelation, authority, tradition, intuition, deductive logic, and empiricism or personal experience. *Scientific* research is something entirely different. It is newer, more tedious in its labor, more diffident in its presentations.

The familiar older methods are usually encountered early in life, and they affect our daily experiences far more. Numerous works on philosophy and knowledge go into the details of the older methods of knowledge acquisition. Here we can only skim the surface of the discussion.

Divine revelation and *authority,* as sources of knowledge, refer to the transmission of information with a mandate to believe. Divine revelation resides in faith in the divinity of the source, accepting it as ultimate authority. Authority may reside in an individual, group, or other source. Knowledge so obtained is not an object of discussion or of comparison. It is so, because it has been so transmitted; doubt is forbidden.

Tradition is simply the accumulated knowledge of the past as transmitted from generation to generation. Accepted lovingly or fearfully, it has proved its function and utility by its survival value. Since one tradition is often in conflict with another tradition, even though both sets of traditions have survived, there is no neutral guide to truth; [3] they are merely different successful accommodations to exacting reality.

Intuition is the existence in the mind of a certainty of something. Its subjectivity forbids direct verification by other individuals in any objective way.

Deductive logic is not truly a way of obtaining new information but rather an analysis of existing knowledge to isolate one, or more, of the intrinsic information elements. The classic example illustrates this point: All men are mortal. Socrates is a man. Therefore, Socrates is mortal.

The first two statements, *premises,* present all the knowledge available. The last statement, or conclusion, merely restates knowledge that is implicit in what is already known. There is no addition to knowledge.

Empiricism is the reliance on personal experience for the acquisition of knowledge. Of course, the fact that memory is often faulty will affect one's recollection of knowledge collected in that way. More important, our perception of experience is affected by our previous experience, by our motivation, our emotions, and our attitudes. Selective perception of experience is a great barrier to accurate information gathering, as is the fact that one's living experience is only a small part of all possible experience.

The method of knowing that is called the scientific approach, or terms of similar import that include the word *scientific* as in scientific research, scientific inquiry, is a more eclectic procedure than any of the classic methods of knowledge acquisition. It does not firmly exclude any of the older methods, but it puts certain skeptical constraints upon them. This skepticism manifests itself in a number of ways. One is that for new knowledge to be acceptable as such, it must pass the test of *replication.* That is, other people must be able to follow the processes—objective procedures and observations—whereby the knowledge was acquired and come to reasonably similar findings.

Until there is actual replication, all evidence tending to support the new knowledge can hardly be called scientific. One-shot cases, lucky guesses, inspired insights, devoted accumulation of data, gifted guru ponderings, however brilliant or useful, are not scientific knowledge. The scientific approach is not without its own value system and assumptions.

It assumes this is a real world, perceivable by the senses or by tangible material mechanisms that can provide evidence perceptible to human beings. Thus, although ultraviolet light cannot be seen, it is perceivable by its effects on certain rocks or in tanning skin, or by registration on a light meter. The same is true of magnetism, revealing itself by its effect on iron filings or the movement of a magnetized needle. The emanations from a television transmitter, not directly perceivable, can be detected by their fluorescence on the screen of the receiver.

Percy W. Bridgman [4] and other scholars have stated that what we *do* defines what we *mean*.[5] Scientific research, with its obsession over possible error, its sedulous diligence in establishing "controls" to locate and prevent mistakes, is definable by what it does. It assigns separate control groups, which are held inviolate, to detect whether the mere act of study has affected the data observed in another group called experimental. It selects samples by a process called randomization. It takes special efforts to avoid bias at every point in its inquiry and mounts a combined assault on a problem with theory and empirical practice as co-equal partners. There are other techniques and devices invented in modern times that are too numerous to list here.

The Methods of Research

Methods of research are so various and specialized to the particular inquiry that reference is made to texts on research method and particularly to those concentrating on techniques adapted to particular kinds of problems. Of course, it is true that the foundations of scientific inquiry are the same in every field. The same assumptions and principles apply, but the techniques adapted to, say, sample selection will be different in criminal justice from those in medical technology, agronomy, or geology. In each case they may deal with issues of sampling, but the specific operationalizing methods used in practice will differ. The basic problem in obtaining a representative sample is the same in all inquiry. Exactly how to do it for seeds, blood samples, rocks, or people's attitudes makes for the differences in techniques.

There is considerable transfer among the behavioral sciences in the techniques that have been found useful for investigations about human beings, their persons, performances, and personalities. However, the relations among people will often depend on accurate research into material objects, which will call for methodologies developed in chemistry, physics, or mechanics.

The overwhelmingly universal technique of scientific inquiry, however, is the use of *inference* as the main analytical tool to examine data.[6] Computation of probability as an aid to inference is the calculus of choice as a foundation for all estimations, speculations, recommendations, and conclusions. We have found no substitute for probability calculations, and although the results must be expressed in probabilistic form, rather than as certainty, we reckon by probability whenever possible, in preference to tradition, authority, or any of the other older methods of knowing.

It has been said that the difference between inference and deductive logic is that inference starts with the particular and goes on to infer, or guess, what the general reality is likely to be, whereas deductive logic starts with a general statement, which is accepted as true, and analyzes the data to clarify what must be true about the particular. Whatever the value of that description, *inference,* also known as induction or inductive logic, is a process of calculated guesses as to what is the fact or what is likely to be the fact in the future.

A large, but relatively simple body of theory has grown up about inference, although the last word has not been said about it by any means. The system of calculation that has been adapted to the use of inference is called probability and, in the opinion of many scholars, is not really within the province of either mathematics, statistics, or even logic. This view sees probability as a distinctly different subject from all others, with all the qualities of simple practicality and abstract philosophy combined. This is a description of the philosophical school known as pragmatism, but it tries, in practice, for a more polished rigor. In some schools it is taught as a separate subject. For our purposes we shall present only a condensed version of inference about past, present, and future facts.

Inference About Past Facts

If a survey of the community by a police manager reveals that a large percentage of the citizens feel that the local police are surly, discourteous, and given to unreasonable use of force, what might he reasonably infer as to the facts that resulted in these findings?

Now, the basic approach to calculating past probability is that what has happened is likely to happen again if the conditions are the same. Specifically, if long observation has indicated that a given event has occurred 95 percent of the time, and the event being researched resembles in all known ways those prior events, a researcher will often anticipate the probability that the event will reoccur about 95 percent of the time in the future.

The application of this approach to the case described is usually very informal, but it need not be so. The police manager, for example, could infer—that is, guess—that the police are surly, or at least have been so in the past, and will continue to be so in the future, and conclude that the best course for him would be to issue orders to remedy this situation. All of this is informal enough and describes a most common managerial problem in police-community relations and a frequently encountered response.

Concealed within the sequenced inferences, however, is the fact that there really is a deductive process going on, based on the premise that the survey respondents answered from personal encounters with police officers who performed as the respondents stated not only in those encounters, but also that the officers habitually so responded to street situations.

That is, the police manager's inferences were founded on the major premise: that all police officers have been discourteous. This, however, is not necessarily the truth. What is indubitably true is that respondents so answered. However, whether they spoke from personal knowledge, hearsay, impressions, or rumor was not determined.

More insightful investigations of public impressions of police behavior have frequently revealed that survey respondents' answers are sometimes more the product of reputation, or rumor, than of actual observation of police behavior.

This is not to say that such public impressions are not important—for they are. However, the inferential sequence should be firmly identified as founded on *reputation*, rather than *observation*, if that is the case.

The correct use of inference by the police manager in the case discussed would be: The past fact that these survey respondents have reported in a certain way leads one to infer that these respondents will probably make similar reports in similar surveys in the future. Quite a bit of difference!

If more specific and detailed information about actual police performance is desired, there should be actual observation of behavior, collected either by outside observers, by asking the survey respondents to report on actual situations observed, or by seeking, and counting a "marker," for example, such "markers" of undesirable police behavior as the number of written civilian complaints against police posted in a given time and place, compared with that in another time and place.

Often the data on which inference is based is incomplete. Additional data is required for proper inference. If this data is available, it should become part of the process. If it is not available, but is merely assumed, as in the above example, where a "marker" represents behavior, that assumption should be clearly in mind as an unproven premise.

Thus the use of inference is not a simple adding up of numbers that estimate probabilities. True, as a general guide it is presumed that no anticipated future event ever is certain, that is, has a probability ratio of one. The probability of an event may have a very high degree of probability, very close to one—but human experience has seen too many "slips twixt the cup and the lip." On the other hand, the assumption is that in the course of human events no event is completely unanticipated. As far as human understanding is concerned, our world, and all the spheres within and without, is not a closed system. As it is commonly put: *Everything is possible,* though the chance of any one thing occurring may be very low, say, $1/10^{1000}$. Since, however, we do not know all possible eventualities, we never really know the denominator of this fraction that estimates probability.

Prior Probability

Prior probability refers to the likelihood of a future event occurring out of a given set of known ways that an event can occur. Thus, if there are 100 ways an event can possibly occur and 65 of those events are favorable to the cause, the probability of occurrence of a favorable event might be estimated as 65 percent, that is, 65 times out of 100.

Note, however, that this calls for a prior knowledge of all "known ways an event can occur." This implies a "closed system" with all possibilities within our imaginings. As was discussed in the section on past probabilities, the real world has not revealed to us all the known possibilities of events in human relations in a given case, though we may assume that we do. Thus the real world of a police-community program may have, in actuality, an infinite number of possible effects.

Hypothesis Testing

The key use of inference in scientific research is in hypothesis testing.[7]

This is the process whereby conjectural solutions to problems, that is, hypotheses, are tested to determine whether they should be accepted or rejected.

It would not be appropriate to go into this matter, which is covered in various texts. We will merely state that no hypothesis in science is ever accepted in the sense that it is considered a "true" statement. Thus all the statements about relationships that were years ago considered invariant and immutably true, the "natural laws," are now considered to be merely relationships that are "useful," as having been observed to occur in such and such a way when observed under such and such a condition. This applies to Newton's laws of motion, Darwin's law of natural selection, the various other laws in mechanics, optics, chemistry, and physics, and, of course, relationships observed in the behavioral sciences—from "the angle of incidence equals the angle of reflection" in optics to "frustration in human beings tends to aggression" in behavioral studies.

Hypotheses are accepted only tentatively, at best. Rejection, however, while never completely a matter of certainty, is conservatively considered to be the safer way to treat a hypothesis regarding a conjectured relationship. The references give a fuller treatment of this technical subject.

The Fallibility of Research

The scientific approach to research, using probabilistic inference, makes no pretense of discovering ultimate truth.[8] It merely arrives at differing degrees of probability that a given relation exists or that an event will occur again. Based as it is on probability, it does not exclude the possibility that scientific "law" or "fact" may not be so. Let us examine an example:

"If rehabilitative program A is applied to a group of 100 juvenile delinquents, 50 percent of them will not be arrested again within five years in 95 out of 100 similar groups of juveniles."

This is an example of what is called a substantive hypothesis put into measurable form. In an action program the director is hoping that infusion of the treatment of the rehabilitation program A into the lives of the youngsters will have the result stated, which we can call B. As more information comes to the director of the project, he may have to modify his hypothesis. He is not so interested in accepting or rejecting the hypothesis as he is in maintaining the program as long as, in his judgment, it is worth the money and effort. He will change his hypothesis to fit his experience. He may decide to substitute rehabilitative program A with another program if he feels the program is not producing the results he hoped for. In the alternative, he may change his expectation of results, the B part of the hypothesis under which he is operating. That is, the general statement of his action hypothesis is, "If A, then B in 95 out of 100 such samples."

He may shift from one program to another program that would be symbolized by, say, from A to A_1, seeking to obtain the same B results. Or, again, he may lower his sights, convinced that only 25 percent of the youngsters can be expected not to be arrested again within five years. That would be symbolized as a shift from, say, B to B_1.

As the director of an action program, he is not interested directly in advancing fundamental knowledge by accepting or rejecting hypotheses, though that may be a spin-off of his work. His main interest is in keeping his youths out of jail by a system of reeducation. He has subsidiary concerns about maintaining funding for his program, advancing the future and prestige of his organization, perhaps, and others. The fallibility of his type of "research," however, is that it is not aimed solely at discovering new knowledge and therefore can be sidetracked easily from that abstract objective for practical reasons, for example, survival of his program.

Going back to the original hypothesis: "If rehabilitative program A is applied to a group of 100 juvenile delinquents, 50 percent of them will not be arrested again within five years in 95 out of 100 similar groups of juveniles," please note that this does not mean the same thing as, "If A, then B 95 percent of the time." Nor does it mean that A is 95 percent effective. It means simply that it has been expected that when A is applied, B is expected to appear (that is, a 50 percent recidivist rate) in 95 out of 100 groups such as the one treated.

As in the preceding chapter, "Evaluation," decision as to whether the action program is valuable, or whether the 50 percent figure is appropriate, is a matter of subjective judgment, based on the director's experience and hopes for his program. Even the figure "95 out of 100 groups such as the one treated" is an arbitrary judgment as to what he deems significant or important. (See Chapter 10, "What Is Significant?")

There are other arbitrary judgments, which add to the fallibility of the findings of such action programs: Whether or not the samples of 100 juveniles are representative, or equivalent to each other and to the general population, or even whether 100 juveniles is the proper size for the sample. All are subjective decisions, with little aid from either mathematics or any other scientific discipline.

The fallibility of research, then, is that, despite its notable record in assisting in developing the most incredibly complex artifacts, machines, and programs, it moves ahead by a narrow focus on a small area, which is made the subject of hypothetical solutions that are tested for acceptance or rejection by a rather technical process, which does not arrive at certain knowledge but only varying degrees of probability: guessing, testing, and guessing again. It admits to fallibility and error and calls for such care in detecting and controlling error that action programmers, out of patience with it and striving for some immediate amelioration of urgent problems tend to move on ahead of the slow-moving pack of scientific researchers.

Continuous Renewal of Research

No area or subject of scientific research is ever considered to be completed, requiring no further work. The way is always open for continuous replication and improvement. Perhaps this perennial renewal is best exemplified by the process of hypothesis testing. As the previous section explained, this is the core of scientific research. It reaches for operationalization of all the previously mentioned assumptions and processes pertinent to science.

The process starts with recognition of a problem and then goes on to identify a *possible* relationship that is relevant to the problem. Thus, if the problem is thought to be: "Schoolchildren do not attend regularly, do not learn when they do attend, and show a marked antipathy toward police," we have made a first step toward solution by putting it in writing. As we discussed in the section on measurement (Chapter 9), the first level of measurement is *nominal,* identifying and *naming* variables, and the quoted sentence does that.

If we then go a step farther and conjecture a relationship that might be a solution to at least a part of the problem, such as: "If an 'Officer Friendly' is installed in Public School No. 1, the pupils will lessen their antagonism toward police," we have gone another step, because here we have stated specifically just what we propose to do: install a certain type of police-community–relations program (Officer Friendly) in a particular school, and we have indicated a definite relationship (antagonism as measured before and after), and have even indicated its anticipated direction (*less* antagonism after the "treatment").

This hypothesis could be further specified, by naming the assigned officer, or officers, detailing their specific duties and daily performances, and citing a specific change in quantitative terms that is predicted in the level of antagonism and, of course, exactly how we will measure antagonism.

There could be other hypotheses set up for other parts of the problem, certainly, but we can concentrate on this one to simplify things.

A plan must be devised to permit us either to accept or reject the hypothesis. This plan, ordinarily, will embrace a means of scaling the trait we have been calling antagonism. What might that be? Ah, there are hundreds that could be devised by any researcher—the question is, which measure will be convincing to the consumer of the research? Should a questionnaire be devised to admit such questions as, "Do you like police?" "Do you hate police?" "Can you take them or leave them?"

Would such a pencil-and-paper questionnaire extract the kind of information that would convince you that the real sentiment of the children is being reached?

Another way would be to use the same questions in an interview schedule presented by a trained interviewer who would ask each child these questions and make notations of the answers.

Still another way would be to count incidents of antagonistic acts before and after the treatment program. Yet another way would be to ask the opinions of teachers before and after the institution of the program. We could continue to devise measures to the limit of our creative imagination: Measuring response to pictures of policemen on a polygraph, Rorschach tests, stimulus-response tests, general attitude measurement tests, eye-dilation tests of pleasure or discomfort, and so on. Each of these tests could be operationalized in particular ways with specific details. As we say, hundreds of tests could be devised. The question as to which test should be selected must be one of judgment: seasoned, educated, even learned and wise, if possible. On the bottom line, however, judgment is subjective, victim to all the bias, preselection of perceptive clues, and error of humans. Of course the decision can be checked and rechecked for various mistakes. We have available measures of internal and external validity, precision, and reliability by experts in such evaluations. If these tests were successfully passed, then the choice of the test would receive the blessing of acceptance.

These tests, however, are devised by the same human process, and we have merely started on a new cycle of doing and checking, modifying, and then doing, checking and modifying, around and around and around again and again.

As we see, the variables involved are susceptible to so many interpretations, of so many different values and magnitudes, under all manner of conditions that the game is one of continual refinement, without ever reaching a point when certainty is claimed and the cycle of renewal can be ended. Research is a process repeated without definite end, each time trying for an ever more accurate result.

Research As Honest Inquiry

As far as community and law agency people are concerned, without going into the numerous details involved, scientific research accepts the obligation to conduct honest inquiry. That obligation is mandated in every aspect of the search for information, for to violate it would negate all the painstaking efforts made.

Although scientific approaches consider that the natural world is without internal values, science has its own value system. It values honest inquiry, as the foundation stone of all its constructs. If any of its other assumptions (see "The Idea of Research") conflicted with honest inquiry, that assumption would no doubt be revised.[9]

Even the assumption that the world is real, objective, and perceivable by the senses is subsidiary to the basic assumption that honest inquiry is the sine qua non of science. Too, such characteristics as replication, the use of probability, hypothesis-testing procedures, skepticism, control groups, data-control measures, the narrow focus on specific questions—all of these, if not dedicated to honest inquiry, must fail as aspects of scientific inquiry.

Inventories of PCR Knowledge

The present state of confirmed knowledge about police-community relations is lamentable. We just do not know what makes for good, bad, or indifferent relations. We do not understand, in a scientific way, how to run societies, cities, or local communities. Some scholars say we do not even know how to run police departments, and that as much, or more, was known about all of these things two or three thousand years ago as is known today.

If true, that would be an argument for the collection and retention of all scientific research records and a careful collation and inspection of them with a view to what might be called a search among research for more fruitful means and methods.

Much of the experience of individual managers and action programmers is eventually lost to those who follow. We have devised no way to retain and organize the bits and pieces of relevant relationships that have so painfully been obtained in myriads of empirical situations, even when they are scrupulously reported by social scientists.

More than six million pages of behavioral science research is published annually, with clear relevance to police-community relations at one level or another. The possibility of developing a classification, storage, and retrieval system that would provide a real inventory of community and police knowledge could be the most exciting project of all. What great value such a bank of information would be!

With monotonous regularity we hear of programs in police-community relations that are brought into being, funded, equipped with human and material resources, vigilantly supervised, having certain effects and consequences on its subjects and operators, and finally ended, to pass into limbo, with no real record available to the rest of the world to scan and learn from their prior experience. On the contrary, much the same project is opened up elsewhere the following year, and the same steps are taken. Intricately complex or simple programs, some with large, even momentous consequences, as well as those with no particularly visible effect —all pass on and are forgotten, full of sound and fury and funding, signifying nothing.

This need not be. That a great storehouse of information could be an ultimate resource to practitioners and scholars is not beyond the realm of possibility. Of course such efforts have been made in the past, but they collapsed under the burden of the ever-widening grasp of human inquiry, which has resulted in overwhelming floods of information, relations, variables, ideas, constructs, theories, generalizations, and approaches to specific facts, both numerical and descriptive.

Today, however, we have at hand at the touch of a button the services of electronic computers, which have storage places that are virtually limitless and a speed of access measurable in billions of bits per second.

The future would seem to hold hope for emphasizing the power of knowledge beyond that ever dreamed by ancients or moderns.[10] For the history of science is science itself, and we are on the edge of making all history a ready tool.

Part IV

Administration

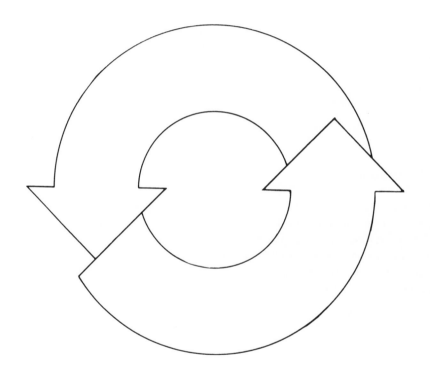

Chapter 12

OPERATIONS

For forms of government let fools
  contest;
What e'er is best administer'd is
  best; . . .
—Alexander Pope, *Essay on Man*

Up to now we have discussed many background matters. Now we w.
see how it all might be put together in the field of operations by
knowledgeable administrators.

Some large rocks in the path of community operations are discussed in the first part of this chapter. Then we come to some tentative solutions and methods of approach and close with the recognition that in the end we are faced with real problems with real human
beings despite, or in realization of, the finest ideals and hopes.

Although many field administrators as well as scholars have
offered their judgment that the prime medium of police-community
relations is *contact* between police and citizen in action operations
in our towns and cities, there have been numerous attempts to
expedite solution to specific PCR problems by special programs to
establish friendship and invite participation in jointly achieving
community and police objectives. This has brought many consequences, some seen as good, some bad.

At one time the United States was a society in which white Anglo-Saxon
middle-class values were paramount. Today we are evolving into a society
where every segment, community of interest, and subculture demands
equal consideration. Our criminal-justice agencies are adjusting to this
new pattern, not without some strain. An acute aspect, adding to the difficulty of adjustment, is the seeming fact that the greater the cultural distance from a central mode of normative actions and beliefs, the greater
the intensity of each group's yearning to retain its little world of private
expectations.

In the face of tenaciously strident diversity, a law-enforcement establishment designed to channel individual members down a mainstream of

compliance is faced with the necessity for rethinking its roles and styles of law enforcement.[1]

If, as we have noted repeatedly in previous sections of this book, policing arrangements today are designed to enforce an imposed behavior on all of the rest, opposition to the very *idea* of policing is only to be expected. *Opposition,* itself, becomes the norm! Although the civil violence of the sixties has passed from the scene, there is considerable evidence that the bona fides of government and its officers are questioned more than ever.

There is a lack of well-founded empirical fact and rigorous scientific research as to the nature and characteristics of the relations between public and government.[2] Pending the arrival of more firmly based findings and conclusions in this area, the police, particularly, would appear to be well advised to seek every opportunity to interact with every community interest for the purpose of sending those messages of support and appeasement we have spoken of so often.

Crime, it has been concluded, by most knowledgeable authorities,[3] cannot be prevented by government agencies. Only community norms and pressures can do that, as all the evidence indicates. Further, it appears that norms develop as a result of local group agreements, fostered by communication processes, some of which are quite well understood.

In the broad view, this is really a philosophy of law that diverges widely from the prevailing utilitarian or positive law concepts. The utilitarian reach for the "greatest good for the greatest numbers" tends toward a disregard of the good of minorities and individuals. Legal positivism, holding that people have only the rights that have been granted by law, constrains the law and its officers in a straitjacket that forbids opening the door to the new freedoms that are demanded by individuals and spearpointed by militant minority leaders seeking new constituencies.

These new communities of unaccustomed interests insist that they are entitled to more consideration than the explicit law grants. Perplexing problems are presented to judges, prosecuting attorneys, and, above all, police. For *the right to be treated as an equal may mean the right to be treated better than equally* [4] is mind twisting to the ordinary law-enforcement officer.

The full development of these outreaching ideas has taken more than two centuries, but it is now here upon us and growing sturdily. Starting at the inception of the nation with legally sustained deprivation of equality for blacks and many other minorities, by the time of the Civil War much of religious discrimination had been meliorated, though the condition of the blacks had in many respects retrogressed. After the Civil War legal sanctions against provable unfairness and inequality increased over the decades until a great leap for verbalized, integrated equality was expressed in the Civil Rights Law of 1964. Today affirmative-action guidelines and procedures are under heavy attack, both for ineffective and overeffective enforcement. Whether or not discrimination in favor of particular minorities will prevail, and if so, to what degree and toward which groups, is unclear. It may be that the entire doctrine will be set aside—certainly modifications and clarifications are overdue.

All of this is too large a pill for the ordinary norm-compliant citizen or officer to swallow. It is even confusing to the extraordinary person. Nevertheless, it is a present reality, and as such is a necessary ingredient in the conceptual armament of every community and criminal-justice manager.

Some scholars see this as merely an updating of the natural-rights theory that guided the eighteenth-century authors of our Declaration of Independence and Constitution. The absolute right to be accorded respect, dignity, and equal opportunities, under all circumstances, with all conditions made equal for all. Today there is argument for envisaging a society that denies all conservative virtues, such as hard work, thrift, even intelligence, talent, and education, as prerequisites for receipt of benefits. The future fact may not go so far, but that is a direction that has not been overlooked. However shocking the idea may be to some current sensibilities, history discloses many societies in which intelligence was scorned, thrift was vice, talent was believed equivalent to witchery and equally condemnable, and hard work was beneath anyone with taste and fine perceptions.

Education was once proscribed, rather than considered virtuous, and no nobleman of the Middle Ages thought it worthy or virtuous to sip too deeply of learning. Intelligence has been scorned as leading to instability, riot, and disorder. Hard work has been disdained in hereditarily ranked societies since they were devised, from ancient Assyria and Egypt to the Spain of the sixteenth century. Thrift, far from being a desirable quality in such societies as the Pacific Coast Indians and among the eighteenth- and nineteenth-century English nobility, was spurned as a narrow-spirited vice. Openhanded generosity to the point of extravagance was virtue.

In a world the uneducated, the stupid, the wastrels, the untalented, and the lazy never made—why should anyone be surprised that they refuse to obey opposing norms? The man-made world constantly devises rules that benefit those who obey those rules made by certain kinds of men, enforced by the same kinds of men.

Probably most who read this book are offended that untalented, lazy, stupid people—as they see them—assert a right to rule. However, there seems to be no evidence in nature's primeval world that early to bed, early to rise, and a long day's work was very much rewarded. On the contrary, most of the anthropological studies of primitive peoples reveal quite different characteristics as being most rewarded. Middle-class values were of no particular survival value in the primitive wild. However much they enabled Plymouth Colony to become economically viable and evolve an industrial empire of material goods, now that the empire is firmly established, we are finding many subgroups that can live quite well with values that exclude the work ethic. Devious dealing, misrepresentation, lying advertising, calculated mislabeling, and promotional schemes are more rewarded than Puritan virtues, it seems. Too, it is quite possible to live in the cracks of our industrial economy without hard work, thrift, or any of the advice from *Poor Richard's Almanac.*

The order changes. Older moral values no longer have the same credibility they once had. Laws founded on moral values—even if they be of a majority of the population—encounter great resistance when imposed on a minority who do not subscribe to such values. Laws for or against legal abortion, gambling, drunkenness, narcotic addiction, or even drug sale seem to be based more on specific value systems than actual physical trauma, hazard of trauma, or avoidance of social or economic disaster. Such laws have always been troublesome to enforce. The issues become even more complex when abortion is declared legal but in practice is denied to those who have the most occasion to need it. There seems something pragmatically moronic about the enforcement of arrangements that not only go against the personal economic stake of individuals, but also that of the society that will have to support the unwanted product of failure to abort —and do so under conditions that are programmed to produce more of the same. When abortion is legal—and presumably moral by legislative fiat— but an anti-abortion stance is taken that negates the law as far as the poor are concerned, for whose benefit, presumably, the law was passed in the first instance, another adversary point of contention is sharpened.

Whether any laws at all should be founded on personal moral judgments is a question that has profound meaning to the relations of our diverse society with its government.[5] None of these problems originates with law-enforcement agencies, except insofar as they participate in the legislative process, usually only on a consultive basis.

It is true that on occasion the efforts of organized prosecuting attorneys and police departments reach a high intensity in lobbying for particular legislation. In the main, however, one must grant that the basic problems are not of police doing. Since the police, however, are not about to abdicate from their law-enforcement role, it becomes the responsibility of every agency and individual in criminal justice to foster cooperative working conditions with every individual with whom contact is made. Of all the units in the criminal-justice system, police departments have the heaviest burdens in this regard because of:

1. The acute emotional content of many police contacts;
2. The tremendous number of people involved in such contacts, amounting to millions of personal citizen-police situations each year;
3. The fact that police-citizen confrontations usually occur when the citizen is without the social support of his relatives and friends;
4. The speed with which such contacts crystallize into violent action;
5. The immediate disposition of confrontations, often with loss of liberty, injury, and even death of the citizen;
6. Finally, the intense interest of the public and mass media in all police news.

In a free country, it is doubtful if police can act with any degree of efficiency without affection, trust, and respect in the people. The degree to which this desirable state of affairs is the consequence of police appeasement behavior, friendliness, and confidence in their secure position in the esteem of the people has not been determined by empirical research. These measures have been laid down exhortatively by writers distinguished as much by humanist, democratic idealism as by concern for impartial inquiry.

A student scanning the literature for value-free findings will finally desist and confess that they are not to be found in respect to matters of possible value to the study of police-community relations. He may reasonably wish for a presentation of relevant facts and relationships that, if not completely value-free, have, at least, as thin a layering of ideology as is humanly possible. To accomplish that, it seems fair to assume that we must try for an encompassing systematic view, rather than a narrowly parochial, pejorative one. What are basic, fundamental, omnipresent variables? People have relations with governments, whatever the pervading ideologies and value systems. What are the factors that are consistently present, in every case, everywhere? How do these factors articulate with each other? What are the verities in every society under all circumstances? This search for ultimate reality has led to what is called systems approaches, which we consider in the next section.

A Systematic Approach

A *system* has been defined as an array of elements in specific relationships designed to achieve an objective according to plan. Only a decade ago, the concept was proclaimed with euphoria in the natural sciences, business, industry, and public administration. Primarily a systems approach is a way of thinking about the job of managing. It calls for visualizing external and internal environmental factors as part of an integrated whole—a whole, that is, which may consist of subsystems, separate and overlapping, containing and contained by subsystems, but all within the entire greater system that is limited only by the manager's vision.[6]

Each of the subsystems is conceived to receive inputs and by an internal process produce outputs. At this point the internal processes are not specified.

This overview approach was a revolt against what had come to be a "cookbook" method of solving problems in government, including police-management problems, by "five simple techniques" or "eight easy steps toward higher performance."

One of the important reasons the systems approach found favor was because of the difficulty of coordinating cooperative effort by diverse disciplines relevant to complex problems. Because the systems approach views all relations with the system in terms of input and output—a communications concept and the common ground between all the behavioral sciences—the translation of diverse concepts and terminology into their communication equivalents constitutes a built-in coordinating process. Thus the systems approach can reach rationally for integrated schemes to deal with ever-widening systems of systems, while maintaining a monitoring feedback to maintain control and coordination of all lesser subsystems. It is an organismic concept, which originally sprang from biology, and like life itself has vitalized new enthusiasms in tackling problems of human management and affairs. There are, however, at least two obstacles: One is that many of the inputs and outputs, even when identifiable, are often unquantifiable. Another is that the systems that are modeled may not be those that are important to the real concerns involved.

An operations commander has two major systems to contend with:

1. His police (or community) unit, with all its resources, present and future; and
2. All other systems, large and small, in complex arrangements.

From this point on, it's any man's game. The commander can see himself as leading his system as an adversary to all the other systems: A two-party, zero-sum game, possibly, and susceptible to analysis by the logic of such games. That is the simplest approach, and to many observers seems to be the way many police chiefs play their role. Though they may never have heard of the theory of games, or Morgenstern and Von Neumann, they often play this game very skillfully and successfully. The rules are relatively simple: The other systems are the enemy. The only benefits one can ever obtain must be wrested from one or more of the adversary systems. To prevent the loss of some benefit, each contact with another such system is to be defensive.

The picture becomes clear, and for lack of space, we shall not go on with it. Further details can be found in the references cited here.

There are any number of systematic approaches, with varying definitions of the systems involved. To mention another one, let us go to the opposite extreme. Imagine a police chief in direct command of the Midville Police Department. His foremost allegiance, however, is as an individual citizen in the larger system, the U.S.A. In this guise his role performance might well be quite different. Again, taking the most extreme example, if he were to find himself in a situation in which the U.S.A. was in opposition to the Midville Police Department, he would—in *this* role—quite willingly sacrifice the lesser system to the greater one. Another factor in his calculation would possibly be the size of the U.S.A., that is, it is such a large system that for all practical purposes it is "open-ended," with unlimited resources and benefits, as well as weaponry and potential for inflicting damages and costs on adversaries.

There are, of course, an unlimited number of systems that can be conceived to be relevant to the manager. The choice is his.

If, of course, the commander is of lesser rank, say, the C.O. of a police-community unit, under an assistant chief, who reports to the police. chief directly, he may reduce his sights and see his role as a "systems player" to be primarily concerned with his PCR unit, within the sphere of an all-encompassing Midville Police Department. His universe of systems goes no further than that, although he does have peripheral, that is, official, contacts with the public as his clients.

One way he might view his field is to examine all the programs ever developed by his police department that appear to him to have a bond with the idea or concept of PCR. Not all of these programs or efforts need have been under the PCR unit. The civil-service commission or the personnel division might have had a program endeavoring to recruit women or black officers, and there may be a number of others. With this in mind, he might make up a list of all efforts made by the Midville P.D. as follows:

I. Personnel programs
  A. Recruitment aimed at
    1. Women
    2. Blacks
    3. Other ethnics
    4. College graduates
    5. College-trained (less than degree)
    6. Residents only
    7. National pool of talent
  B. Promotion programs aimed at: All above, plus?

II. Specialized training programs
  A. Police
    1. Crisis intervention
    2. SWAT
    3. Safe streets
    4. Sensitivity training
    5. Trigger-word seminars
  B. Civilian
    1. Neighborhood watch training
    2. Ride-along Program
    3. Prevent Burglary Program
    4. Know-a-Cop Program

III. Image building
  A. Newspapers
  B. Television
    1. Cooperation with TV crews
    2. Liaison with scriptwriters
  C. Public
    1. All involvement programs
    2. Public Information Office phone
    3. Visit Headquarters Program
    4. School Resource Program
    5. Speakers' Bureau
  D. Other Agencies
    1. City: None found
    2. State: None found, except reports
    3. Federal: Reports to FBI, applications to LEAA

IV. Attempts at a dialogue
  A. Precinct Councils
  B. Politeness Pays Program
  C. Safe Streets Program
  D. All programs involving citizens

Each system can be idealized as a unit with an *input* and an *output*. Systems analysis endeavors to quantify all inputs, rationalize and perfect the system's "treatment" of that input, and finally outputs. It is quite difficult, of course, to get everyone's agreement as to the quantification of goals, especially of a police system. It is equally difficult to quantify a police systems output in relation to those goals.

In systems analysis all subsystems are similarly quantitatively analyzed, using mathematical simulation models when applicable, statistical procedures, and computers. Some of the techniques are quite advanced, and the assistance of experts is usually useful, but police managers should closely observe systems analysts to become familiar with arbitrary judgments that are made in selecting measures and procedures and to protect the decision-making authority in his department, which might otherwise be appropriated by the technicians.

Systems analysis (S/A) can be used to develop procedures for handling current routine information and to present the numerical substantiation for various options in operations, that is, managerial analysis. From that array of choices, the operations commanders can make their decisions. S/A can also be used in exceptional circumstances that call for an important and specific decision. This is often called staff analysis. When these important studies are to be made, it is often wise to call in outside consultants, who are not too close to the job of policing or community relations, with all the occupational bias and identification common to close contact over long periods. That does not mean that the police-community–relations manager is locked into the conclusions or recommendations of such a study. Not at all. Conclusions and recommendations, by whomever made, are "guesstimations." The police or community manager may find them incompatible with his larger objectives. In such a case, he should quietly put them aside or even postpone their public review until he has had a chance to reevaluate the entire study.

The View From the Top

The responsible manager of a criminal-justice agency, today, is not overly impressed with the imperfect body of knowledge and experience thus far gathered about police-community relations. Too much is mere assumption to be comfortable.

It is everywhere assumed that law enforcement is easier if the police department is believed to be honest, fair, helpful, and courageous. Another assumption is that police can always improve their reputations in those directions by close adherence to regulations and the law. These assumptions have been given credence in formal policing for more than one hundred years.

Community-relations programs based on the above two assumptions have been a part of traditional police wisdom at least since 1829 when the London Metropolitan Police Department was formed. The efforts by police departments on both sides of the ocean and, in fact, in all the English-speaking countries have vigorously projected that image to the best of their ability by close and friendly cooperation with the community. This included citizen tours of headquarters and police museums, providing stories, both factual and fictional to all the media, police visits to schools, and speeches at civic functions. As far as top police management was concerned, perfecting the image was what police-community relations were all about. Community leaders had no different vision. Public relations, also known as press relations, were concerned with simply image building and polishing.

Specialized units devoted to community relations started to flourish in the 1950s, which brought citizen committees into regular discussions about community issues. In the late 1950s some of the larger departments encouraged their personnel to take courses in psychology and human relations.

Despite this, in the 1960s the image of the police deteriorated rapidly. Television coverage, books, articles, newspaper stories, speeches, and street demonstrations often put the police in a very bad light. They were portrayed as lawless, tyrannical, brutal, corrupt, and even of being connivers and accomplices in murders and bombings.

The methods and the assumptions upon which public relations were predicated did not provide the successful results to which the police were accustomed. Something was missing—or happening—but it was difficult to discover what it was. Innumerable commissions, four of them presidential, could offer nothing more substantial than to recommend more police-community–relations programs and units. Countless studies, speeches, learned articles, and books reflected on the matter, but in sum, their suggestions, in retrospect, seem to have been more of the same.

Attention was given to poverty and to lack of education and opportunity as causes of deteriorated relations. Such matters, however, were not within police or even local community control. In any case, there was no more poverty, ignorance, or lack of opportunity than previously in the community. As far as the police were concerned, they were more educated than ever before in history.

Community efforts at developing dialogues with police departments have not been overly successful. When they have taken the route of civilian review boards, they have generally been strenuously resisted. Police endeavors at reaching into neighborhoods via storefront offices have had a spotty success, and even that has tended to become vitiated with time.

Most programs have been conducted under the advice and guidance of specialized units, separate from the units that perform the regular police functions of patrol and crime detection. There appears, from surveys conducted by researchers, to be considerable friction and dysfunctional resentment between the specialists in community relations and the regular force.

Training, too, has tended to be separate from the military-type emergency-response skills that are the major preoccupation of police training. It is quite customary for community-relations units to require college degrees for their members, although this is a rare qualification, indeed, for the rest of the force.

Commitment to community-relations programs has generally been conspicuous during a crisis and for a short time afterward. The tension and crisis-oriented nature of all police administration perhaps best describes, as well as explains, the lack of concern noted about community relations between disasters.

There is little hard data to indicate that even the above observations are critically relevant, let alone that they provide any real guide toward organizational or procedural improvement. There we have the view from the top. It is not much—but that is all there is.

"Hidden Persuaders"

Examination of police-community–relations efforts that have been labeled as such reveals four major thrusts:

1. Attempts at a *dialogue*
2. *Image* enhancement
3. Specialized *training*
4. New *personnel* programs

These efforts, almost invariably, have been instituted as a result of a crisis of one sort or another and centralized in specialized programs or even separate units. As an administrative device, to try to produce change in an existing organization without disrupting ongoing practices, these programs have usually been organizationally separated from the rest of the department, even when they were nominally under a field commander. Whatever the position in the table of organization, community-police assignments come to be filled by specially interested and trained personnel. Often they have developed specific projects that have reached into the community. They have not been so successful, as a rule, in reaching the community of their own department.

In any case, their efforts have been evaluated as having only peripheral value. As they, on occasion, have acquired a temporary credibility with local communities, they have lost credibility with their own departments. They have been called slackers, goldbricks, and even stool pigeons by the other officers, too ready to incite complaints against police.

Nevertheless, some community-relations officers have been very talented and dedicated people. When they have been supported by their chief, they have commanded measurably more cooperation from other members of the department and have operated with more claimed success. Because there is rarely any objective evaluation, claims of success are as much speculation as anything else. The consensus of most of the commissions and scholarly groups that have studied the matter is that, although they may have cooled the fires of great crisis and helped smooth matters after serious local disturbances, on the whole, their success has not been as great as hoped for by their proponents.

The separateness of community relations has been deplored by many commentators, and it has tended to be a factor in the continuing marginal value of community-relations programs to police departments and their regular operations. The objectives of these programs and units have been unclear, except that they may serve to keep the chief informed of levels of tension in the community and to provide a continuing visible administrative response to any negative criticism, or complaint, of lack of sensitivity to the community.

The difficulties of evaluation being what they are (Chapter 10), there has been practically no realistic evaluation of police-community relations in terms of identifying realistic objectives and measuring the degree to which these objectives have been reached.

Some police-community–relations units have instituted training programs for policemen, and they have frequently given lectures at recruit and in-service training sessions. In addition, they have developed panels of outside speakers, experts in the fields of human relations, sociology, psychology, and crisis intervention, to conduct seminars, lab sessions, and various other training programs, often called workshops. The total impact on police departments seems to have been minimal, according to those in a position to know.

Considering that each police officer in every rank has a full day of learning experiences in his daily work, none of which necessarily confirms the sermons of people who seem to him to be impractical theorists, it is no wonder that the results have not been spectacular. If a police officer learns on the street that it is safer and more emotionally satisfying to remain impersonal when issuing a traffic citation, no amount of pleading by an alleged expert who "hasn't been there" is going to convince the officer that friendliness is the better tactic. Everything we have discussed in this book from the very first chapter—as well as reported field experiences—indicates that this type of training session is ineffective. Loudly berated by a motorist and confronted by his refusal to produce his driver's license, a police officer is in an embarrassing situation, with high levels of anger, frustration, and aggression building in him. When he discovers that the simplest and quickest way to handle the situation is to overawe, with a show of power or an arrest, he will no longer be in a receptive mood to listen to lectures on other ways to handle the issue, ways that involve long drawn-out patient listening, the swallowing of insults, and smiles in the face of abuse. On a simple operant-conditioning level there is less reward and more punishment in being the kind of officer the "expert" suggests, rather than the kind of policeman the situation seems to demand.

These experiences are the "hidden persuaders" that have militated against success in the programs that heretofore have been instituted. What is clearly so logical and provable under the relatively aseptic conditions of the laboratory does not provide sufficient reward in the field situation. Their experiences, on or off duty, teach otherwise. Nor do laboratory-developed procedures necessarily work well in the field. However, the failure of close fitting theory to practice does not mean that one is error.

On the contrary, it merely indicates the incomplete description of one or of both. There is no reason why descriptions of both theory and practice should not jibe with operationalized versions of reality.

In communications terms (once again!) the police officer is quite obviously more influenced by his job experiences than by a preachment by outsiders, who do not suffer the fatigues and frustrations of dispute settlement and patrol day after day. The teachers are not "significant others," who might serve as models for identification to the officers, nor are they respected charismatic figures or leaders of opinion or influence. They see the teachers, surveys indicate, as "emperors without clothing" and even severe punishment could not make them deny the nakedness they perceive.

Whether this analysis is correct is still to be seen. There has been no experimental research credible enough to settle the issue of what kind of training will be effectual. The realities of the communication processes involved in the continuing job experiences of officers are the "hidden persuaders" that nullify the efforts of "trainers" and human-relations courses. Police officers are persuaded to do the job as they do it, rather than as others may want them to perform, by far more efficient means than passive classroom artificialities and charades. The training that has changed them and keeps them persuaded is the street-situation, tensions, bitterness, embarrassment and frustration. These persuaders are hidden only from the laboratory situation and the classroom.

If this analysis offers any suggestion for improvement, one would believe that it is: Not to make more believable game plans for the class, but rather to make the job situation the scene of the lessons to be learned. On-site credible street situations should be the learning scene.

Reaching the Community

Police-community relations just are—it is not a matter of responsibility. It is just a fact of modern life that police and the communities interact and relate. The judgment of what is *good* or *bad* community relations is a subjective one. What will appear "good" to one commander or community of interest may appear quite "bad" to another.

The prevailing attitude among most scholars is that keeping a minority "in its place" is bad. There are any number of eminent commentators on the current scene who decry such an attitude as being un-American, unfair, and even inhuman. That may be so—at least no one in public life in this country will quarrel with that judgment today. It is a private, personal judgment, nevertheless, and studies and commissions that do not announce this attitude as a prejudgment tend to obfuscate their objectivity and distort their findings.

American police are expected to uphold "democratic values." It would be difficult to find anyone to deny that normative obligation. Again, however, that is a judgment, not a statement of fact, particularly when "democratic values" are well-nigh undefinable in operational terms for a criminal-justice agency.

It might be more productive to try, at least to a reasonable degree, to separate objective descriptions, data, and findings from judgmental conclusions of "'good" or "bad," "improvement," or "deterioration."

Thus, "reaching the community" is considered a "good" thing, and a "progressive" police chief will try to do so with all his might. This type of conclusionary thinking is, perhaps, a handicap to discovering facts. It contains within it vague philosophic implications that, somehow, the community is good, that communicating with it on its own terms is desirable, that if a government agency will do so, it will be performing its functions better, and a host of other prejudicial matters all of which are possibly "good" but not necessarily founded on an impartial review of the facts.

A part of this philosophy appears to present the idea that if large amounts of information about the police department and its policies, practices, and records were made available to the public, in some manner, there would be an automatic "improvement" in relations between police and public. In hypothetical form: "If more information, then better relations." Research has not confirmed this myth.

The relationship between monitoring information and public satisfaction is complex. Certainly it is not a simple linear positive one. Historically, the more known about a formal policing organization the greater the public dissatisfaction. Study after study, when properly analyzed confirms this, and common observation agrees.

When there was little *independent* information obtainable about the Federal Bureau of Investigation and the Central Intelligence Agency in the years before Watergate, there was almost universal admiration and support for both agencies.

Since that time, there have been senatorial investigating committees, wide-ranging press investigations and reportings, all conducted outside of the purview of the agencies under investigation. In these cases more information about the real FBI and CIA lowered prestige and presumably worsened "relations." And the above-stated hypothesis must be rejected.

One could object, "If the agencies had been found to be 'lily-white' the hypothesis would have been accepted." But "lily-white" is a judgment, not an observable fact. In any case, that was not the judgment, and going only by the observations of fact alone, on the basis of the listed investigations the hypothesis must be rejected.

Whether a similar investigation of the Midville Police Department would produce the same conclusions as to the hypothesis? Since it has not been done, we just do not know.

Some of the "improvements" that are promised to lead to "better" police-community relations are:

1. Faster police response to emergency calls
2. "Exhibition of sympathy and compassion" by police officers
3. Higher "efficiency and effectiveness"

Of this list the only one that is clear is the first: faster police response to emergency calls—and as to that, until we go out and try it, we really do not know whether that is a variable affecting police-community relations at all. It may be utterly irrelevant, of very little relevance, or— we really do not know.

The "exhibition of sympathy and compassion" and "efficiency and effectiveness" have not been operationalized by any specific statement, thus, we do not know exactly what is meant. We can't even express an opinion as to their possible relevancy, let alone undertake an impartial, empirical investigation.

Another suggestion that is repetitively offered to "improve" police-community relations is the theory that when police know and understand the origins of community tension they will be able to avoid crisis responses.

However, knowledge of existing tension hardly implies motivation on the part of police to lessen it—even if they could. Despite this, the advice continues.

There is constant insistence in the literature on police and community behavioral patterns that the training of police in community problems and of community members in police problems will spontaneously lead to better relations.

Even the "common sense" of the practical, long-experienced police officer that communities of interest can be "reached" and made content simply by providing a professional police service, meaning, a well-educated police, who respond speedily and are willing to engage in service activities, seems not be be supported by experience.

There remains, however, one thing that seems quite certain: Widely different community compositions result in equally varied issues, expectations, and responses.

In the last analysis, then, we are reduced, at the present time to one-on-one problem-solving situations. Each police authority and community leader must assess the particular problems faced by himself. This is not necessarily reducing the approach to "fire fighting," or waiting until a crisis occurs and then reacting to it. It is more like community-crisis-prevention.

Functional Analysis

Procedures likely to sufficiently cope with problems at this level would seem to be quite like research techniques, as adapted by agencies charged with crisis prevention: public health, environmental control, central intelligence agencies, military staffs, and even fire-insurance companies. These procedures are easily presented as a sequence.

1. *Factual objective assessment* of "relations" between police and communities of interest, real and imaginary, by listing each event of communication with any PCR involvement, especially if recorded in permanent form.
2. *Evaluation* of each of the above events as negative or positive.
3. *Recording of conclusions and recommendations* of observers and experts as indicative only of their *opinion*.
4. *Recognition* that the opinions of observers and experts can become substantive facts only when and if they are reacted to as if really factual. In that case they do become a "self-fulfilled prophecy."
5. *Planning* to meet the conditions discovered by functional procedures (1) through (4).
6. *Implementation* of plans by regular operations units, under their regular commanders or leaders, police or community.

Those who have read this far will recognize the above as a model that tries to operationalize previously discussed ideas.

Examination of police departments with "satisfactory" relations with communities reveals them to be those in which the communities do not feel threatened by their police. This has been called, in the communication model, the transmission, consciously or subconsciously, of messages of support and appeasement to the public in credible form.

In a very special sense, "reaching the community" is the prime function of the entire police department. To restrict this outreach to a limited community-relations project or to a community-relations unit in a police department is placing what should be a burden of all on the shoulders of a few.

The N-Square Factor

From the days of Napoleon, mathematical analysis has indicated the enormous and disproportionately cumulative advantage given by superiority of numbers in attacking a problem. Called the N-Square Factor it can be summarized as: Bring all available assets to bear on a problem in order to maximize success and minimize losses, especially if each asset has a multiple and continuing positive effect.[7]

The calculations for N-Square analysis will be found in the references cited for this chapter,[8] but the concept is so apt to "fire-fighting" and crisis-oriented approaches that it suggests that empirical evaluation, when we can do it impartially, may reveal that perhaps some of the current practices of police administration are not so ineffective in the use of available resources as has been supposed by various theorists.

Waiting for an emergency to arise, and then bringing all available personnel and other resources into play appears to have mathematical substantiation, under certain conditions. Following that principle, we can readily agree that *operations,* if supplied for only those services that have been demanded and no others, will extend the effective value of resources. Also, this operational strategy will develop spontaneous innovation in response to crisis pressures and reassure the public with messages of support and appeasement.

Continuing the N-Square concept: It agrees that "reaching the community" is the proper task of the *entire* police department. To isolate this mission to the narrow precincts of a specialized unit becomes a waste of unused resources. The weak thrust of the few members of the unit cannot compare with the cumulative impact on the community if each member of the department emits multiple messages of appeasement and support. The references cited, if imaginatively examined, may change the point of view of students of police administration, and community guidance in significantly new directions.

Opinion Leaders

All of the knowledge that communications research has discovered about *opinion leaders* and the two-step flow of influence (see Chapter 5 and references) can and should be used in operations in police-community relations. It has been the practice in many police departments to locate local people of influence and keep their identities and information about how they can be reached quickly in emergencies on file in local station houses for use by local commanders. In this day of mass media, opinion leaders can have regional and even national impact, and this information should be part of the matters managed as a subdivision of the "community-intelligence-assessment function." Of course, community leaders should create and conserve these intelligence resources, too.

The maintenance of information and constant updating of contacts with groups and individuals are critically relevant to community relations. It is not merely a matter of filekeeping. It is necessary to refresh the commitment of all persons on this file by regular contacts on a personal, informal basis. Of course, the rule of "diminishing returns" will place an upper limit on the time, money, and effort devoted to this task.

Settling for Less

It is unrealistic to assume that any of the community demands are nonnegotiable or that the police department's requirements are not amenable to compromise. If the demand made cannot stand any reduction, it probably is because the demand was not high enough in the first place. Negotiation means giving up something and accepting less. Sometimes less is more. Especially when the alternative to less is *nothing!*

Every good negotiator must have something with which to negotiate. Therefore, all demands should be very carefully phrased so that they will be amenable to modification, reduction, alterations, and new arrangements. It is in the discussions with adversary parties that these matters become the core of negotiation.

A series of "No's" on both sides is not negotiation but rather confrontation, awaiting solution by either withdrawal or force. Actually, it is a species of aggressive behavior.

Thus the anticipation in negotiating matters in police-community relations must be always to hope for more but be ready to settle for less.

Hoping for More

In negotiating, it is rare that a stage is reached where, even in really hard-nosed bargaining, more cannot be attained. Even when the negotiations have reached a point of mutual agreement, experience reveals that the toughest negotiators are still "in there" trying to obtain yet another advantage. It is not a case of being dishonorable. The fact is that even when basic agreement has been reached there is still so much to be done that one must pose the question: Can I do more now? If so—do it!

Even if there is nothing that can be done on your own side, for your own protection, you must be aware that your adversary is asking himself, "Are there any odds and ends, conditions, or other matters that should be straightened out now?" This may be the best time for both sides to pursue negotiations just a bit further. When the issues involve matters of great moment, too many negotiators are overhappy to have attained the bulk of their side's requirements, and complete the settlement without getting that "little bit extra." That is faulty negotiation. It is usually easier to get "that little bit extra" at that time. It can save endless, tedious hours of wrangling at a later date.

Coming to Limited Agreements

When groups are representative of diverse, contentious elements, as most communities of interest are, it would be futile to try to include detailed statements in the written agreement or on tape. The key is: When opposed by or representing groups that are divided against themselves, do not be specific.

Certainly it would be the height of folly to try to particularize every facet of every part of the agreement. Consent from one of the subgroups would meet with opposition from another splinter group, often rupturing the nascent compact between department and community.

No, it is far better to reach only limited agreements, which can be interpreted by each subelement as being in its favor. In effect, then, the agreements are merely agreements to agree, rather than rigid listings of rights and obligations, each one an arguing point at a later time.

Let the phrasing be general and pleasant, supportive of fine sentiments and matters easily consented to. We are all against sin—we can agree to that—although our definitions of *sin* might be quite different.

Admittedly, this advice is in opposition to the legal training of lawyers, who try to itemize each jot and tittle in laborious detail. Their experience has shown that to be the best practice when lawyers are in charge on each side of litigious parties. The lawyer's task is to maintain control of his client, so that an orderly settlement of issues can be completed. If he cannot maintain control, the lawyer will usually resign from the case. Thus it is useful to cite each point that can be picked out from the entire case and settle it, item by item—when both parties are controlled.

Agreements made with diffused social groups and people who are temporarily associated with each other with no binding organization, authority or control are in a different class. Agreements made under such conditions between police and communities of interest are usually best when they discuss only generalities. After all, they are not contracts ordinarily binding on each member of all groups. It is unrealistic to try to devise detailed documents binding on every splinter group and party member unless the documents are to be enforceable in a court of law. Since community/police agreements rarely are of this kind—be general!

Stop, Look, and Listen!

The essence of negotiation is *listening*. Listening implies recognition of the value and importance of what the other fellow has to say. It is appeasing and submissive in style but not in substance. It encourages the hopes of the other side and sometimes make him overambitious in his demands—but at least it keeps the negotiation open.

There comes a time when listening is no longer the appropriate tactic —after you have established rapport and you know you have something the other side wants. Be alert to signals that your time for listening is over. You discover this by *looking* at the discussants on the other side and all the obtainable evidence. Sometimes this is revealed by open admission or other clear information. Sometimes it is revealed only by his style or manner. At this point stop him from talking, as you have already stopped your listening.

It is your turn to talk—to keep him listening to one argument after another, ceaselessly. Ignore or gently override his interjections. Keep bringing up different reasons why he should comply. He already knows the best reason—his own decision, unformed on his tongue but clamoring in his brain. The reasons you recite keep his attention and act cumulatively on his will. Were you to let him talk, he would refresh his recollection of all the opposing arguments he has. Further, you may reveal some sign that he will interpret as giving in to him and be reinforced in his own cause. Or, if you refuse to give him that sign of recognition, he may become offended and retreat to a nonnegotiating stance.

Keep talking to the end, keep giving your reasoned arguments. After you leave, you lose control of the situation. As long as you are presenting your case you are selling your merchandise. Never, however, overlook the crucial fact that you must first sell yourself as a reasonable, fair, appeasing, and supportive friend.

Impervious Groups

The maintenance of contacts with persons and groups does not mean that they will be passive receivers of influence from the police, which they will supinely pass on to the community. On the contrary, their influence on the police may be far greater than any possible influence the police may have on them.

There is, of course, the possibility of mutual changes under influence by this interaction, particularly as both sides see common goals and means within reach.

On the other hand, there are certain groups and individuals who are totally impervious to police influence. Some groups are designed to be so—that is one of their cardinal goals. Their purpose is to resist outside influence from the police and, on the contrary, to spread their own influence. Sometimes this includes actions to influence the police by direct or indirect action. The various international terrorist groups are prime examples of organizations of this type.[9] Although some will announce their antagonism, that is not always the case. Sometimes the long-term goals of these groups are concealed.

Aside from groups, there are emotionally disturbed individuals who are beyond rationality or who have only a limited perception of their own motives. In either case—individual or group—they are impervious to outside influence and are ready to provide any amount of input to the police department and often to society in general in the desire to exert as much influence as possible either to expedite or to interfere with the department's short-term or long-term goals.

When these individuals and groups can be identified, it is tempting to take the position that it is pointless to communicate information or any input whatever to them. This is inadvisable, because, on a theoretical basis at least, as long as they receive information input some influence will exist, even if only minimally. The problem is to try to direct that influence along channels toward a productive end. Also the actions involved in communicating to these groups can be made visible to other groups and individuals who are not impervious. The public example shown will often expedite information and influence flow to these other groups, as long as there are guards against appearing to exhibit an unwarranted submission to the influence of these impervious groups.

Often impervious groups will present nonnegotiable demands. Usually this is done in highly dangerous situations, with hostages in their possession or when they occupy some sensitive, crucial building or other physical installation, and exploit their power over life and property to extract concessions from both community and police.

The matter has been the subject of a great deal of study in recent years and, although there are no foolproof tactics for dealing with impervious types, the basic strategy is to keep negotiating, despite their refusal to admit that is what is being done. As long as the parleys continue, there is always hope for an improvement in the situation. It takes time for negotiations to take effect.

As to PCR with impervious types, the greatest profit seems to be in demonstrating to uninvolved third parties that the police, despite provocation, remain cool and poised, with an invariable calm posture of willingness to interact with everyone in order to accomplish their mission.

The Analysis of Tension

It is important in all analysis to separate fact from *opinion*, however the latter may be named: *estimation, judgment, recommendation, conclusion*. Granted that in a profound philosophical sense the underpinnings of facts, as observed by humans, do have a subjective element, the difference in the level of subjectivity between "I saw the two men in the room" and adding ". . . the two men were angry with each other" is obvious.

Following usual rules of evidence, we call the last phrase opinion, of low evidentiary value and not admissible in a court of law. The statement "I saw two men in the room" is considered quite admissible, as testimony of the evidence of one's senses. The attempt to testify as to their state of mind, "angry," calls for a speculation on the part of the witness. He would, however, be permitted to describe their words, the loudness of their voices, perhaps even the quality of tones, as sensory perceptions.

We often make these speculative, conjectural conclusions about another person's state of mind, intentions, or attitudes. As we have seen in Chapter 11, even with the best available instruments, such conclusions are suspect. Off-the-cuff, spot judgments are even more likely to be in error.

Our guess as to the state of tension in another person, his state of anger, potential aggression, is subject to the grossest miscalculations. In fact, our opinion of another's state of mind is probably more indicative of our own emotional or cognitive attitude than of his. This is particularly so when we are intimately involved as part of the interactional and emotional patterns in an ongoing confrontation.

Because police-community relations take this very predicament as the archetype of its concerns, it should be the core of its study at the tactical level, and that is what has been the center of our discussions all along. Face-to-face confrontation between individuals calls for the tremendous reserves of tact and forbearance that are the result only of long experience in the successful application of these two virtues. However, in those situations that can be prepared for in a more leisurely fashion, we have available a number of additional resources.

First, we can have present at the meeting experts trained in crisis intervention, experienced negotiators, and skilled human-relations counselors. Although it would be inappropriate here to try to delineate all their methods and strategies, there has been developed an interesting approach that has often been of use in clarifying issues between communities of interest and police managers (Figure 12–1). Actually, the technique is too simple to make any great claim for its efficacy. It is offered here for whatever use might be made of it, as having been used by many organizations to sooth ruffled feelings, relieve tensions, and calm troubled tempers so that more important matters could be approached with an eye to resolving fundamental differences between community and police.

Reconciling Dissidents
As has been pointed out, to enter into program planning or implementing with incompatible groups is a chancy thing and very probably should be avoided.

Nevertheless, the real world does not always provide people and groups that are so united in philosophy and normative structure, in aims, ambitions, and dreams, as to render unnecessary the need for accommodating dissidence. Even if there were no differences at the inception, they would soon develop. Therefore, ways of handling such discord often must be attempted.

One method that was first presented in the 1950s and has since been used in a number of police and community projects is called the normative sponsorship theory. Simply, the proposition is that to achieve success a program should be sponsored only by persons and groups who have similar norms. This has special importance in regard to the goals of the proposed project. Up to this point, it seems merely common sense. A project will reasonably maximize its likelihood of success if it has the full participation and involvement of every member of the groups involved. The more they like each other—and are alike—the greater the pleasure and satisfaction in personal interaction. This legitimate consensus is reached by identifying as many consensus points as possible between each individual and between each group.

The identification of consensus points is done at the very beginning, when getting the group together, and at every crisis that may occur later on to put a stop to minor irritations that might rip through a community with increasing dissension with each convert to one side or another.

One authority summarizes the process as follows:

1. Identify leadership—including opposition leadership
2. Bring leaders of relevant systems together

3. Identify areas of agreement and disagreement
4. Implement the program
5. Quality control, continuous program development, and updating.

The sequence appears to fit in with all our previous discussion except for item 3. Identify areas of agreement and disagreement. The method that is recommended is to prepare a matrix as follows (Figure 12–1):

Do We Agree or Disagree?

Ideas Held About

Ideas Held By:	Police Department	Community A	Community B	Community -n
Police Department	Fill in: 1. Norms? 2. Attitudes? 3. Actual behavior? 4. Kinds and amount of normative behavior? 5. Kinds and amount of deviant behavior? 6. Problems? 7. Alternative solutions? 8. Ultimate goals? 9. Acceptable means? 10. Unacceptable means? 11. Solutions "they" offer?	(Fill in: 1 through 11)	(Fill in: 1 through 11)	(Fill in: 1 through 11)
Community A	(Fill in: 1 through 11)	(Fill in: 1 through 11)	(Fill in: 1 through 11)	(Fill in: 1 through 11)
Community B	(Fill in: 1 through 11)	(Fill in: 1 through 11)	(Fill in: 1 through 11)	(Fill in: 1 through 11)

Figure 12–1

The various communities, A, B, and so on, refer to the communities relevant to the particular project involved. Although these communities may be almost endless, only those most significant would be included in the matrix, for example, local neighborhood, community councils, black associations, other police agencies, prosecuting attorney's office, social welfare organizations, and so on.

It need not be as extensive as it appears. Even the beginning effort should clarify issues. Of course, in practical use, each set of eleven questions should be reproduced on an 8½ by 11 sheet of paper, with sufficient space for each answer. The matrix is presented merely to aid in keeping the various returns in order and for presentation in compact form. Too, the questions need not include all eleven—or, in the alternative, questions could be changed or more questions could be added.

If the differences among the groups are not too great and there is a strong area of agreement on important matters, sometimes dissidents can be reconciled sufficiently to agree to go ahead on a joint mission, with their reservations clearly stated, and with mutual respect for the right to differ in opinion. Often an analysis, such as this matrix facilitates, will identify this possibility.

Chapter 13

POLICE-COMMUNITY–RELATIONS UNITS

All other men are specialists, but his specialism is
omniscience.
> —Sir Arthur Conan Doyle,
> *The Return of Sherlock Holmes*

Although many authorities have pointed out that every police officer
is at all times involved in police-community relations—every time he
talks or is even seen by a member of the public—there have been
many attempts to organize specially.

To expedite the total effort and to provide a cadre of specialized
talent able and willing to concentrate, more than the average police
officer, on making a closer bond with the community, specialized
police-community–relations units have been set up in most large
police departments.

The functions of these specialized units vary with each department, some maintaining only a staff-service function to the chief and
to other units, others performing line-operational duty with citizen
clients in the neighborhoods.

Specialization and Generalization

The phrases "Community-Relations Unit," "Police-Community Relations
Unit," and "Police-Community Unit" refer to an organizational unit
within a police department with the mission of enhancing the quality of
police-community relations. It seems a simple enough and direct enough
way to approach the problem, but the consequences are manifold.[1]

Specialization, as a principle of organization, has been known and
used since prehistoric times. In various parts of the United States, Germany, Britain, and many other places, certain localities were centers for
concentrated, specialized work on repetitive tasks that required special
skills, training, and interest. A worker performing the same task, even the
same motions, over and over again becomes highly skilled, acquiring
an ability, sureness, and accuracy that vastly increases output and quality
of product. Thus, certain areas in both the New and the Old World

became the scene for Stone Age factories manufacturing flints for spears and arrows. In other places, pottery, basketware, and other ancient manufactories prevailed and prospered.

The restriction of personnel and organizational units to a single function, grouped under one head, is a classic approach toward improved performance. The important thing about specialization in community relations is that it brings decision making to the place where it can be made most expertly. For decision making is a skill, and practice here makes perfect, as surely as for arrowhead flintchippers, telephone installers, and surgeons.

Thus, it is reasonable to expect that community-relations specialists would become highly skilled at communicating with local leadership, cementing personal relations, and making friends among the neighborhoods. PCR personnel can be carefully selected for special educational backgrounds, trained skills, and natural talent at getting along with people. It is not, however, a one-way street. There are drawbacks: Once people in the specialized staff units start to make decisions about field operations, the field commanders and their people are not going to like it. Trouble is latent, at first, perhaps, as friction, then squabbles, then conflicts, and sometimes a clear breakdown in articulation of operations.

Traditional principles of organization such as unity of command and command responsibility are not so old-fashioned as to be completely unreliable guides to a smooth administration. A field commander—and even his subordinate—will be resentful of intrusions from a headquarters staff unit venturing to make field decisions on their turf.

Of course, there are valuable special skills that can be of great use in human-relations work, skills that would not ordinarily be found in officers in patrol or in other field assignments. There is no need to deprive departments of the services of such refined natural or trained abilities. It is merely a matter of successfully channeling the specialists' talents toward department objectives.

Field personnel, almost by definition, tend toward being generalists in skills and orientation. Especially is this true of police patrol officers. Their field commanders are responsible for making the major decisions that will result in police success in the geographic or functional areas that are their responsibility. It is quite customary for field commanders to have in their command specialist individuals, from clerical staff, summons men, plainclothesmen, juvenile and police-athletic-league specialists, just as a military commander will have reconnaissance, tank, antitank, sappers, and field kitchen people and units. All that is theory, what is the record?

The history of separate specialist police-community units is replete with stories of their ostracism by the rest of the department, their futility in affecting the course of either police image or more fundamental police-community relations.[2] As working police officers, however, they have, as a group and individually, shown the highest degree of dedication to their tasks. Their record on staff work has been outstanding—exceptional in quality and in quantity. They have made breakthroughs in establishing rapport with community people under harsh and unfavorable circumstances with remarkable success. In doing so, however, they have often lost the goodwill of their own department.

On theoretical and on practical grounds, then, one is tempted to be guarded about advising a department to institute a police-community–relations unit that is to have field responsibility or command.

Centralization and Decentralization

Centralization and decentralization is another issue that seems to have been current in social organizations from earliest times. A manager, giving directions in a face-to-face communication, is in centralized control of the organization over which he has such face-to-face contact with all the members.

When the organization becomes large, with many persons involved, covering a wide area of space so that communications become diffused, distorted, or destroyed, the top manager does not receive the facts necessary for decision until the time for decision is past. At that point, centralization must give way to a degree of decentralization in decision-making that is proportionate to the communication-distance from point of decision to high level commander.

The variables involved are complexity of decision, degree of familiarity with topical or local information, intervening levels of supervision, urgency of the time factor. These appear to be the conditions that demand increased decentralization, permitting decisions to be made on the basis of input received in time for the decision to be effectual.

To determine the degree of decentralization of control and decision making that is necessary, machinery must be devised to provide input regarding the delay in correct decision making, whether or not delay affects the decisions adversely, and if so, how much. With that information in hand, the question of whether more decentralization is needed can be weighed. An argument for increased staff assistance could be made if instantaneous decisions are not needed but complex analyses are necessary before decision can be made. Whether this would be *central* staff or separate, technical staff assigned to the decentralized field commander would depend on such considerations as kind and amount of such assistance required.

The Best of All Worlds

Tables of organization, formal organizational structure, and the design of organizational communication networks—all of which are much the same thing—have been called a stopped-motion photograph of a dynamically flowing set of channels carrying information and orders. At any one time, the patterns that can be discerned are the organizational "structure."

Because, however, no still photograph or graphic outlining of boxes with interconnecting lines can ever show how the patterns change from day to day, or how the quality of communication subtly modifies from hour to hour, such efforts at freezing organizational structure, although helpful to understanding, are not very representative of the living organisms of a complex association such as a police department. In addition, the *informal* lines of information and influence defy delineation.

Nevertheless, it is interesting to study some of the organizational charts that have been devised in attempts to crystallize all information in one package. They remain, however, unarticulated frameworks.

The hope for perfection in organizational charting is probably a dead end. The epigraph at the beginning of Chapter 12 is in point:

> "For forms of government let fools contest;
> What e'er is best administer'd is best; . . ."

Basic Philosophies

Since 1955, when police-community relations was conceived as separate from general police work, scholars have emphasized the creation of specialized units in police departments whose main, if not only, task was to administer community relations.

Historical evidence is conclusive that police departments, before 1955, considered themselves in the business of handling community relations on a department-wide basis, as part of their job.

The new direction was pursued in 1955, after the National Institute of Police-Community Relations, was sponsored by the School of Police Administration and Public Safety of Michigan State University. Focusing on the interaction between law-enforcement agencies and communities, the institute took a dim view of the dangers that ensue when a high level of antagonism is permitted to exist between them.

The National Institute of Police-Community Relations tried to aid police in becoming aware of the need for insight and technique to improve their relations with the communities they contacted. This conceptual approach has remained as a trend in this country. Many departments have PCR specialists who preach the necessity of having only college-trained personnel in their elite units, which are supervised by a commander who has immediate and direct access to the chief of the department. Many exhibit a high level of style and presence in private and public discourse. They are magnificent public speakers, able to deal on the platform with large audiences of wealthy and prestigious citizens, covering themselves and their departments with honor as they demonstrate that police officers are not necessarily boors and brutes.

A large number of other institutes, seminars, and conferences, with the generous support of much media coverage, followed the NIPCR. Almost every department of any size appears to have acknowledged the value of some aspects of this special approach to PCR as giving impetus to both police and community for greater understanding.

This has been a continuing theme, as we have seen, as a means to higher production. Too, since World War II, "Administration" had become a college discipline. The number of professional and academic schools providing courses in the subject has risen spectacularly. Many schools by 1955 were devoted to specialized aspects of administration: business administration, public administration, hospital administration, and many others. Since then, the trend has accelerated.

Administrators had always sought ever more control. Their traditional preoccupations were mechanistic rational supervision and management: "unity of command," line and staff, time and motion, central planning.

Then came the discoveries, in the 1930s, by Elton Mayon and other human relations counselors, that human performers could make or break an organization. Human participants had sentiments, emotions, attitudes, and drives that must be considered for maximum performance.

Cost/benefit analysis was invented by business, but the vast expenditures for defense during the Cold War and various "police actions" opened an inquiry as to its relevance to the military establishment.

As cost/effectiveness measures became ascendant, primed by then Secretary of Defense Robert S. McNamara and his covey of experts and systems planners on the national scene, the approach was extended to the first police cost/effectiveness studies, and the military model of outward deportment became standard. Repeated infusions of personnel trained in military forms of organization and behavior, after the wars in Korea and Vietnam, expedited this trend.

Thus the so-called ideal organization of a police department's PCR is today seen to be in a specialized unit, reporting directly to the chief, which provides him with staff studies. Data from information surveys, which are usually quite informal, provide a barrier against charges of non-recognition of community relations. This jurisdiction-wide unit is given a localized focus by allowing district commanders to appoint at least one police officer to special duty with the community at the neighborhood level.

Thus, the basic philosophy seems to be to reach as much as possible for every administrative device in keeping with the current wisdoms in administration. It is doubtful if the state of the art at present permits any better organization.

It is puzzling, however, that, whereas Taylor [3] and Mayo [4] were empirical researchers who sought justification for their theories in real situations, today there are many theories about organizational matters that seem to evade empirical study. "Arguments" are made for or against various administrative procedures on the basis of *logic, representation,* or "ever better" happenstances such as quicker *responsiveness* and *efficiency.* Such diffused terminology tends to an inexactness that is intolerable in a scientific sense.

The never-ending dispute about military versus nonmilitary models of organization is a prime example of the guesswork that serves in place of scientific inquiry even on long-standing issues. One form this disputation (instead of investigation) has taken is the listing of claimed advantages for one model or the other.[5]

Claimed advantages of the military police model:

1. Officer is denied the arbitrary and capricious application of his personal value system on others;
2. The model is conducive to an orderly approach to conditions and emergencies of all kinds;
3. The high degree of centralization ensures responsiveness to the department's policies toward the community;
4. The internal discipline of the military model holds officers to a responsibility to the civil community, as it does the military forces;

5. Incompetent, erratic, politicized, and overemotional persons are discouraged from employment;
6. Constant internal self-criticism, leading to higher and better performance, results in a steady advance in methods and techniques of police work;
7. A high degree of centralization is necessary to ensure responsiveness to the police department's policies toward the community in regard to members with widely divergent attitudes toward minorities and ethnically identifiable community members;
8. Constant in-service retraining encourages a generalist attitude, flexible performance and assignment;
9. By assignment of only police to all police tasks, identities of complainants and informants is secured, and rights of privacy regarding personal histories are protected;
10. Criminal information is securely protected by limited access, lest it be used for improper purposes by police members and other persons.

Amazingly enough, the same allegations are turned around and made into *disadvantages* of the military approach in much the same words: [6]

1. The rigid concept of order makes it difficult for officers to be flexible in dealing with a heterogeneous community;
2. The model denies the officer the basic freedoms and values of the democratic society he is expected to sustain;
3. The officer is handicapped in the exercise of responsible discretion and judgment;
4. Lack of discretionary judgment tends to deny the claim of police to be members of a profession;
5. Regimentation discourages competent innovative persons from seeking employment with police;
6. Self-criticism is discouraged, closing off improvement;
7. The model's high degree of centralization tends toward an insensitivity to the need to be responsive to individual communities;
8. Interchangeable assignments ignore the special skills and distinctive qualifications of members best adapted for different aspects of police work;
9. The use of police for secretarial and filing duties is costly and less efficient than use of nonpolice personnel;
10. Military control of criminal and other information limits its use by police officers on field duty and patrol.

Such contradictory conclusions without a data base have been the bane of practical people trying to accomplish their mission in police and community relations. Actually, we do not know the best way to organize for community relations, although we might be better equipped to recognize a bad arrangement by reason of its failure to produce the way we want it to. In short, the relative advantages or disadvantages of the military model versus some other model, the advisability of centralization against decentralization of decisions, or even whether specialization is better than generalist attacks are unknown to us.

Frankly, we only recognize good organizational practice when we succeed at what we want to do, and then, in a Pavlovian conditioned-response sort of way we conclude that it was the organizational structure that did it. *Post hoc ergo proper hoc* (after the fact therefore because of the fact), an ancient Roman folly, is still common today.

Perhaps we cannot decide between all these options because none of them is truly germane to the issues to which they have been applied. Is it, rather, that we have not had enough scientific research, not tried hard enough to *measure?* Instead, we are still at the stage of arguing the matter.

The basic philosophy today is to try to do everything for all people at all times—it follows then, that we try to use all methods. We reach for both specialization and generalization—a little of each, a *balance* as they say. Police-community relations is centralized at high levels of command, and it is also recommended that local commanders have special powers and responsibilities. The military model is the usual mode, but it is modified in regard to police-community–relations personnel as to styles of address, the encouragement of friendly, informal contracts, and, often, with a civilian as the nominal head.

In the hope that it will be helpful, let us try to return to fundamentals. We have had a long series of discussions in this book, and it appears that we are being led by data and by necessary assumptions to the following: First, policing arrangements do exist, and will exist, in and among all groups of humans.

Second, the policing that will be successful will be only what is normative to the group, that is, those methods consented to by the group as being the natural order of things, utterly to be expected and beyond any question, because there is no other reasonable or comfortable way. In a word, the policing arrangements that can hope for success are only those that have become completely *acculturated.*

Third, acculturation starts in the child's very earliest years. The normative responses developed then can be changed only with difficulty, and with many failures of attempts at reprogramming.

Fourth, the policing arrangements that will have the highest probability of success will be those that are perceived as persuasively related to basic normative values of the persons who will be policed.

Fifth, because a police manager is presented with a police department and a public of communities of interest that were in existence before he came upon the scene, he is, perforce, faced with preexisting normative configurations in all these groups.

Sixth, in view of the fact that each of these communities of interest has political power—that is, in this country they vote the way they wish and can and do influence others to vote in accord with these wishes—the police manager is forced to seek accommodation among the contending normative structures.

Seventh, as long as the police manager remains in a managerial position he retains some power to influence, some power to move people and events toward the goal of his police mission and to retain his managerial position. For if he is in constant danger of losing his position, there can be no continuity in policing arrangements such as is necessary to the normative legitimacy of such arrangements.

Eighth, if the contending forces change in their power relationships too quickly, there will be no generally acceptable normative structure to be policed.

Ninth, in such an unstable state, the police manager's job becomes one of constant vigilance to discover the state of the normative net surrounding him.

Tenth, and finally, the only "correct" organization for police-community relations is one that is equipped to change in any direction indicated by community input. Further, the most important function of a police-community–relations unit is to perceive as completely as possible all norms, changes in norms, trends in attitudes of the various communities of interest, and to report on these matters to the chief. If they can, additionally, provide staff assistance to the chief and line units to cope with the new normative situation, they will have earned their keep.

The basic assumption in all the above is that policing arrangements should be adapted as completely as possible to the prevailing situation. Under present-day circumstances, the situation is never what it was, even a little while ago, but never quite what new input seems to indicate, because of "influence lag" in the community.

A few last points: The power of the police chief to change the public is minimal, although he does have sufficient power to affect the normative structure of small communities of interest in regard to peripheral normative behavior, for example, a department-wide effort to enlist a substantial part of a community of interest in a school program that encompasses school crossing guards, traffic safety, block home units, and block watchers. This is a situation in which the existing norms of the community are sustained by massive influence toward slightly modified normative behavior.

The power of the chief, however, is much greater over his own department. If he can be patient, over time, he can greatly modify the overt performance of his personnel. Basic attitudes, however, will probably be unchanged during the course of one administration.

Training programs of many kinds have been instituted. They have not been found to be very successful in changing either attitudes or values. It is possible that the low success rate is due to the fact that a training program is ordinarily scheduled for a relatively short time, and long-rooted basic normative attitudes slowly formed early in life will take a correspondingly longer training period to change successfully the attitudinal patterns of adults. That it can be done, however, by extended exposure to new normative patterns seems quite certain. Attitudinal change is especially obtainable when situationally supported by peer pressure. "Total immersion" is the term applied to such situational exposures as prison, military organizations, and even within the police community itself, where a notable change in attitudes and values in the police officer has been noted, as he moves from job applicant, through successive stages of police candidate, rookie, first-year police officer, experienced police officer, to grizzled veteran.

Attitudinal change in police officers over the years has been shown repeatedly. The question of directing that change, according to the evidence, would seem to be a function of control of the street situation, the promotion and reward system, and peer pressure to sustain the new direction desired.

Problems of Elites

One of the major problems of establishing new levels of education, higher qualifications, and distinctive abilities in a police sub-unit is that the rest of a large organization senses a serious disturbance and threat. The consequent evil done to organizational goal achievement is serious.

Police-community–relations specialized units often seek only college-trained people, particularly those with training in psychology, sociology, human relations, and social work. The professional orientation of this group is at odds with that of the rest of the force, who feel this and resent it. The entire police-community unit becomes, in short order, an isolated enclave, unable to enlist substantial support from the rest of the department and having a minimal effect on them.

The impression that there are "strangers in the department" is reinforced when it appears that the newcomers are cooperating with civilians to make complaints against police. The close communication the PCR people have with the public, especially that part of the public that criticizes police, appears to the ordinary police observer to be the alliance of the PCR unit with enemies. Viewed as consummate treachery, open warfare is a frequent result.

The situation is not aided by the close-knit group identification developed by PCR members with their own units. They feel that their special training and education have given them recognition on a professional level with others of equal training in colleges and private life and that they are not appreciated by the rest of the department. However great their trained skill in interpersonal relations, it often will not be enough to compensate for the handicap of being in a situation that is impossible of simple resolution.

One attempt to reduce this problem to manageable size has been to assign the PCR members who provide information to the field branch to assist the field officers on raids and arrests initiated by their information. This is not an unalloyed success—for many practitioners have pointed out that by doing so they prejudice their own natural constituency, their specific community of interest.

Another route is to rotate assignment to the PCR unit at regular, short intervals. Some small departments assign as much as 10 percent or more of their sworn officers to the PCR unit and rotate them every three months or so.

The question of the PCR constituency has sometimes been resolved by setting up as PCR targets:

1. The community that is disaffected with the police, and
2. The members of the police community who for reasons of disaffection, or other, are a source of anti-community incidents or sentiment.

These are two very narrow paths to travel. The militantly estranged community often sees PCR members as false ambassadors, lying in their teeth. The police community considers the unit's efforts at listing "trigger words" and "advice" about community relations an arrogance of assumed moral superiority, which is resented. These problems may be behind the basic rationale of seeking a civilian head for such units: avoidance of charges of elitism at the highest level.

A Review of the Field

Police departments have tried both polar extremes of organization:

1. The chief of police keeps all community-relations matters under his direct control (see Figure 13–1)
2. Local police commanders handle all relations with the community (see Figure 13–1)

In usual practice there is somewhat of a blend of these two. It would be impractical to do otherwise, but the degree to which the emphasis is on having top-level or local-level concern varies from department to department, with infinitely small variations between departments. There are changes in each department over time, as community conditions change, and as new programs are phased in and old programs out.

The number of police departments in this country appears to be decreasing as mergers of political entities and functions continue. This decrease is probably more than matched as private police organizations increase in number—and develop equivalent community-relations problems.

Another dimension by which we can analyze departments is by separating operations from support aspects of police-community–relations efforts. *Operations* in PCR consist of staffing and operating storefront station houses, control and supervision of all neighborhood community involvements, such as block watchers, block houses, coordinating councils, civilian radio-taxi patrols, civilian observation patrols, senior-citizen escort services, community councils, crime-reporting programs, Operation I.D. programs, anti-burglary surveys, and the many others that police and community ingenuity can devise.

Supporting services in PCR consist of maintaining files of all community contacts, continuing regular contacts with all persons of influence in the community, establishing speakers' bureaus and acting as agents to book speakers for community audiences, providing statistical and geographical analyses as required, as well as demographic analysis of communities of interest important to PCR, and maintaining a staff trained and equipped to handle planning and research in PCR.

If we were to consider only the two dimensions mentioned, our descriptive summary of the field might be summarized as in Figure 13–1.

The extreme of centralization would be concentration of both operations and support in the chief's office. The extreme of decentralization would be the delegation of all operations and support to local command-

Police-Community Relations Control and Function

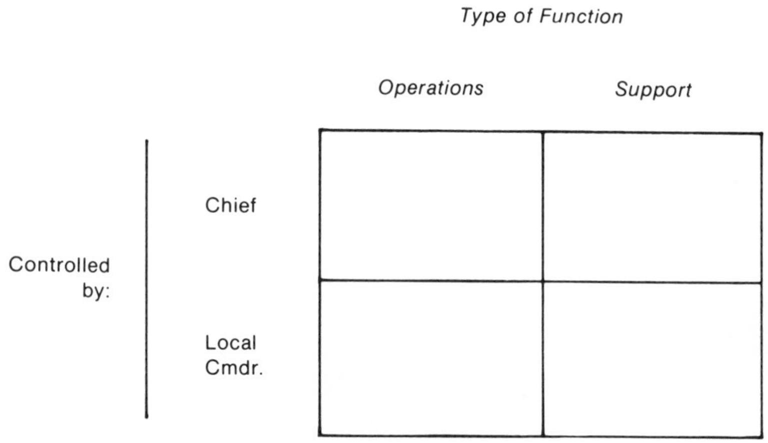

Type of Function

	Operations	*Support*

| Controlled by: | Chief | | |
| | Local Cmdr. | | |

Figure 13–1

ers, or even to individual police officers. It has been theorized that support services should probably be retained in the chief's office, where trained personnel, communication facilities, and data storage and retrieval can best serve the entire department, whereas operations should be decentralized to field comamnders, geographic and functional, to the maximum. That is, commanders and subordinates should have geographically outlined responsibilities, such as precincts, zones, districts, posts, boroughs, sections, or divisions, and be held responsible for the good order of their community relations insofar as their areas are concerned. Functional commanders and subordinates, such as detectives and other line personnel with city-wide responsibilities, should be required to maintain their community relations with particular reference to their specialties.

Theories are often persuasive. They remain, however, just theories until tested with empirical fact. The kind of research on organization and administration of police-community relations that would provide answers to this and similar questions has not been done. It is appropriate at this time to take a glance at some typical police departments' arrangements for handling community relations.

New York City Police Department
The New York City Police Department is commanded by and under the

general direction of a civilian police commander. Directly under him are the chiefs of the uniform and the detective forces and a number of civilian deputy commissioners charged with various duties. The deputy commissioner in charge of community affairs can be, and often is, appointed from the general public and need not have had any previous police experience. He is a civilian and is expected to have a large number of contacts with influential citizens at the highest as well as all intermediate levels. With the recent budgeting problems, there has been a reduction in the number of personnel he supervises, as well as a substantial reduction in budget allotments for all community outreach by the department. This has motivated members working in one capacity or another in community affairs to seek out financial backers for various worthwhile programs.

The deputy commissioner has an executive officer who serves as the direct operating contact with three major divisions on the next echelon:

1. Administrative Section (Division)
2. Youth Aid Division
3. Community Affairs Division

There is an attempt to use terms that will denote the level in the hierarchy to which a branch pertains. Thus, "division" indicates the level just under the executive officer. Ordinarily a division head will be of a certain police rank, with salary and privileges that pertain to that rank. However, because of a small number of personnel assigned or a relatively low level of importance, a lower-ranking officer may be put in charge, or a division-level operating branch may be called a section, or even unit, even though it is at the division level, that is, reporting directly to the executive officer.

In order of rank, the levels are division, section, and unit.

As can be seen, the Administrative Section just under the executive officer is division-level. However, because its functions are mainly office management and communications and correspondence for the office of the executive officer and the deputy commissioner, it is considered less important than the other two major branches that report to the executive officer: the Youth Aid Division and the Community Affairs Division.

It can be seen that the use of "division" in the title of these branches is useful in that it differentiates them from "community affairs" as used at the deputy commissioner's level.

The terminology is not a hard and fast thing, however, as we see by the table of organization (Figure 13–2). Co-equal with "unit" are branches called "program," "squad," "team," and even "dialogue."

New York City Police Department

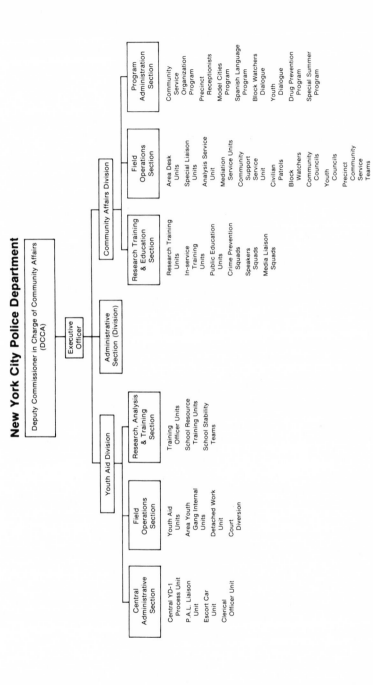

Figure 13–2

244 POLICE AND THE COMMUNITY

As must be the case always, organizational formalization and rationalization must be flexible when faced with field operating conditions. It is quite apparent that top administration, in assigning the various names, is trying to clarify unit assignments and job descriptions.

Of particular interest to the student of community relations are the two units called Block Watchers. Both of them are in the Community Affairs Division, but one reports to the Field Operations Section and the other reports to the Program Administration Section. The subunit called simply Block Watchers, in the Field Operations Section, in a system of thousands of neighborhood housewives and other persons who watch in their neighborhoods and report suspicious persons or incidents to the police. They work alone, as widely separated individuals, who are supported in the field by the Community Support Service Unit.

The unit called Block Watchers Dialogue, however, is an in-service training and research-type effort endeavoring, among other things, to talk to the block watchers to obtain feedback from them as to their problems, difficulties, worries, and fears—as well as the matters that have given them satisfaction. Too, it seeks to provide them with a more general support, from the entire police department, as well as recognition for the excellent work they have done. For this reason, although the unit is directly under the Program Administration Section, it is called a *dialogue*. In short, the officers are *listening,* not *directing.*

It would take the major portion of this book to go into the details of any community-relations program of any large city, especially that of our largest, New York. However, as an example of the maximum in specialization, and extensive outreach, New York City's program is relevant to all cities.

The entire New York City Police Department frequently changes its organizational structure in major and minor aspects as it creatively tries to cope with situations as they arise both within and without the department. At one time the department consisted of some thirty-six thousand personnel. At the present time it is down to approximately twenty thousand, as a result of attrition, layoffs, and other reasons, mainly the present austerity in budgeting. Many dedicated officers and civilian employees have worked longer hours than required by their assignments in the sheer joy and enthusiasm of their interest in the human problems involved in all community relations. This has gone so far as to actively seek the aid, financial and personal, of lay people and large corporations to help support such programs as the Civilian Radio Taxi Patrol, the Civilian Patrol (both of these are patrol by civilians in radio-equipped autos, closely supervised by the police department), Senior Escort Service, Precinct Community Councils, and many others.

The size of the problems—and the attempts at solution—in New York City are awesome. There are thirty thousand block watchers, thousands of youth volunteers employed in the summer programs, as many thousands of adult volunteers in various civilian patrols, contributing not only their time but also their expenses.

To this must be added civilians who volunteer for duty on precinct, community, and youth councils and in the dozens of other programs, some of which continue as others are phased out in a never-ending panoplied flux of communities of interest of every national origin and shade of education, culture, and occupation. One survey counted seventy-seven different nationalities among the unpaid volunteers in the community-affairs programs of the New York City Police Department.

Most of the civilians who eventually participate are recruited through local precinct station houses or via a special mailing address to the department called Box 466.

As one dedicated sergeant assigned to full-time duty in community affairs put it, "Community-minded people always involve themselves as much as they can. But the people I want are those who usually sit back and let others do it!"

Chicago Police Department

The Chicago Police Department's very tightly organized approach to police-community relations has recently been reorganized. Perhaps the fairest way to present their arrangements is to reproduce the general orders, which succinctly describe the entire plan. Figure 13-3 reproduces the general orders for the current Bureau of Community Services. The precision and specificity of this directive is typical of the way the Chicago Police Department handles its internal communications. Figure 13-4 is their current table of organization.

At the practical level, there is a constant and strong effort to decentralize part of the community thrust to the neighborhood. This is explicitly set forth by another general order (Figure 13-5), which very clearly outlines their District Community Service Program as to purpose and objectives as well as the itemized duties of the sergeant assigned to neighborhood relations.

Political administrations in Chicago show great concern about neighborhood affairs. Although the order is dated "22 April 1977," Chicago's police department has for many years emphasized neighborhood relations,

Chicago Police Department
General Order, 16 April 1977

CHICAGO POLICE DEPARTMENT

GENERAL ORDER

	DATE OF ISSUE	EFFECTIVE DATE	NO.
	15 April 1977	16 April 1977	77-11

SUBJECT
ORGANIZATION AND FUNCTIONS OF THE
BUREAU OF COMMUNITY SERVICES

DISTRI- AMENDS
BUTION
C

RELATED DIRECTIVES   RESCINDS
General Order 73-2 Organization for Command
General Order 77-12 District Community Service Program

I. PURPOSE
This order defines the organizational structure and functions of the Bureau of Community Services.

II. ORGANIZATIONAL STRUCTURE AND FUNCTIONAL RESPONSIBILITIES OF THE BUREAU
A. The Bureau of Community Services, commanded by a Deputy Superintendent who reports directly to the Superintendent, consists of the following:
   1. Neighborhood Relations Division
   2. Preventive Programs Division
   3. Public and Internal Information Division
   4. Reproduction and Graphic Arts Section
   5. Program Development and Evaluation Unit
B. The Bureau of Community Services assists in the formulation of Department policy relating to police-community relations and, through continuous evaluation of Department policy, recommends changes when required. The Bureau studies conditions, incidents, statistics, and locations to determine areas where improvement in police-community relations are needed.
C. The Bureau develops short-range and long-range plans and programs designed to:
   1. indicate that law enforcement and the maintenance of social order are a combined police-community responsibility.
   2. encourage citizens to participate in crime prevention programs and to assist the police in the identification and prosecution of offenders.
   3. analyze and evaluate police-community relations programs and projects.
D. The Deputy Superintendent for Community Services:
   1. coordinates and directs the activities and resources of the Bureau to provide police-community services.
   2. utilizes the Program Development and Evaluation Unit, to initiate innovative concepts, to measure effectiveness of current practices, and recommend procedures designed to cultivate a viable relationship between the Department and the community.
   3. is the Chairman of the Executive Steering Committee of the Beat Representative Program. The Executive Steering Committee is the policy-making body of the Beat Representative Program. The Deputy Superintendent, as Committee Chairman:
      a. represents the Chicago Police Department in formulation of program policy.
      b. provides direction to the Executive Committee.

    c. insures that the policy and procedures of the committee are carried into effect.

    d. coordinates program development.

    e. provides guidance in program operation and procedure.

    f. oversees the operation of the program to the extent that the established goals and objectives are achieved.

E. Neighborhood Relations Division

The Division, commanded by a director, coordinates the Department human relations programs, establishes and participates in student programs in schools, and maintains staff supervision and liaison with the district neighborhood relations sergeants. The division consists of the following sections, each commanded by a lieutenant:

1. The Human Relations Section:

    a. receives, records, analyzes and disseminates information within the Department on racial, religious, and nationalistic incidents.

    b. investigates and reports violations of statutes and ordinances regarding civil rights.

    c. coordinates the Department's Human Relations activities by establishing and maintaining communications with community organizations and their leaders; reports and investigates tension situations within communities on a city-wide basis.

    d. assists the Chicago Police Department's Training Division regarding police-citizen relations training needs.

    e. provides representatives to participate in community meetings.

    f. provides a lecturer/instructor on social change for the Training Division.

2. The School Visitation Section:

    a. administers, participates, and provides on a staff level, the Officer Friendly program in the elementary and secondary schools; administers the Explorer Posts Law Enforcement Program.

    b. provides resource information and citizenship programs.

    c. provides staff assistance for the city's youth summer program.

3. The Staff Assistance Section:

    a. develops community relations programs to provide the public with insight into police problems and to gain support, cooperation and acceptance of the police effort.

    b. works closely with the deputy chiefs of patrol and district commanders and maintains liaison with the Commander of the Youth Division, Director of Public and Internal Information Division, the Director of the Labor Relations Section and the Safety Education Section of the Traffic Division to establish police community relations programs.

    c. maintains liaison with the leaders (officers of civic, service and religious groups; educators, social workers, and clergy) within the district.

    d. schedules and administers the use of buses and the exhibit cruiser assigned to the Bureau of Community Services.

    e. arranges speaker engagements on all aspects of the Department's operations through the Public and Internal Information Division.

    f. provides staff supervision and liaison with the neighborhood relations sergeant in each district.

F. Preventive Programs Division

The Division, commanded by a director, provides a means for police-citizen communication, directed toward developing and applying crime prevention measures. The Preventive Programs Division consists of the following three sections, with one lieutenant, designated as a section leader, in charge of the three sections.

1. The General Crime Prevention Section operates six service centers within selected areas of the city with three sergeants as area supervisors. Each center is supervised by a police officer and staffed with uniformed Community Service Aides. This section:

    a. assists Business and Youth Crime Prevention Sections in conducting crime prevention workshops and seminars.

      b. arranges and conducts safety programs, crime prevention seminars and workshops for senior citizens.

      c. conducts bicycle registrations, bicycle safety, youth recreational, and tutoring programs.

      d. assists members of the Bureau in Department sponsored crime prevention programs by acting as crowd control ushers or guides and distributes department literature.

      e. assists community organizations, block clubs, church groups, etc., in planning and implementing civic projects and crime prevention programs. Also reports hazardous conditions, i.e., abandoned buildings, unsafe sidewalks and streets.

      f. arranges and conducts projects as a group and/or assists in other Department sponsored projects.

      g. assists the Department in identifying or locating lost children and in recovering stolen autos.

      h. provides personnel to visit the elementary schools regularly to establish rapport with the children. Programs to combat vandalism are arranged and conducted by section members in the schools and with PTA's.

2. The Youth Crime Prevention Section:

      a. conducts specifically structured workshops for young people. These workshops include the following subjects:

        (1) Safety education excluding traffic safety, the dangers of drug abuse, and crime prevention.

        (2) Positive action for avoiding crime involvement.

      b. coordinates with the neighborhood relations sergeant on athletic, cultural, and educational programs.

      c. conducts employment referral operations.

      d. conducts complete physical surveys of residential premises, including comprehensive written reports.

      e. arranges and conducts crime prevention seminars and workshops, including drug abuse programs for block clubs, churches, and other community groups.

      f. assists the community by providing guidelines for forming Citizen Band Radio Patrol units and conducts regular meetings to lend continued training and coordination to their operations.

3. The Business Crime Prevention Section:

      a. provides a central source which businessmen may contact for information, guidance and advice in business crime prevention.

      b. provides speakers on Business Crime Prevention.

      c. promotes and conducts both local and citywide seminars on business crime prevention and industrial safety in conjunction with the Criminal Investigation Division of the Bureau of Investigative Services.

      d. conducts complete physical surveys of business premises, including comprehensive written reports.

      e. prepares and exhibits crime prevention displays and crime prevention literature.

G. Public and Internal Information Division

The Division, commanded by a director, is responsible for the dissemination of information to Department members and to neighborhood organizations, public and private agencies, and other groups. The Division consists of three sections, each supervised by a sergeant.

1. The Special Activities Section:

      a. provides assistance to the families of officers seriously injured or killed and files appropriate claims for the officer or his dependents under the Federal Employees Compensation Act, Public Safety Officers' Benefits Acts of 1976, and the Law Enforcement Officer's and Firemen's Compensation Act.

      b. is responsible for the submission of pertinent reports to the City Council Finance Committee relative to line of duty deaths.

      c. serves as a liaison with the Hundred Club of Cook County.

    d. administers the Mid-America Red Cross Blood Program for Department members, their families, and retirees.

    e. arranges and conducts police promotional events, awards and police recognition ceremonies.

    f. serves as a liaison for outside agencies involved in police projects; promotes and conducts various programs of interest for Department members.

    g. maintains liaison with retirees to provide assistance whenever possible (including providing job opportunities upon requests).

2. The Publication Section is responsible for writing the following publications which are disseminated to the public, Department members and their families.

    (1) the annual statistical summary

    (2) the Chicago Police Star Magazine

    (3) the Police Community News

    (4) crime prevention pamphlets and brochures.

3. The Public Interest Section:

    a. arranges and conducts tours of Department facilities, answers inquiries from the public concerning Department operations, arranges for speakers for neighborhood organizations, public and private agencies, schools, businesses and other groups.

    b. administers the ride-along program for other than news media representatives.

H. Reproduction and Graphic Arts

The commanding officer of this section reports directly to the Deputy Superintendent for Community Services. This section acts in a staff capacity to the Deputy Superintendent. Employing the technical abilities of its personnel, this section provides the following services:

1. composition, layout and reproduction of wanted circulars, Daily, Special and Supplementary Bulletins, Department directives and other Department publications.

2. criminal sketches, illustrations, beat maps, signs, charts, graphs and displays.

3. photocopies, identification photos and multi-media presentations.

4. various types of duplicating equipment and camera repairs.

5. addressograph services.

Superintendent of Police

84-76 WPB

Figure 13–3

Chicago Police Department Bureau of Community Services

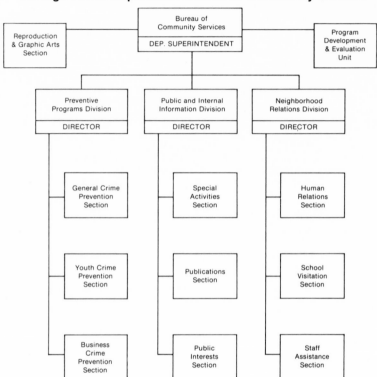

Figure 13–4

administering a special division with subdivisions for human relations, school visitation, "Officer Friendly" programs, police-community workshop programs, and many other locally oriented projects.

One program that is very well received is their Beat Representative Program. A beat representative is a community person who lives or works in his particular police district. The beat representative works as a catalyst for neighborhood involvement, "reinforcing the fact that only an alerted, aroused citizenry can thwart crime." The beat representatives do not remain anonymous. On the contrary, they must become known to the community and serve as a communication link with the community in which he or she lives or works.

Chicago Police Department
General Order, 22 April 1977

CHICAGO POLICE DEPARTMENT

GENERAL ORDER

	DATE OF ISSUE	EFFECTIVE DATE	NO.
	21 April 1977	22 April 1977	77-12

SUBJECT   DISTRI- AMENDS
DISTRICT COMMUNITY SERVICE PROGRAM BUTION
                                           C

RELATED DIRECTIVES   RESCINDS
General Order 77-11, Organization and Functions of the   General Order 72-7
Bureau of Community Services
Special Order 75-20, Beat Representative Program

I. PURPOSE
This order:
A. continues the Department's District Community Service Program which extends the present community relations, crime prevention, human relations, and public information staff operations by assigning neighborhood relations sergeants and neighborhood relations officers to assist district commanders in accomplishing their community relations function.
B. identifies the function and responsibilities of the neighborhood relations officer.
C. continues liaison between the Patrol Division and the Bureau of Community Services.

II. OBJECTIVES OF THE PROGRAM
The District Community Service Program is:
A. dedicated to broadening the opportunity for police service through close study of the problems of individual communities.
B. directed at easing social tensions in the city and developing better understanding and cooperation between the police and various segments of the community.
C. designed to better acquaint Department members and the community with each other's poblems and to stimulate action aimed at solving these problems.
D. aimed at encouraging cooperation between the community and the Department in a concerted effort to reduce crime.

III. NEIGHBORHOOD RELATIONS SERGEANT
A. A neighborhood relations sergeant is a member of the Patrol Division assigned to each district with the exception of the First District, who functions as an aide to the district commander in dealing with community relations problems. He will receive his assignments from and report directly to the district commander.
B. The neighborhood relations sergeant will:
1. maintain communication through the district commander with the following divisions of the Bureau of Community Services:
a. Neighborhood Relations Division
b. Preventive Programs Division
c. Public and Internal Information Division

2. attend district community workshop meetings, follow up on issues raised during workshop meetings, and report to the workshop what action was taken.
3. assist the district commander in expanding community relations workshops programs in a particular police district with special emphasis on the specific needs and problems within the district.
4. maintain liaison with community leaders (officers of civic organizations, religious groups, educators, and social workers) within the district to generate interest in crime prevention programs.
5. disseminate information to the community about available activities in the area, such as:
   a. programs sponsored by the Park District, social agencies, etc.
   b. programs sponsored by the Chicago Housing Authority.
   c. police programs, such as Junior Police Officer, Explorer Posts, and the exhibit cruiser, etc.
6. promote, stimulate, and support recreational activities where they are needed within the community, and promote off-duty police participation in them.
7. maintain liaison in his district with field units and workers of the Human Relations Commission, Human Services, the schools, the YMCA, Boy Scouts, and similar agencies so that their resources will be directed toward the elimination of tension in the community.
8. keep the businesses in the district apprised of how they can contribute to the stability of the community.
9. develop and maintain liaison within the district between the police and all elements of the community. For example:
   a. Maintain contact with neighborhood groups
   b. Assist individual officers in solving community relations problems.
   c. Conduct roll call training sessions on community and human relations problems, based on current Department policy as approved by the district commander.
10. stimulate the organization of neighborhood advisory committees to meet regularly with Department representatives to discuss matters of mutual interest between the police and the community.
11. assist in promoting the policy of encouraging the recruitment of minority group members into the Department.
12. be alert to job opportunities for youth in the community.
13. give direction to and supervise the performance of the neighborhood relations officer and coordinate his activities with other field operations in the district.
14. maintain liaison with neighborhood newspapers for the dissemination of newsworthy information and crime prevention programs.
15. keep his district commander and watch commanders informed of existing and potential problems and problem areas.

IV. NEIGHBORHOOD RELATIONS OFFICER
A. The neighborhood relations officer is a police officer assigned to the district who will receive his assignments from and report directly to the neighborhood relations sergeant. He will be in constant contact with community conditions which need to be and can be corrected. The number of neighborhood relations officers assigned to each district varies according to the needs of each particular district. Neighborhood relations officers are not assigned to the 1st District.
B. The neighborhood relations officer will:
1. with the guidance of the neighborhood relations sergeant, relay to the proper authority complaints that are not of an emergency nature such as but not limited to: badly maintained parks; school playgrounds closed when most needed; uncollected garbage; building code violations; rodents; broken sidewalks, pavement and curbs; defective street and signal lights, etc. Notify complainants of the action taken whenever a referral has been made.
2. assist in promoting special Department campaigns such as "Operation Crime Stop," "Help the Police Help You," "Operation Identification," etc.

3. maintain close contact with the youths in the neighborhood.
4. cooperate with the beat officers in matters of community services.

V. PATROL DIVISION LIAISON
The Chief of Patrol will facilitate liaison between the neighborhood relations sergeants and the Bureau of Community Services. The Staff Assistance Section of the Neighborhood Relations Division will perform the liaison function by guiding and counseling the neighborhood relations sergeants. The Staff Assistance Section will review and disseminate to all neighborhood relations sergeants information on programs found to be successful in other areas.

Superintendent of Police

Indicates new or revised item.
32-77 F Mc

Figure 13–5

Another position, called Block Captain, requires the same general involvement, but anonymity is retained.

We immediately note that the New York P.D. Community Affairs Division is headed by a civilian and the Chicago P.D. Bureau of Community Services is led by a police official. Otherwise New York and Chicago departments are similar: centralized staffing and control, with a constant push to involve people at neighborhood levels. Too, both community-relations divisions report to the head of the department directly, indicating the importance with which it is viewed.

Los Angeles County Department of Sheriff
Other departments in other towns do things differently. The Los Angeles County Sheriff's Department, which is a police department in every functional way within its geographical jurisdiction, separates its Community Services Bureau by three intervening levels from the head of the organization, as shown by accompanying charts (Figures 13–6 and 13–7). It is quite interesting to note that the command level above the Community Services Bureau also controls internal and special investigations, as well as organized crime.

Los Angeles County Department of Sheriff

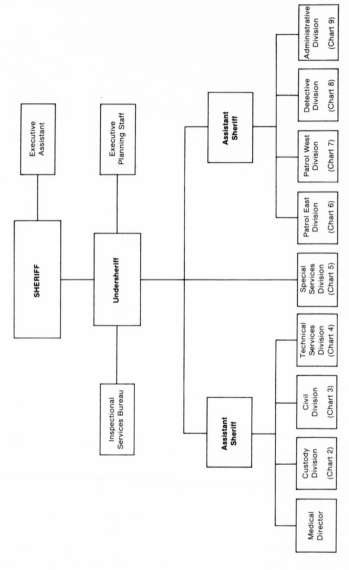

Figure 13–6

Los Angeles County Department of Sheriff
Special Services Division

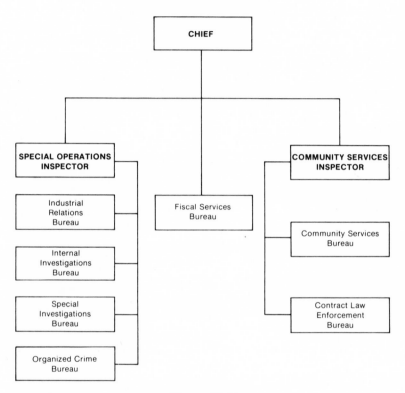

Figure 13–7

The Los Angeles County Sheriff's Department administers a variety of programs, from Adopt-a-Deputy (a variation of "Officer Friendly" programs) to sponsoring "Boys' Day in Government" and other special "holiday"-type programs, some addressed to the Chicano population. The programs are quite innovative, and a new program being enthusiastically supported is called Vial of Life. Designed to aid senior citizens and other people who require frequent medical attention, the Vial of Life program provides a printed form on which all pertinent medical information—

Los Angeles Police Department Organization
of the
Administrative Office — Community Relations

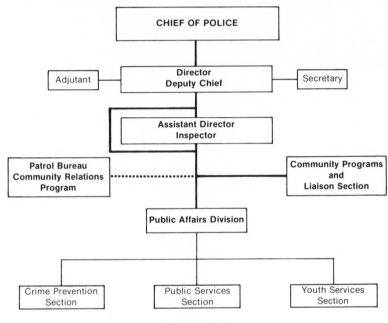

Figure 13–8

family doctor, hospital preference, type of medicines required—is listed and a vial in which to store the list. The vial is placed in the refrigerator, to be found by those reporting in an emergency situation. With the information stored in the vial at hand, officers, paramedics, and ambulance attendants have a head start in treating the sick and injured.

City of Los Angeles Police Department

The City of Los Angeles Police Department resembles the Sheriff's Department of the county in that both groups locate community-police matters at the fourth level of administration in 1969 (Figure 13–8). In the city's department, however, a new quality of separate control was introduced: police-community matters were separated into three divisions with three separate commanders. This, however, was unsatisfactory in 1974, and now the Community Relations Section has a single commander, although he is still in the fourth echelon from the top (Figure 13–9).

The City of Los Angeles Police Department conducts a number of programs similar to those of other community-affairs departments of equivalent size, listing, in addition, such innovative programs as Police-Clergy Council, Medical Safety Officer, and such special events as Mexican Independence Day, boys' and girls' summer camps, and regular fund-raising affairs.

Throughout the country, surveys indicate that practically every police department of any size has concerned itself with specific organizational structure and procedures for improving the police image by creating special units for expediting and ameliorating community relations. There is, however, a wide divergence of practice as to just what the organization should be and how it should work. Writers and academics deeply concerned with police-community relations insist that whoever is in charge of PCR should report directly to the chief, because of the importance of the PCR unit's function. Others, often line commanders, point out that PCR is everyone's business—especially every police officer's—and as such should be disseminated throughout the entire department as an integral part of police obligation in a free society.

The International Association of Chiefs of Police, who have been in the forefront of many improvements in the entire institution of policing in this country, in 1966 presented five "model" organizational plans for cities varying in population from 1 million to 10,000. In each organizational plan the PCR unit was placed at the second echelon down from the chief, and were otherwise similar as well.

One year later, the President's Commission on Law Enforcement and the Administration of Justice recommended a model in which the community-relations office reported directly to the chief (Figure 13–10).

Many police departments have a PCR office reporting at a high level—either directly to the chief or to the second echelon. In addition, one or two officers are selected by local district station houses to handle PCR at the neighborhood level, reporting to the local commander, with copies to the central PCR office. Because the local commander chooses these officers and can remove them from this assignment at any time, the responsibility and power are retained at the local or district level, which is,

Organization of the
Los Angeles Police Department

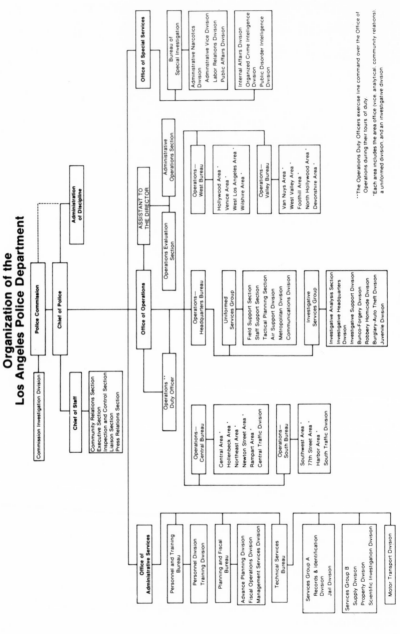

Figure 13–9

Police Commission

Chief of Police

Administration of Discipline

Commission Investigation Division

Chief of Staff
- Community Relations Section
- Executive Section
- Inspection and Control Section
- Liaison Section
- Press Relations Section

Office of Special Services

Bureau of Special Investigation
- Administrative Narcotics Division
- Administrative Vice Division
- Labor Relations Division
- Public Affairs Division
- Internal Affairs Division
- Organized Crime Intelligence Division
- Public Disorder Intelligence Division

ASSISTANT TO THE DIRECTOR

Administrative Operations Section

Operations— West Bureau
- Hollywood Area '
- Venice Area '
- West Los Angeles Area '
- Wilshire Area '

Operations— Valley Bureau
- Van Nuys Area '
- West Valley Area '
- Foothill Area '
- North Hollywood Area '
- Devonshire Area '

Operations Evaluation Section

Office of Operations

Operations '' Duty Officer

Operations— Headquarters Bureau

Uniformed Services Group
- Field Support Section
- Staff Support Section
- Tactical Planning Section
- Air Support Division
- Metropolitan Division
- Communications Division

Investigative Services Group
- Investigative Analysis Section
- Investigative Headquarters Division
- Investigative Support Division
- Bunco-Forgery Division
- Robbery Homicide Division
- Burglary-Auto Theft Division
- Juvenile Division

Operations— Central Bureau
- Central Area '
- Hollenbeck Area '
- Northeast Area '
- Newton Street Area '
- Rampart Area '
- Central Traffic Division

Operations— South Bureau
- Southwest Area '
- 77th Street Area '
- Harbor Area '
- South Traffic Division

Office of Administrative Services

Personnel and Training Bureau

Personnel Division
Training Division

Planning and Fiscal Bureau
- Advance Planning Division
- Fiscal Operations Division
- Management Services Division

Technical Services Bureau

Services Group A
- Records & Identification Division
- Jail Division

Services Group B
- Supply Division
- Property Division
- Scientific Investigation Division

Motor Transport Division

'' The Operations Duty Officers exercise line command over the Office of Operations during their tours of duty.

' Each area includes the area office (vice analytical community relations) a uniformed division, and an investigative division

**Law Enforcement Assistance Administration's
Table of Organization of
"One Form of a Well Organized Municipal Police Department"**

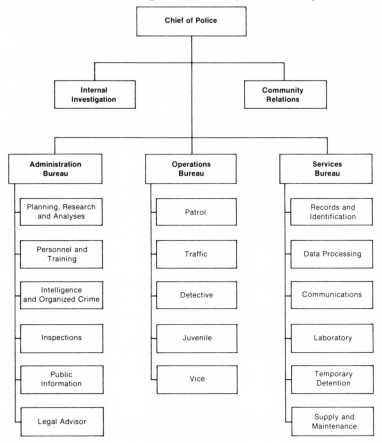

Figure 13-10

as with other police responsibilities such as crime, patrol, and often investigations, where it usually is.

At this stage of the art, we just do not know what is best. It is not a matter of taking a guess; it's more a matter of meeting specific situations head-on with rational response and reviewing constant feedback from the scene to modify all ongoing efforts until we learn better what to do and how to do it.

Part V

Review
and Recapitulation

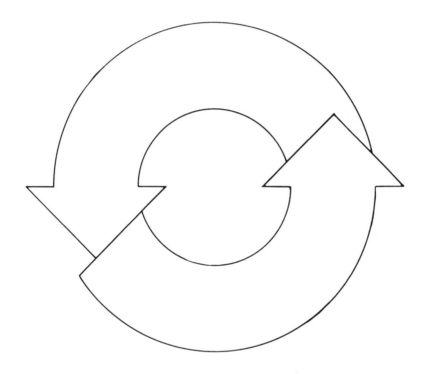

Chapter 14

A TOTAL VIEW

If liberty and equality, as is thought by some, are
chiefly to be found in democracy, they will be best
attained when all persons alike share in the government to the utmost.
—Aristotle, *Politics*, Book IV

To view the totality of everything—that is, *you*, the *community*, and
the *police*—is beyond our capacity with the present state of knowledge. We can only review the past and infer some of the things that
are likely to happen. Above all, we await the results of further research in police and community and what they can and should be
to themselves and to each other.

After having covered so many subject areas, all related to police-community
relations, we might pause a moment to recollect the objectives in mind
at the inception of this book: to examine society as a whole and, in
particular, to explore options and variables in the hope that exploration
might lead to improvement in the quality of life and police-community
relations. Where has this path led us?

Above all, one is impressed with the apparent omniscience of the public about its police, and its relations with various communities. In the
last analysis, all police-community relations are public knowledge, by
their very nature. Generally, the less actual contact a formal police force
has with a community, according to scholarly reports, the better its relations, as measured by lack of complaints. Americans, it appears, com-
plain of police whenever they are noticed. People made conscious of being
supervised, watched, or controlled object strenuously. Their outcries are
most bitter after personal confrontations with officers.

The objections take the form of resentment and complaint in a high
percentage of contact situations, which are interpreted to the disfavor of
the police agency. Harsh words are felt as police brutality. Mere dis-
courtesy is sensed to be unlawful use of force.

Americans barely tolerate formal policing agencies, and then, only to
hold *other* individuals in check. Almost everyone feels police are ac-

ceptable for use against "strangers." Personally they will not submit easily to police supervision.

There does not seem to be much difference in the public reaction in other countries, except in degree. However, most other countries have less mobile populations and stronger primary, face-to-face permanent group relationships that serve to maintain norm compliance at relatively high levels. The more totally the social environment monitors behavior, the stronger the norm-compliance structures that develop.

Terror works well to enforce norms, especially for the short term. It must be exerted, however, with utterly demoralizing ferocity, up to and including the extinction of the offending persons. Those who survive without submission, however, are reinforced in their norm deviation.

Arm's-length contractual agreements—quid pro quo persuasion, as it were—works for an even shorter term. People quickly become accustomed to receiving regularly allotted awards or rewards and revert to their "natural" state of normative behavior, despite gifts or emoluments for norm change.

Constant supervision and physical force that exact norm compliance work well, but at the expense of a deterioration of the kind of cooperation in police and community relations that we have come to feel is the democratic and proper approach. Over the course of generations, however, this can be changed, it appears, and the most forceful, repressive measures will no longer be resisted. They will have become "fitting and proper." Any attempt to ameliorate repressive means will then be deemed inappropriate and strangely foreign. At that juncture the people themselves may oppose remission of punishments and repression. However, human beings are still separate entities, culture-bound though we be, and a few, isolated exceptions to any normative pattern have always appeared.

As far as the present normative pattern of United States is concerned, there is but one basic measure of police effectiveness: *satisfaction of the public with their policing arrangements.*

If the level of satisfaction is not extremely high, with relatively few and isolated instances of dissatisfaction, norm deviation will acquire ever greater acceptance by the general public with consequent internal strife and polarization and a steadily decreasing effectiveness of policing arrangements.

In this country, the first words of the United States Constitution declare sovereignty to reside in "We the *People* . . ." However, we have not yet found techniques to maintain equal sovereignty, and to allow

240,000,000 separate individuals, fractionated and diverse, to share in the government, as enjoined by Aristotle, quoted in the epigraph at the beginning of this chapter.

We have found, however, some policing arrangements in which the *People* have been given a certain respect and recognition—by redundant messages of appeasement and support, as their due—and consequently have reached a much higher level of acceptance and success in their community relations. Generally the smaller the group being policed, the easier it is to obtain that optimum state. Other factors that require minimization include the number of norms to be enforced, the intensity of the required enforcement, the number of deviations in a given group within a given time, and the visibility of the enforcement machinery.

If public consent is obtained to policing arrangements, all measures of the police become successful in a practical sense, with or without the arts of police science or administration. "Public consent," however, is not a bare majority. The consent that is demanded is widespread acceptance, at least on a verbal level, to the point that the policing arrangements have the moral force of a norm or of mores.

Consent such as this appears to be obtainable in the ways described in the previous chapters. The picture is obscured, however, by temporary agreements that can be reached by various techniques used in advertising, public relations, politics, and even in police work. Though we may be aware of this art and science, we are not immune from it. This influence, however, does not last long. Credibility gaps quickly develop between strangers. It is only with primary loved ones that credibility remains firm. In the long run, those who emit an aura of diffused danger are enemies, taken as such and hated as such.

It seems reasonable to conclude that the average American citizen is, in the ordinary course of his daily affairs, not too interested in police. But when an incident forces police on his perceptions, he feels they are a harsh, unknown quantity, rather than a symbol of service as proclaimed by police executives in press releases. The kind of information channels that make police and citizen either friends or straight-out enemies has not evolved. They remain strangers. Each side senses a subtle menace in the other's presence far too often. Hanging over all the relationships of citizen and police is a pall of wariness, if not militant alienation. Police officers, supervised by inscrutable internal-affairs superiors, know this feeling well.

The smaller the town, the more informal the police-community relations, and thus the less need for special attention to maintaining communications redundant with messages of appeasement, friendship, and support.

The improved technologies that have become available in the last two decades—two-way radio for each officer, closed-circuit television monitoring of places and people, helicopter patrol, sophisticated weaponry, and tactical maneuvers—have not been used in ways that improve police-community relations, except insofar as admiration for technical skill has abounded.

There is a brighter side: There is a rising awareness of all the matters cited. Image making no longer is an acceptable government ploy. Now high officials decry the practice. There are hundreds, thousands of scholarly treatments of the subject of government relations with the people and police relations with community in particular. Too, the subject is a regular course of study in ever more universities and colleges, as well as in community and in internal police discussions and seminars.

Research in communities and in police relations is increasing, and communities and police departments are sincerely seeking credible solutions. The prospect for improved police-community relations becomes better each day. Much will depend on serious inquiry by scholars and practitioners to lead the way.

Appendix A

THE NINE PRINCIPLES OF POLICE OF THE LONDON METROPOLITAN POLICE FORCE, 1829

1. To prevent crime and disorder, as an alternative to their repression by military force and severity of legal punishment.
2. To recognize always that the power of the police to fulfill their functions and duties is dependent on public approval of their existence, actions and behavior, and on the ability to secure and maintain public respect.
3. To recognize always that to secure and maintain respect and approval of the public means also the securing of the willing cooperation of the public in the task of securing observance of laws.
4. To recognize always that the extent to which the cooperation of the public can be secured diminishes, proportionately, the necessity of the use of physical force and compulsion for achieving police objectives.
5. To seek and to preserve public favour, not be pandering to public opinion, but by constantly demonstrating absolutely impartial service to Law, in complete independence of policy, and without regard to the justice or injustice of the substance of individual laws; by ready offering of individual service and friendship to all members of the public without regard to their wealth or social standing; by ready exercise of courtesy and friendly good-humour; and by ready offering of individual sacrifice in protecting and preserving life.
6. To use physical force only when the exercise of persuasion, advice and warning is found to be insufficient to obtain public cooperation to an extent necessary to secure observance of law or to restore order; and to use only the minimum degree of physical force which is necessary on any particular occasion for achieving a police objective.
7. To maintain at all times a relationship with the public that gives reality to the historic tradition that the police are the public and the public are the police; the police being only members of the public who are paid to give full-time attention to duties which are incumbent on every citizen, in the interest of community welfare and existence.
8. To recognize always the need for strict adherence to police-executive functions, and to refrain from even seeming to usurp the powers of

the judiciary of avenging individuals or the State, and of authoritatively judging guilt and punishing the guilty.

9. To recognize always that the test of police efficiency is the absence of crime and disorder, and not the visible evidence of police action in dealing with them.

The above "Nine Principles" were incorporated in the first working manual for Constables of the London Metropolitan Police District, established in 1829 under the authority of Parliament. The "Principles" themselves, while not specifically attributable to anyone, have been cited as being clearly the work of the draftsmanship of Commissioner Richard Mayne.

Appendix B

A MODEL FOR PCR PROGRAM DEVELOPMENT

Models have been discussed in Chapters 4 and 5 as devices that might expedite understanding and decision making. A model for PCR program development that might be considered is to commence with the translation of all PCR issues into communication terms. There are any number of ways this translation could be effected. Here is one of the simpler ways:

I. Identification of PCR Issues Affecting the "XYZ" Department
  A. *Opinion Analysis:* The matrix presented in Chapter 12 (Figure 12-1), when properly executed, will identify transmitters and receivers of significant PCR messages. It can be modified to fit the needs of any department, as the communities of interest may appear. These may be town executives and agencies, judicial figures, news-media offices, citizens' groups, locality groups, individuals, and others who have, or might have, opinions that would affect the social reality of PCR communications by whatever channel.
  B. *Fact Sheets:* Each community of interest listed in the executed opinion analysis is assigned a fact sheet, which lists each occasion in the past year that a PCR communication, that is, each official and unofficial comment of approval or disapproval of the police department, has actually appeared. These comments can be summarized under appropriate headings as to locality, nature of comment, to whom comment made, and disposition (if a complaint).

      Particular attention should be paid to media comment, with headings for date and time, where made, by whom, to whom, nature, how and why made, so that the entire picture can be seen in summary form.
  C. *Summaries* of the above data (if voluminous) so as to put *opinion* in context with the *facts.*

      Include summation of favorable and unfavorable positions taken, on balance, by each community of interest together with an estimation of the net assessment of the community relations of the department. For example:

    1.   Interest shown by the following groups and individuals;
    2.   Support from the following groups and individuals;
    3.   Disinterest evinced by the following groups and individuals;
    4.   Opposition shown by the following groups and individuals.
This last group will probably be the major source of PCR problems. If so, effort should be concentrated there, as the present problem in the community.

II. Action Options
   A. Identify the various programs or performances that would focus department effort at turning opposition into support. The "N-Factor" principle of Chapter 12 can often be usefully applied here. One way to specifically apply this principle is to provide answers to the following question:
       1.   Is any response necessary? What are the consequences if no action is taken?
       2.   Will the problem recur or continue? What will be the consequences?
       3.   What are the alternative ways recurrence or continuance can be prevented?
          a.   Are "engineered" options available? What are they, and what are the consequences of each?
          b.   Are "educational" options available? What are they, and what are the consequences of each?
          c.   As a last resort, what are the "enforcement" options? Whom do they affect? What are the anticipated PCR consequences of each specific enforcement option?

The purpose of this scheduling of programmatic options and their consequences is to identify the choices that minimize the negative aspects of PCR and maximize supportive, positive, and appeasing relations with the community. No two departments will have exactly the same mix of problems, issues, transmitters and receivers of messages with PCR content. The effort to articulate a communication model such as this, however, should clarify issues and options in program development.

NOTES

Chapter 1 Introduction

1. These are only some of the commissions that have been concerned with police and community problems: U.S. President's Commission on Crime, 1965–1966, U.S. President's Commission on Law Enforcement and Administration of Justice, 1966–1967, U.S. President's Council on Youth, 1969, U.S. President's Task Force on Prisoner Rehabilitation, 1970, U.S. National Advisory Commission on Civil Disorders, 1969, U.S. National Commission on Criminal Justice Standards and Goals, 1974, U.S. National Commission on Urban Problems, 1974, U.S. National Commission on the Causes and Prevention of Violence, 1969.
2. The "three E's" of enforcement, education, and engineering have been used by police traffic specialists as guidelines to reduce accidents for more than half a century.

Chapter 2 Identification of Relevant Variables

1. Donald T. Campbell, "Factors Relevant to the Validity of Experiments in Social Settings," in *Problems in Social Psychology*, Carl W. Backman and Paul F. Secord, eds. (New York: McGraw-Hill, 1966). See H. W. Smith, *Strategies of Social Research* (Englewood, N.J.: Prentice-Hall, 1975), for separation and analysis of problem areas into qualitative typologies, pp. 245–7.
2. H. W. Smith, ibid. For a specific case as an example of modern approaches, see Claire Sellitz, Lawrence S. Wrightsman, and Stuart W. Cook, *Research Methods in Social Relations*, 3rd ed. (New York: Holt, Rinehart and Winston, 1976), pp. 456 ff.
3. Gary T. Marx, "Alternative Measure of Police Performance," in *Criminal Justice Research*, Emilio Viano (Lexington, Mass.: D. C. Heath, 1975), pp. 179 ff. John Dewey, *How We Think* (Boston, Mass.: D. C. Heath, 1933), pp. 106–18, discusses the difficulty of coming to grips with the variables of a problem. Sellitz, op. cit., pp. 44–5.
4. Daniel E. Bailey, *Probability and Statistics* (New York: John Wiley & Sons, 1971), Chapter 1, "A Conceptual Foundation," emphasizes the *facts* and the *guesses* one has about nature, and the probability that they are adequate and correspond with nature. Dennis P. Forcese and

Stephen Richer, *Social Research Methods* (Englewood Cliffs, N.J.: Prentice-Hall, 1973), pp. 3–6. Aristotle, *Physics,* Book II, Chapter 7, beseeched mortals to seek *causes.* The scientific approach has lowered its sights to merely seeking useful information by detecting critically relevant variables. See also M. Turner, *Philosophy and the Science of Behavior* (New York: Appleton, 1967), passim, and W. C. Guenther, *Concepts of Statistical Inference* (New York: McGraw-Hill, 1965).

5. This is called *nominal* measurement. For a short discussion of the various amounts of information contained by various levels of measurement see Robert S. Clark, *Fundamentals of Criminal Justice* (Lexington, Mass.: D. C. Heath, 1977), pp. 56–9.

6. Sellitz, op. cit., Chapters 8, 9, and 10.

7. Sir Ronald Fisher is the giant in modern probabilistic approaches to scientific inquiry, see his *The Design of Experiments* (London: Oliver & Boyd, 1935) and *Statistical Methods for Research Workers* (London: Oliver & Boyd, 1935). A simpler approach is M. Sidman's *Tactics of Scientific Research* (New York: Basic Books, 1960).

8. David Nachmias and Chava Nachmias, *Research Methods in the Social Sciences* (New York: St. Martin's Press, 1975), is an excellent comprehensive exposition, valuable for anyone who wants a review of scientific inquiry.

9. A. J. Cameron, *A Guide to Graphs* (London: Pergamon Press, 1970), is one of many good sources available.

10. Fisher, op. cit., is the prime source here. Simpler treatments include F. N. Kerlinger, *Foundations of Behavioral Research,* 2nd ed. (New York: Holt, Rinehart and Winston, 1973); Richard P. Runyon and A. Haber, *Fundamentals of Behavioral Statistics* (Reading, Mass.: Addison-Wesley, 1971).

11. Donald R. Weidman, John D. Waller, Dona MacNeil, Francine L. Tolson, Joseph S. Wholey, *Intensive Evaluation for Criminal Justice Planning Agencies,* (Washington, D.C.: LEAA, 1975). G. C. Helmstadter, *Research Concepts in Human Behavior,* (New York: Appleton-Century-Crofts, 1970).

12. For those students who have been "turned off" statistics, a small booklet by Stanley S. Blank, *Descriptive Statistics* (New York: Appleton-Century-Crofts/Meredith, 1968), may be just the difference. It is in programmed form, requiring solution of each problem before going on to the next, in sequenced form. For those who want a more usual form but still an interesting presentation for a nonmathematician, see George H. Weinberg and John A. Schumaker, *Statistics: An Intuitive Approach,* 3rd ed. (Monterey, Calif.: Brooks/Cole, 1974). A more formal and complete presentation is Samuel B. Richmond, *Statistical Analysis,* 2nd ed. (New York: Ronald Press, 1964). Of course these are only a few titles out of many to choose from. A book that takes out much of the anguish, while presenting the basic logic of statistical inference, is Elijah P. Lovejoy, *Statistics for Math Haters* (New York: Harper & Row, 1975).

13. For those who would like to obtain a probabilistic model of prob-

lem solving, M. F. Rubinstein, *Patterns of Problem Solving* (Englewood Cliffs, N.J.: Prentice-Hall, 1975), is an interesting, easy to comprehend presentation. If a more intensive inquiry into probability is desired, D. E. Bailey, *Probability and Statistics: Models for Research,* is very good. Simpler, with direct reference to measurement errors, is L. G. Parratt, *Probability and Experimental Errors in Science* (New York: Dover, 1961). This is an elementary survey suitable for students.

Chapter 3 The Intelligent Use of Experts

1. J. Von Neumann and O. Morganstern, *Theory of Games and Economic Behavior* (Princeton: Princeton University Press, 1944), is the classic work in game theory. The literature on game theory is growing rapidly, and there are many simpler works in the field. M. D. Davis, *Game Theory: A Nontechnical Introduction* (New York: Basic Books, 1970), is as good as any and has an introduction by O. Morganstern, which describes how game theory developed out of problem analysis.
2. W. B. Gallie, *Peirce and Pragmatism* (Harmondsworth, England: Pelican Books, 1952), interprets the essential responsibility one has to meet nature on its own terms. Percy W. Bridgman's many works in which he defined and detailed his views about "operationalization" fill the void between the theorist and the practitioner.
3. G. Zaltman, P. Kotler, I. Kaufman, *Creating Social Change* (New York: Holt, Rinehart and Winston, 1972); W. G. Bennis, K. D. Benne, and R. Chin, eds., *The Planning of Change* (New York: Holt, Rinehart and Winston, 1964). These two books can be very helpful to a manager desiring to effectuate police-community–relations changes. The first edition of the Bennis book has more material relevant to the manager's problems than the newer second edition.

Chapter 4 Models and Modeling

1. Nan Lin, *Foundations of Social Research* (New York: McGraw-Hill, 1976), Chapter 3, which discusses modeling theoretical social structures in a way different from the method described in this book.
2. A. Blumstein, K. Kamrass, and A. B. Weiss, eds. *Systems Analysis for Social Problems* (Washington, D.C.: Washington Operations Research Council, 1970), presents systematic models from a dozen different perspectives; N. M. Amosov, *Modeling of Thinking and the Mind,* trans. by Leo Finegold (New York: Spartan Books/Macmillan, 1967), is an example of the power of modeling.
3. Robert K. Merton and R. Nisbet, *Contemporary Social Problems,* 3rd ed. (New York: Harcourt Brace Jovanovich, 1971); S. K. Weinberg, *Social Problems in Modern Society,* 2nd ed. (Englewood Cliffs, N.J.: Prentice-Hall, 1970).
4. L. Coser, *Masters of Sociological Thought: Ideas in Historical and Social Context* (New York: Harcourt Brace Jovanovich, 1971), is a good beginning for a student who wants to grasp the sociological model as it has developed historically, with many obvious applications to police-community relations. Max Weber, of course, is the basic source for

models of authority, legitimate and illegitimate. A very readable translation is by H. H. Gerth and C. W. Mills, *From Max Weber: Essays in Sociology* (New York: Oxford University Press, 1958).
5. L. Broom and P. Selznick, eds., *Sociology* (New York: Harper & Row, 1968), is a good set of readings with flashing insights via the sociological model.
6. R. Bierstedt, *The Social Order,* 3rd ed. (New York: McGraw-Hill, 1970), presents a lucid explanation of all these concepts.
7. A. Etzioni, *A Sociological Reader, in Complex Organizations,* 2nd ed. (New York: Holt, Rinehart and Winston, 1969), offers several different ways of adapting the sociological model to police departments and other bureaucracies.
8. J. C. Coleman, *Abnormal Psychology and Modern Life,* 3rd ed. (Glenview, Ill.: Scott, Foresman, 1970), presents a variety of psychological models of personality from Freudian psychoanalytical models through stimulus-response models to "self" models.
9. M. Deutsch and R. M. Kraus, *Theories in Social Psychology* (New York: Basic Books, 1965).
10. A. Freud *The Ego and Mechanism of Defense* (New York: International Universities Press, 1946).
11. Coleman, op. cit.
12. J. Bentham, *Introduction to the Principles of Morals and Legislation,* J. H. Burns and H. L. Hawt, eds. (London: Athlone Press, 1970), presents the legalistic equal-punishments-for-equal-crimes doctrine, which was immensely influential almost one hundred years ago and appears to be returning to favor today.
13. There is not much material on the economic aspects of police-community relations—nothing comparable with C. J. Hitch and R. N. McKean's *The Economics of Defense in the Nuclear Age* (New York: Atheneum, 1967), or the much more sophisticated treatises on cost/benefit analysis that have appeared since then in regard to organizational problems.
14. R. D. Lee, Jr., and R. Johnson, *Public Budgeting Systems* (London: University Park Press, 1973).
15. Zero-based budgeting is having its period of favor in the reach for the businessman's ethic of having every process and program prove itself in measurable dollar terms. The high interest in planning-programming-budgeting systems of the late 1960s appears to be lessening in government. The basic emphases and concepts associated with PPBS appear to be implicit in zero-based budgeting. The U.S. Department of Agriculture in 1962 was an early experimenter in zero-based budgeting, but the department abandoned the effort after only a short trial as being wasteful of administrative time, as old issues are rehashed interminably. Many programs were found to be politically mandatory and could not be dismantled no matter how compelling the data and the analysis, see A. Wildavsky and A. Hammann, "Comprehensive Versus Incremental Budgeting in the Department of Agriculture," *Administrative Science Quarterly,* 10 (1965), pp. 321–46.

16. C. Wiltse, *The Jeffersonian Tradition in American Democracy* (New York: Hill & Wang, 1960). In this country the democratic political model is the theme. This appears to consist of the belief that ". . . whatever they may be led to do in moments of stress or passion or fear, people have in the long run enough intelligence, enough morality, enough wisdom to govern themselves, not merely passably, but well," p. vii.
17. Walt Whitman, Preface to *Leaves of Grass*, 1st ed., 1855.
18. H. Jacob and K. N. Vines, *Politics in the American States*, 3rd ed. (Boston: Little, Brown, 1976). For a quantitative research orientation see, S. A. Kirkpatrick, *Quantitative Analysis of Political Data* (Columbus, Ohio: Charles Merrill, 1974).
19. Walt Whitman, *Democratic Vistas*, 1871.
20. R. Pound, *An Introduction to the Philosophy of Law* (New Haven: Yale University Press, 1922). P. G. Chevigny, *Police Power* (New York: Random House, 1969); J. Skolnick, *Justice Without Trial: Law Enforcement in a Democratic Society* (New York: John Wiley & Sons, 1966); American Bar Association, *The Urban Police Function* (New York: American Bar Association, 1973); all take a legalistic approach to police and its relations with communities.
21. R. Quinney, *The Social Reality of Crime* (Boston: Little, Brown, 1970) and *Criminology* (Boston: Little, Brown, 1970).
22. M. R. Konvits, *Bill of Rights Reader*, 3rd ed. (Ithaca, N.Y.: Cornell University Press, 1965); G. Berkley, *The Democratic Policeman* (Boston: Beacon Press, 1969).
23. H. James, *Crisis in the Courts* (New York: David McKay, 1977), discusses the negative impact that court maladministration has on the community.
24. Warren E. Burger, Chief Justice of the United States Supreme Court, "Agenda for 2000 A.D., Need for Systematic Anticipation," address given before the National Conference on the Causes of Popular Dissatisfaction with the Administration of Justice," in St. Paul, Minn., April 7, 1976.
25. After-the-fact court supervision of the legality of police action has appeared to exacerbate rather than heal police-community relations. A. R. Coffey and E. Eldefonso, *Process and Impact of Justice* (Beverly Hills, Calif.: Glencoe Press/Collier Macmillan, 1975).
26. C. W. Mills, *The Marxists* (New York: Dell, 1962).
27. K. Marx, *The Eighteenth Brumaire of Louis Bonaparte* (New York: International Publishers, 1964), gives explicit examples from history illustrating his thesis that the nonproductive establishment controls and exploits the labor of the community and is, therefore, inherently in a confrontation with the guardians of the status quo.
28. R. Hofstadter, *The American Political Tradition* (New York: Knopf, 1948); J. McGinniss, *The Selling of the President, 1968* (New York: Trident Press, 1969). The sequence shows changing views of democratic models. It would be useful to compare the nuances of those models with that in *The Federalist Papers*, the celebrated collection of essays by Alexander Hamilton, James Madison, and John Jay (New York: New American Library, 1961).

29. C. M. Wiltse, *The Jeffersonian Tradition in American Democracy* (New York: Hill & Wang, 1935).
30. C. Rossiter, *The American Presidency* (New York: New American Library, 1956).
31. A. Lincoln, "Address at Gettysburg, Pennsylvania," November 19, 1863.
32. E. Long, J. Long, W. Leon, P. B. Weston, *American Minorities: The Justice Issue* (Englewood Cliffs, N.J.: Prentice-Hall, 1975).
33. E. Allbright, M. A. Baum, B. Forman, S. Gems, D. Jaffe, F. C. Jordan, Jr., R. Katz, and P. A. Sinsky, *Criminal Justice Research: Evaluation in Criminal Justice Programs* (Washington, D.C.: U.S. Government Printing Office, 1974).
34. E. Cleaver, *Post-Prison Writings*, R. Scheer, ed. (New York: Random House, 1969).
35. R. Goodwin, *The American Condition* (New York: Doubleday, 1974).
36. R. K. Merton, *Social Theory and Social Structure*, 2nd ed. (Glencoe, Ill.: The Free Press, 1957).

Chapter 5   The Communication Model

1. C. Cherry, *On Human Communication*, 2nd ed. (Cambridge, Mass.: M.I.T. Press, 1966).
2. W. Gore and J. W. Dyson, eds., *The Making of Decisions: A Reader in Administrative Behavior* (New York: The Free Press, 1964).
3. L. A. Dexter and D. M. White, eds., *People, Society and Mass Communications* (New York: The Free Press, 1964).
4. C. E. Shannon and W. Weaver, *The Mathematical Theory of Communication* (Urbana, Ill.: University of Illinois Press, 1949); L. Brillouin, *Science and Information Theory* (New York: Academic Press, 1956).
5. Cherry, op. cit.
6. C. E. Shannon and W. Weaver, *The Mathematical Theory of Communication* (Urbana, Ill.: University of Illinois Press, 1949). G. K. Zipf, *Human Behavior and the Principle of Least Effort* (Cambridge, Mass.: Addison-Wesley, 1949).
7. D. E. Broadbent, *Perception and Communication* (London: Pergamon Press, 1958).
8. N. Wiener, *Cybernetics*, 2nd ed. (Cambridge, Mass.: M.I.T. Press, 1961).
9. Cherry, op. cit., presents a simplified mathematical treatment. Shannon and Weaver, op. cit., of course, is the classic presentation, but much more difficult.
10. S. Goldman, *Information Theory* (London: Constable, 1953).
11. M. A. P. Willmer, *Crime and Information Theory* (Edinburgh: University of Edinburgh Press, 1970).
12. S. Winograd and J. D. Cowan, *Reliable Communication in the Presence of Noise* (Cambridge, Mass.: M.I.T. Press, 1963).
13. J. R. Davitz, ed., *The Communication of Emotional Meaning* (New York: McGraw-Hill, 1950).
14. J. Reusch and W. Kees, *Non-verbal Communication* (Berkeley: Univer-

sity of California Press, 1964). E. T. Hall, *The Silent Language* (Garden City, N.Y.: Doubleday, 1959).

15. H. Quastler, *Information Theory in Psychiatry* (Glencoe, Ill.: The Free Press, 1955).
16. E. Katz and P. Lazarsfeld, *Personal Influence* (New York: Free Press, 1955).
17. E. Emery, P. H. Ault, W. K. Agee, *Introduction to Mass Communications,* 2nd ed. (New York: Dodd, Mead, 1965).
18. G. A. Heise and G. A. Miller, "Problem-Solving by Small Groups Using Various Communication Nets," *Journal of Abnormal and Social Psychology,* 46 (July 1951), pp. 327–35.
19. W. B. Gallie, *Peirce and Pragmatism* (Harmondsworth, England: Pelican Books, 1952).
20. Cherry, op. cit.

Chapter 6   Interaction

1. A fact that is often overlooked is that in any group of more than two members there are more groups that are potential communities of interest than there are individuals in that group.

A simple computational formula is:

$$C_p = 3^n - 2^{n+1} + 1$$

Where:

C_p = Potential communities of interest

n = Number of individuals in the group

Thus, considering only the communication-interaction situation of a single police department or officer with a group of varying numbers of citizens, the directional reactions will potentially be for a group of only two, of which the police are designated as A and the citizen as B. $A \rightarrow B$; and $B \rightarrow A$—a total of only two directional reactions. But for a group of three, $A, B,$ and C:

A	→ B	B	→ A
A	→ C	C	→ A
B	→ C	C	→ B
A	→ BC	BC	→ A
B	→ AC	AC	→ B
C	→ AB	AB	→ C

The total number of directional reactions is 12. For a group of four, $A, B, C,$ and $D,$ the number of such possible communication patterns rises to 50. For a group of ten persons the number jumps to more than 57,000. For a group of 100 persons the number is approximately 516 followed by 44 zeros. And for 1,000 persons the total communication patterns soars to 132 followed by 475 zeros!

Since each one of these directional-interactions is a potential community of interest, with a specific impact on a police department, the implications are profound. This is discussed again in connection with the N-Square Factor in Chapter 12 and the related footnote.

2. R. F. Bales, *Interaction Process Analysis: A Method for the Study of Small Groups* (Reading, Mass.: Addison-Wesley, 1950).
3. CRM, Inc., *Society Today* (Del Mar, Calif.: Communications Research Machines, Inc., 1971), pp. 127–8; J. W. Thibaut and H. H. Kelley, *The Social Psychology of Groups* (New York: John Wiley & Sons, 1959).
4. D. Cartwright and A. Zander, *Group Dynamics* (New York: Harper & Row, 1960).
5. G. C. Homans, *The Human Group* (New York: Harcourt Brace and World, 1950). "Special Issue on Small Group Research" was a high point in small group reporting on research, *American Sociological Review*, 19:6 (December 1954).
6. E. Goffman, *Encounters: Studies in the Sociology of Interaction* (Indianapolis, Ind.: Bobbs-Merrill, 1961).
7. M. Deutsch, R. M. Kraus, *Theories in Social Psychology* (New York: Basic Books, 1965); J. C. Coleman, *Abnormal Psychology & Modern Life*, 3rd ed. (New York: Scott, Foresman, 1964).
8. E. J. Green, *Psychology for Law Enforcement* (New York: John Wiley & Sons, 1976).
9. Coleman, op. cit., p. 361.
10. L. Festinger, *A Theory of Cognitive Dissonance* (New York: Harper & Row, 1957).
11. L. Bryson, *Symbols and Values* (New York: Harper & Row, 1954).
12. E. Sapir, "Symbolism," in *International Encyclopaedia of the Social Sciences*, 14 (New York: Macmillan, 1934), pp. 493 ff.
13. E. Nagel, "Symbolism and Science," in L. Bryson, et al., *Symbols and Values: An Initial Study*, 13th Symposium of the Conference on Science, Philosophy and Religion (New York: Harper & Row, 1954), pp. 39–71.
14. C. Kluckhohn, *Culture and Behavior* (New York: The Free Press, 1963), pp. 289 ff.
15. D. Krech, R. S. Crutchfield, and E. L. Ballachey, *Individual in Society* (New York: McGraw-Hill, 1962), pp. 137 ff.; p. 189.
16. R. A. Nisbet, *The Sociological Tradition* (New York. Basic Books, 1966), Chapter 7.
17. D. G. Dean, "Meaning and Measurement of Alienation," *American Sociological Review*, 26 (October 1961), pp. 753–7. CRM, op. cit., p. 474.
18. M. DeFleur, W. V. D'Antonio, L. B. DeFleur, *Sociology: Man in Society* (Glenview, Ill.: Scott, Foresman, 1972), p. 298; M. Harrington, *The Other America* (New York: Macmillan, 1962).
19. D. Bell, *The End of Ideology* (New York: The Free Press of Glencoe, 1960), pp. 335–97.
20. M. DeFleur, W. V. D'Antonio, L. B. DeFleur, *Sociology: Man in Society* (Glenview, Ill.: Scott, Foresman, 1972); E. Gross, "Industrial Relations Reward Systems," *International Encyclopedia of the Social Sciences*, vol. 7 (New York: Macmillan/Free Press, 1968), pp. 250–1.
21. E. Fromm, *Marx's Concepts of Man*, trans. by T. B. Bottomore (New York: Ungar, 1961).

22. Blauner, *Alienation and Freedom* (Chicago: University of Chicago Press, 1964). But a new wave of anti-Marxist intellectualism has arisen, particularly in France, out of the 1968 student riots in Paris and the revelations of Aleksandr Solzhenitsyn, which reject rationalism and progress as well as Marxism. This may be a return to the ideas of freedom of a generation ago, e.g., Jacques Maritain, Simon Weil, and George Bermann.

Chapter 7 Confrontations and Conflicts

1. L. Coser, *The Functions of Social Conflict* (New York: The Free Press, 1956).
2. K. Lorenz, *On Aggression,* trans. by Marjorie Wilson (New York: Harcourt Brace, 1974), pp. 137, 253.
3. R. Clift, *Toward a Professional Police* (Santa Cruz, Calif.: Davis, 1974), is one of a number of attempts to open a dialogue on ritualization or ceremonialization of behavior between police and citizen, but does not appear to go as far as it might toward fundamentals.
4. K. Lorenz, op. cit., pp. 261 ff.
5. E. J. Green, *Psychology for Law Enforcement* (New York: John Wiley & Sons, 1976).
6. F. Wertham, *The Show of Violence* (New York: Eton Books, 1948).
7. M. Symonds, "Policemen and Policework: A Psychodynamic Understanding," in Arthur Niederhoffer and Abraham S. Blumberg, *The Ambivalent Force* (Hinsdale, Ill.: Dryden Press, 1976).
8. A. Niederhoffer and A. Smith, *New Directions in Police Community Relations* (Hinsdale, Ill.: Dryden Press, 1974), p. 35.
9. Ibid., p. 38.
10. K. Davis and W. E. Moore, "Some Principles of Stratification," *American Sociological Review,* 10 (1945), pp. 242–9.
11. G. Myrdal, *An American Dilemma: The Negro Problem and American Democracy* (New York: Harper & Row, 1962).
12. A. de Tocqueville, *Democracy in America* (Garden City, N.Y.: Doubleday, 1955).
13. W. Burger, op. cit., on the fact that we have a right to a "systematic anticipation" of improvement in justice as an essential element in a superior quality of life.
14. Lorenz, op. cit.

Chapter 8 Sociopolitical Processes

1. A. Burgess, *A Clockwork Orange* (New York: Ballantine, 1976).
2. *Newsweek,* July 18, 1977, p. 9.
3. R. Bierstedt, *The Social Order,* 3rd ed. (New York: McGraw-Hill, 1970), offers a different typology of the same general import.
4. England has had the same organization and much the same policies for more than 100 years. The vaunted success of their police, however, seems to be questioned more now than ever before, under the impact of ethnic problems that the previously homogeneous population had never encountered, see D. Humphrey, *Police Power and Black People* (London: Granada, 1972). The British authorities, however, remain unperturbed:

The Ditchley Conference on Police Community Relations in 1970, cited in this book, came to no definite conclusions. Less propagandist in tone and better documented is E. Krausz, *Ethnic Minorities in Britain* (London: Granada, 1972).

5. Bierstedt, op. cit., is followed in the main here. However, C. J. Friedrich, *Authority* (Cambridge, Mass.: Harvard University Press, 1958), is acknowledged as having been profoundly influential in formulation of this section, as were the implicit philosophies in G. Rude, *Wilkes and Liberty* (Oxford: Clarendon Press, 1962).

6. *Cambridge Ancient History,* Vol. I (Oxford: Oxford University Press, 1934), for the most primitive era; Vol. II, for the earliest kingdoms, and Vol. III for Hammurabi, Solon, and Solomon's Codes of Justice.

7. A. Hamilton, J. Madison, and J. Jay, *The Federalist Papers* (New York: New American Library, 1961), is considered to be a most authoritative presentation of the thoughts of the Founding Fathers.

8. A good summary of liberal thought in this country up to the 1950s, with many apt references, is J. R. Pennock, *Liberal Democracy* (New York: Rinehart, 1950).

9. J. Hector St. John (pseudonym de Crèvecœur), *Letters from an American Farmer,* 1782 (New York: Dutton, 1957).

10. C. M. Wiltse, *The Jeffersonian Tradition in American Democracy* (New York: Hill and Wang, 1960).

11. A. F. Tyler, *Freedom's Ferment* (New York: Harper & Bros., 1944).

12. J. Bryce, *The American Commonwealth,* 3rd ed. (London: Macmillan, 1909).

13. J. Harvey and L. Bather, *The British Constitution* (London: Macmillan, 1966).

14. A. Barth, *The Price of Liberty* (New York: Viking, 1961).

15. O. Handlin, *Boston's Immigrants,* rev. ed. (Cambridge, Mass.: Harvard University Press, 1959), comments that immigrants built "a society within a society," p. 176; N. Glazer, "Ethnic Groups in America: From National Culture to Ideology," in M. Berger, T. Abel, and C. H. Page, eds., *Freedom and Control in Modern Society* (Cambridge, Mass.: Harvard University Press, 1940).

Chapter 9 Planning, Implementing, and Monitoring

1. M. G. Ross, *Community Organization* (New York: Harper & Row, 1955).

2. R. S. Clark, *Fundamentals of Criminal Justice Research* (Lexington, Mass.: D. C. Heath, 1977); E. Webb, D. Campbell, R. Schwarts, and L. Sechrest, *Unobtrusive Measures* (Chicago: Rand McNally, 1966); J. Nunnally, *Psychometric Theory* (New York: McGraw-Hill, 1967); L. Thurstone and E. Chave, *The Measurement of Attitude* (Chicago: University of Chicago Press, 1929).

3. D. Nachmias and C. Nachmias, *Research Methods in the Social Sciences* (New York: St. Martin's Press, 1976).

4. B. S. Phillips, *Social Research: Strategy and Tactics,* 3rd ed. (New York: Macmillan, 1976).

Chapter 10 Evaluation

1. E. A. Suchman, *Evaluation Research* (New York: Russell Sage Foundation, 1967).
2. C. Weiss, *Evaluation Research* (Englewood Cliffs, N.J.: Prentice-Hall, 1972).
3. R. Wasserman, M. P. Gardner, and A. S. Cohen, *Improving Police-Community Relations* (Washington, D.C.: Law Enforcement Assistance Administration/National Institute of Law Enforcement and Criminal Justice, June 1973).

Chapter 11 Research

1. A. Neiderhoffer and A. Smith, *New Directions in Police Community Relations* (Hinsdale, Ill.: Dryden Press, 1974); W. R. Jones, *Finding Community: A Guide to Community Research* (Palo Alto, Calif.: James E. Freel, 1971).
2. A. N. Whitehead, *The Function of Reason* (Boston: Beacon Press, 1929); A. Przworski and H. Teune, *The Logic of Comparative Social Inquiry* (New York: John Wiley & Sons, 1970).
3. G. C. Helmstadter, *Research Concepts in Human Behavior* (New York: Appleteon-Century-Crofts, 1970.
4. P. W. Bridgman, *The Intelligent Individual and Society* (New York: Macmillan, 1938).
5. J. Z. Young, *Doubt and Certainty in Science* (London: Oxford University Press, 1951); W. James, *Pragmatism* (New York: World, 1955); A. N. Whitehead, *Science and the Modern World* (London: Penguin Books, 1952).
6. L. G. Parratt, *Probability and Experimental Errors in Science* (New York: Dover, 1961); I. J. Good, ed., *The Scientist Speculates—an Anthology of Partly-Baked Ideas* (London: Heinemann, 1962).
7. R. S. Clark, *Fundamentals of Criminal Justice Research* (Lexington, Mass.: D. C. Heath, 1977), pp. 103 ff.
8. W. C. Dampier, *A History of Science,* 4th ed. (London: Cambridge University Press, 1948).
9. A. N. Whitehead, *Adventures of Ideas* (New York: Macmillan, 1933).
10. N. Wiener, *The Human Use of Human Beings* (Garden City, N.Y.: Doubleday, 1954).

Chapter 12 Operations

1. Advisory Commission on Intergovernmental Relations: A Commission Report, *State-Local Relations in the Criminal Justice System* (Washington, D.C.: U.S. Government Printing Office, 1971), p. 33.
2. E. Bittner, *The Function of the Police in a Modern Society* (New York: Aronson, 1975).
3. H. Mannheim, *Criminal Law and Penology,* in Morris Ginsberg, ed., *Law and Opinion in 20th Century England* (Berkeley: University of Cal-

ifornia Press, 1959); R. Quinney, *Criminology* (Boston: Little, Brown, 1970); K. Mannheim, *Ideology and Utopia* (New York: Harcourt, Brace and World, 1936); *Freedom, Power and Democratic Planning* (New York: Oxford University Press, 1950).

4. The necessary conclusion of those who are familiar with the history of blacks in this country comes to this: Unless blacks receive more aid than that given to whites, the existing disparity in rights, accomplishment, and privileges will persevere for another hundred years, see *The Negro in American History*, prepared by the Board of Education of the City of New York and printed by the State University of the State of New York, State Education Department, Bureau of Secondary Curriculum Development, Albany, N.Y., 1965.

5. C. J. Friedrich, *The Philosophy of Law in Historical Perspective* (Chicago, Ill.: University of Chicago Press, 1963).

6. A. Blumstein, M. Kamrass, and A. B. Weiss, eds., *Systems Analysis for Social Problems* (Washington, D.C.: Washington Operations Research Council, 1970).

7. Frederick William Lanchester, "Mathematics in Warfare," in *Aircraft in Warfare* (London: Constable, 1950), reprinted in *The World of Mathematics*, vol. 4, James R. Newman, ed. (New York: Simon & Schuster, 1956); Antoine Henri Jomini, *Precis de L'art de la Guerre* (Paris, 1836). As staff officer to Napoleon, Jomini formulated Napoleon's use of concentrated forces against inferior units as a main principle of field operations. See short discussion in R. S. Clark, "Guidelines in Scientific Research #22, The N-Square Law," in *The Police Chief*, 44:11 (November 1977), p. 82.

8. The principle of concentration of forces has been rather clearly enunciated since the days of Napoleon and his staff analyst, Jomini. French Admiral Suffren, however, called such operations by the English as being under the "veil of timidity," which resulted in his defeat.

Napoleon, himself, had no such compunctions and repeatedly concentrated his forces to divide an enemy.

As this principle may be applied to police-community–relations administration, one may view the multiplicity of negative messages about the police as building up an increasing influence on the public.

These messages are opposed by positive messages of aid and support by the police department.

It must be noted that negative as well as positive messages can be issued by the police department.

If we consider these multiple, discrete messages as mutually opposed, and in the long run as canceling each other out on a one-for-one basis, the *sources* of these messages, in effect, eliminate each other as credible sources. The relationship can be expressed as:

$$Y = \sqrt{\frac{r_x}{r_y}(X^2 - X_o) + Y_o^2}$$

in which Y represents *sources* of multiple positive credible messages.

Y_o = Original number of credible sources of positive messages

X = Number of credible sources of
    multiple negative messages

X_o = Original number of credible sources of
    multiple negative messages

r_x = Rate of negative message production

r_y = Rate of positive message production

That is, sources of credible positive messages will combat sources of credible negative messages and extinguish them at a rate that will vary as the square of the proportions between them.

In practice this means that if the sources of bad impressions of police are more numerous than good, the bad image will prevail very quickly and overwhelmingly. The reverse, of course, is also true: if the sources of positive, favorable impressions and messages are more numerous than the unfavorable, the police will quickly become the public's darling.

The relationship can be illustrated graphically, showing the tremendous advantage that the preponderance of message sources can give in shaping the information base of public opinion.

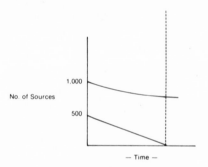

The diagram indicates that the numerical advantage of having twice as many credible positive sources of communications quickly results in, granted ideal conditions, a great increase in the ratio of favorable over unfavorable messages. This is so, even if the theoretically possible extinguishment of unfavorable sources' credibility does not come to pass.

Many other incidental applications come quickly to mind, e.g., the advantage of political campaign contributions to purchase more than a proportional share of advertising.

9. Anthony Burton, *Urban Terrorism: Theory and Practice* (New York: The Free Press, 1976).

Chapter 13   Police-Community–Relations Units

1. A. C. Filley and R. J. House, *Managerial Process and Organizational Behavior* (Glenview, Ill.: Scott, Foresman, 1969); O. W. Wilson and R. C. McLaren, *Police Administration,* 3rd ed. (New York: McGraw-Hill, 1972);

A. Etzioni, *A Sociological Reader on Complex Organizations* (New York: Holt, Rinehart and Winston, 1969).
2. "Historical Perspectives on the Police Community Service Function" by Jack E. Whitehouse in A. Cohn and E. C. Viano, eds., *Police-Community Relations: Images, Roles and Realities* (New York: Lippincott, 1976) p. 101–9; P. F. Cromwell, Jr., and G. Keefer, *Police-Community Relations* (St. Paul, Minn.: West, 1973).
3. F. W. Taylor, *The Principles of Scientific Management* (New York: Harper, 1911).
4. E. Mayo, *The Human Problems of an Industrial Civilization* (New York: Macmillan, 1933).
5. R. Trojanowicz and S. L. Dixon, *Criminal Justice and the Community* (Englewood Cliffs, N.J.: Prentice-Hall, 1974), p. 220.
6. Ibid., pp. 220 f.

INDEX

Abnormality, 94–95
Abortion laws, 206
Absolutism, 138
Acculturation of norms, 236, 264; lack of, 205–206
Accused, rights of, 45–46
Action programs, 171, 187; evaluation, 177–178, 195–196
Adams, Sam, 141
Adaptation: modes of, 161–163, 165; stages of, 164
Adler, Alfred, 142
Affirmative action, 120, 145, 205
Aggressive behavior, 106–107, 116–118, 123–124, 221; phylogeny of, 107; survival value of, 106, 117
Agreements, 220–222
Alcoholism, 94, 98
Alienation, 103–105
Allport, Gordon, 91
American Bar Association, 13
American Psychiatric Association, 98
Analysis: defined, 5; functional, 219; graphic, 10; N-Square, 219–220; quantified, 32, 211 (*see also* Quantification); relevant variables in, 5–6; statistical, 14–16, 178, 211. *See also* Data analysis; Factor analysis; Systems analysis
Anomie, 38
Antisocial personality, 98–99
Antisocial reaction, 98
Anxiety, 89–90, 91
Appeasement behavior, 109–110, 116, 123–124, 204, 207, 219, 220, 265, 266; survival value of, 124
Aristotle, 3, 42, 125, 263, 265
Arithmetic mean, 15, 94
Associational groups, 130, 132–133
Associational norms, 33, 34, 132; conflict with communal norms, 34–36; conflicts between, 36
Associations, 32, 37, 38, 130–131, 132–133; *vs.* institutions, 37, 133
Attack dogs, 108
Attitudes, 103; classes of (conscious, automatic, technical), 165; defined, 102; measurement, 102, 103, 151, 162, 196–198
Attitudinal change, 75–76, 103, 164–165, 238; role of age in, 77; stages of, 164; "three levels of difficulty" concept of, 164–165; time requirement, 164
Authority, 32, 38, 132; in apposition to liberty, 140; Bible quoted on, 44–45; historical survey, 138–140; as institutionalized power, 38–39, 139; as source of knowledge, 188–189
Average(s), 93–94; index of, 15

Banton, Michael, 13
Beat representative program, 250
Behavior: abnormal, 94–95; classes of (conscious, automatic, technical), 165; critically relevant variables in, identification, 6, 11; deviant, 94; education for, 3; enforcement of, 3, 34, 35, 72, 204, 264; engineering of, 3; hostile, evolution of, 117; motivation, 98–100, 102; motivation analysis, 112–113; normal, 94; in various theories of personality, 89–92. *See also* Aggressive behavior; Appeasement behavior; Normative behavior
Behavior modification, 99, 126, 164–165, 237–238; stages of, 164; techniques, 3, 31; "three levels of difficulty" concept, 164–165

Behavioral science, 89–105, 233; concepts and terminologies of, 32–38, 208
Biased samples, 180
Bible, 44, 88–89, 140
Bilingualism, 79
Biological models, 143
Bismarck, Fürst Otto von, 137
Black Power, 49, 104, 118–119, 128
Blacks, 118–122, 204–205
Block watcher programs, 240, 244. See also Crime-reporting programs
Bridgman, Percy W., 78, 190
British Parliament, 142
Bryan, William Jennings, 61
Budgets, municipal, 42
Bureaucracy, ritualism in, 162
Bureaucratic groups, 130–131, 132–133
Butler, Nicholas Murray, 19

Candidates, political, 74, 76, 111; incumbents, 50
Carter, Fred, 118
Carter, Jimmy, 3
Cellini, Benvenuto, 101
Central Intelligence Agency (CIA), 43 217
Centralization, 231–232, 236, 240–241, 253, 257–259
Change: modes of adaptation to, 145–146, 159–163; resistance to, 162, 165; stages of, 164; "three levels of difficulty" concept, 164–165
Channels, in communication theory, 52, 58, 60–61
Charisma, 76–77
Chicago Police Department, 245–253; Beat Representative Program, 246, 250; organization, 245, 250; PCR functions, 245, 246–253
Citizen complaints against police, 116, 118, 239, 263
Citizen-police confrontations, 108–109, 113, 115–117, 207
City in History, The (Mumford), 13
Civil demonstrations, 36, 46, 114–115, 126, 204
Civil Rights Law of 1964, 205
Civil rights movement, 128
Civilian patrols, 240, 244–245
Civilian radio taxi patrols, 240, 244
Civilian review boards, 213
Class consciousness, 122
Class distinctions, 110, 118

Clemenceau, Georges, 160
Combat-style approach tactics, 115
Communal norms, 33–34; conflict with associational norms, 34–36
Communication: basic elements of, 52, 58; channels of, 52, 58, 60–61; defined, 56; vs. influence, 56, 58 (see also Influence); in police-community relations, 67–68, 72–77, 78; probabilistic inference in, 54; process diagrammed, 54–55; receivers of, 52, 58, 60–61, 64–70; reinforcement, 77; transmitters of, 28, 52, 60–61; verbal, 54–56, 58, 60–61; written, 58, 60–61
Communication models, 50, 51–56, 73, 74–75, 143; mathematical description possible, 54
Communication theory, 52–82, 164–165; adaptive reaction, 67; alphabets, 57, 64–65; basic principles of, 58–62; channel competition, 73–74; channel selection, 61–62; coding process, 54, 59–60; decoding process, 54, 67; definitions, 57–58; filtering, 67; information content, 54, 56, 57, 58–59; information rate, 53, 54; language, 79–80, 100–101; mathematical descriptions, 53, 54, 56; message comprehension, 56, 58–59, 64–65; "noise," 53, 54, 69, 77; nonmathematical description, 53–54; "nonstationary" signal statistics, 52–53; perceptual rate of information intake, 68–69, 73; recall, 66; recognition, 68, 69–70; redundancy in, 53, 56, 58, 59, 62–64, 68–69, 117, 123; selective perception, 67, 73–74; signal, 54–56, 58, 60, 62–63; signal analysis, 54; signs, 58–60, 64–65, 80–81, 100; "stationary" signal statistics, 52; time dimension, 53, 60; universals, 66; words, 80–82, 100
Communities of interest. See Factions; Interest groups
Community-crisis prevention, 219–220
Compliance, 164, 264. See also Norm compliance
Computer model, 32
Computer programming languages, 63
Conclusions, 16–18, 171, 211, 219, 225; defined, 16; vs. findings, 16–17, 175; in probabilistic form, 17–18
Conflict, 106–112, 122–124; cause elimination attempts, 108; functions

and benefits of, 106–108, 122–123; levels of, 115–118; between norms, 34–36, 117; phylogeny, 107; suppression of, historical examples, 108; survival value of, 106, 117, 123
Conformity, 161
Confrontation, 106–112; in American society, 110–112; citizen-police, 108–109, 113, 115–117, 207; community-government, 108–109; functions and benefits of, 106–108; vs. negotiation, 221
Consensus, 70; between dissidents, 226–228
Constituencies, 49
Constitutional rights, 141–142; vs. crime control requirements, 31, 45–46, 142
Control groups, use of, 179, 190
Cooley, Charles Horton, 70
Cost/benefit analysis, 42, 187, 234; example, 183
Crèvecoeur, Michel Guillaume de (J. Hector St. John), 43, 120, 141
Crime control requirements, vs. constitutional rights, 31, 142
Crime prevention, 204
Crime-reporting programs, 180–183, 240, 244–245
Criminal conspiracy, 129
Criminality, limitations of social choice by, 134, 145
Crowd psychology, 39
Cue, in S-R theory, defined, 90
Culture of Poverty, The (Lewis), 13
Curfews, 108
Customs and folkways, as unwritten norm, 33, 34, 35

Darwin, Charles, 194
Data analysis, 9–13, 178–184; descriptive, 9-11; error typology, 179–180; findings, 13–16, 178; graphic, 10–11, 15; inferential, 11–13, 179, 191–193; statistical, 14–16, 178; tabulation, 10, 15
Data collection, 9–10, 14–15, 178
Data processing, 15
Decentralization, 231–232, 236, 240–241, 245, 257–259
Declaration of Independence, 140, 205
Deductive logic, 189, 191
Defense mechanisms, 90
Definitional models, 44–47

Democracy, 42–43, 46–47, 49, 109, 139, 263, 264–265
Democratic models, 30, 46
Democratic Vistas (Whitman), 43
Descartes, René, 78
Descriptive data analysis, 9–11
Deviant personality and behavior, 94
Discrimination, 118–119, 145, 205
Dispersion, index of, 15
Displacement activity, 109, 117
Dissidents, dealing with, 167–168, 226–228
Divine revelation, 188–189
Divine right of kings, 138–139, 166
Dollar democracy, 47
Doyle, Sir Arthur Conan, 229
Drive (life-energy), 142, 143; primary vs. secondary, 90
Drug addiction, 94, 98
Dyssocial reaction, 98

Economic models, 30, 41–42, 143. See also Politico-economic models
Education, in value systems, 205
Ego, 89–90; defined, 40, 89
Election campaigns, 111. See also Candidates, political
Elections, trend of defeating incumbents in, 50
Empiricism, 189, 220, 234
Enforcement: of behavior, 3, 34, 35, 72, 204, 264; law, history of systems, 138–140. See also Law enforcement
Equal-interval measurement, 157
Equality, 42–43, 46, 204–205; of opportunity, 110, 205
Error typology, 179–180
Essay on Man (Pope), 203
Ethnic groups, 119–120, 121–122, 130, 145; defined, 119
Ethos, 85, 87, 97–98
Evaluation, 169–185; of action programs, 177–178, 195–196; cost aspects, 171, 176; criteria for, incorporation in plan, 170, 173; defined, 169–170; design of, 178–180; empirical, 220; error typology, 179–180; example of, 180–184; independence and objectivity required, 173, 174–175, 177–178, 184; judgmental bias in, 178, 180–184; vs. monitoring, 170, 173; of PCR units and programs, 169–185, 214, 219; purpose of, 175, 179; quantification in, 171;

reasons for, 176; reports, 171, 174, 175, 185; validity of, 177–178
Evolution, 145–146
Existential theories of personality, 91
Existentialism, 91, 142
Experimental model, 179
Experts, use of, 19–20, 22, 23–27

Face-to-face contacts, 60–61, 71, 73, 75, 132, 207, 225, 231
Fact, findings of. *See* Findings of fact
Factions, 49; political, 111, 143–145. *See also* Interest groups
Factor analysis, 93
Federal Bureau of Investigation (FBI), 217
Federal grants, 47–48, 169
Federalist Papers, 143
Findings of fact, 13–16, 171, 178; *vs.* conclusions, 16–17, 175; defined, 13, 16; descriptive, 13; examples, 14, 16–17; non-statistical presentation of, 16; in probabilistic form, 18; statistical presentation of, 14–16
Folkways and customs, as unwritten norm, 33, 34, 35
Force: as sociological term, 37–38, 134; threat of, as power, 134–135
Franklin, Benjamin, 169
Freedom, 43, 46, 48, 85; American ideal, 140–143; in apposition to authority, 140; as cause of factions, 143–144; conflicting goals, 110; in personality theories, 88–89, 91. *See also* Individual liberties
Frequency distribution, 15
Freud, Sigmund, 89–90, 100, 142
Fromm, Erich, 91
Functional analysis, 219

Galileo Galilei, 154
Game theory, 209
Gay Power, 49, 104, 128
Generalization *vs.* specialization, 229–231, 236
Generation gap, 111–112
Ghettoization, 108
Gough, John Bartholomew, 106
Government: Bible quoted on, 44–45; communication with public, 217; democratic, 263, 264–265 (*see also* Democracy); factions and vested interests, 111 (*see also* Factions); local, confrontation with community, 108–

109, 126–127; malfeasance and corruption in, 111, 115; present public attitude toward, 50; separation of powers, 141, 142
Grant applications, 47, 169
Graphic analysis, 10; frequency distribution in, 15
Greece, ancient, 139
Group compliance, 35, 86
Group personality, 85–88
Groups, 32, 35–36, 86, 87–88, 129–133; associational, 130, 132–133; bureaucratic, 130–131, 132–133; categories of, 130–131; dissident, dealing with, 167–168, 226–228; goal attainment phenomenon, 86, 87; impervious, dealing with, 223–225; internal control phenomenon, 86; loyalty to, 119; "personality" of, 96, 98; "power" groups, 49; social, 130; societal, 130; sources of power (people, organization, assets), 136–137; statistical, 130; status systems, 96–97. *See also* Constituencies; Factions
Guns, police, 115–116

Hall, Edward T., 166
Handcuffs, 115
Hawthorne experiments, 180
Hegel, Georg Wilhelm Friedrich, 5
Heidegger, Martin, 91
Herrick, Robert, 186
Hierarchical systems, 138–139, 140
Hitler, Adolf, 61
Hobbes, Thomas, 28
Holmes, Oliver Wendell, 100
Home rule, 142
Homosexuals, 122. *See also* Gay Power
Hume, David, 140
Hypothesis testing, 193–198

Id, 89–90, defined, 40, 89
Identification, in behavioral or attitudinal change, 164
Impervious groups, 223–225
Implementation of plans, 149, 159, 166–168, 219
Imprisonment, 108, 134; solitary confinement, 101
Incentives, 98, 102. *See also* Motivation
Indexes, statistical analysis, 15
Individual liberties, 43, 45–46, 48–49, 99, 141–144, 204–205. *See also* Constitutional rights

Inductive logic, 191. *See also* Inference

Inference, 7–9, 11, 66, 191–194; defined, 7, 191; and hypothesis testing, 193–194; probabilistic, 8–9, 11, 17–18, 54, 191–193, 194; use of, 7–9, 191–194

Inferential data analysis, 11–13, 179, 191–193

Influence, 56–57, 61, 64, 74–76, 85, 135–136, 223–224; *vs.* communication, 56, 85; face-to-face relations, 71, 73, 75; of "legitimizers," 71–72; of mass media, 70–71, 72–73; of power, 134; *vs.* power, 135–136; receiver's input, 74, 75; two-step flow of, 70–77, 164, 165, 220

Influence lag, 237

Information, defined, 58

Information bureaus, police, 78, 115

Information content, 54, 56, 57, 58–59, 64

Information diffusion, 77–78

Information distortion, 77

Information intake, perceptual rate of, 68–69, 73

Information rate, 53, 54

Innovation, 159–160, 161–163. *See also* Change; Planning

Input, in analysis, 31, 183, 208, 211

Insanity, 145

Instinct, 89

Institutions, 32, 37; *vs.* associations, 37, 133; defined, 37; *vs.* norms, 37, 133

Interaction, 85–87, 132, 223–224; defined, 85; symbolic, 100–102

Interaction error, 180

Interest groups, 35–36, 49, 70, 80, 111, 119–121, 129; agreements with, 222; Madison on, in *The Federalist*, 143. *See also* Factions

Internalization, 164, 166–167

International Association of Chiefs of Police, 257

Intuition, 189

I.Q. scores, 156, 158

Irish Catholics, 119

Jackson, Andrew, 141

Jefferson, Thomas, 46, 141

Jews, 119, 139

Judiciary, 141

Jung, Carl, 142

Juvenile delinquency, 77, 94, 104

Keats, John, 85

Kierkegaard, Sören, 91

King, Martin Luther, Jr., 61

Knapp Commission *Report*, 13

Knowledge, sources of, 188–190

Language, 79–80, 100–101

Latin Power, 121

Law: conflicting values, 205–206; origins of, 139; philosophy of, 204–205, 206; Roman, 139–140; as written norm, 33, 34, 35

Law enforcement, 203–204, 206–207; history of systems, 138–140

Leaders, training by confrontation and conflict, 107, 108. *See also* Opinion leaders; Political leaders

Learning theory, 90

Legal models, 30, 45–46

Legal positivism, 204

Legislative branch of government, 141, 142

"Legitimizers," 71–72

Leviathan (Hobbes), 28

Lewis, Oscar, 13

Liberty. *See* Freedom; Individual liberties

Library resources, 19, 20–21

Life-force, 142, 143

Lincoln, Abraham, 46

Living New Testament, 44

Locke, John, 140

Logic, deductive *vs.* inductive, 191

London Metropolitan Police Force, Principles of, 212, 267–268

Long, Huey, 61

Looting, 104–105

Lorenz, Konrad, 13, 72, 113, 124

Los Angeles City Police Department, organization and PCR functions, 256–258

Los Angeles County Sheriff's Department, organization and PCR functions, 253–256

Luther, Martin, 140

McNamara, Robert S., 234

Madison, James, 143, 187

Majorities, 136; rule of, 143, 144

Management, systems approach in, 208–211

Mao Tse-tung, 136

Marx, Karl, 104, 122

Marxist models, 30, 46

Maslow, Abraham, 91, 142
Mass media, 61, 80, 207; influence of, 70–71, 72–73, 76, 111; investigations of official malfeasance by, 111, 115
Mathematical models, 28, 29
May, Rollo, 91
Mayne, Richard, 268
Mayo, Elton, 233, 234
Mead, Margaret, 13
Mean, arithmetic, 15, 94
Measurement, 149–158; after-the-fact, 169–172 (see also Evaluation); of attitudes, 102, 103, 151, 162, 196–198; equal-interval, 157; error probability in, 151, 179–180; kinds of, 154–158; limits of, 153–154; natural zero in, 158; nominal, 155; numerical counting, 152, 155; ordinal (rank ordering), 155–156; in PCR, 152–153, 162–163, 196–198; of performance, 149, 166–167, 172–173 (see also Evaluation; Monitoring); ratio-level, 157–158; real-time, 172–173; research aspects of, 174, 177, 178–179, 184, 196–198; standards for, 150–151, 152; of variables, 13–14, 154–158, 196–198
Mechanization, 104
Median, 94
Mental illness, 94–95, 145
Merton, Robert K., 50, 161, 162, 165
Message, defined, 58
Message comprehension, 56, 58–59, 64–65
Message distortion, 59, 77
Michigan State University, 233
Minorities, 106, 121, 204–205; "keeping in place," 216; protection of, 144, 145. See also Blacks
Models, 28–50, 51; appraisal of, 47–50, 53; biological, 143; communication, 50, 51–56, 73, 74–75, 143; definitional, 44–47; economic, 30, 41–42, 143; experimental, 179; kinds of, 30; legal, 30, 45–46; mathematical, 28, 29; political, 30, 41, 42–43; politico-economic, 41–43; psychological, 39–41, 143; religious, 30, 44–45; social-psychological, 39; sociological, 30, 32–39, 143; socio-political, 143; systematic, 30–32; tripartism in, 164
Monarchism, 138–139, 166
Money power, 137
Monitoring, 149, 159, 166–167, 173; vs. evaluation, 170, 173

Montaigne, Michel Eyquem de, 140
Montesquieu, Charles de Secondat, Baron de la Brède et de, 140
Moral anxiety, 90
Moral principle (superego), 40, 89
Mores, as unwritten norm, 33, 34, 35
Morgenstern, Oskar, 209
Motivation, 102, 112–113; of antisocial personality, 99; in psychosocial context, 98–100
Motivation analysis, 112–113
Motives, conscious vs. unconscious, 99–100
Motor patterns, 113; "sets," 102–103
Multilingual communities, 80
Mumford, Lewis, 13
Municipal budgets, 42

National Institute of Police-Community Relations, 232–233
Natural laws, 194
Natural rights, 205
Negative reinforcement, 90
Negotiation, 221–222, 223, 224
Negro, term, 119
Neighborhood watch projects, 180–183, 244–245
Neurotic anxiety, 89–90
New York City Police Department, 241–245; Block Watchers, 244; organization, 241–244; PCR functions, 242–245, 253; personnel strength, 244; use of handcuffs, 115; use of sidearms, 115–116; volunteer services, 244–245
News, mass media and, 61, 72
Newspapers, 50, 72, 73–74
Newton, Sir Isaac, 194
Night sticks, 108
Nominal measurement, 155
Norm(s), 32–36, 70–71; acculturation of, 236, 264; associational, 33, 34, 36, 132; associational vs. communal, 34–36; communal, 33–34; conflicts between, 117, 205–206; conflicts between, as source of instability, 36; defined, 32–33, 94; enforcement of, 3, 34, 35, 204–206; historical perspective, 205–206; vs. institutions, 37, 133; lack of (anomie), 38; prescriptive, 33, 34–35, 163; proscriptive, 33, 34, 35; religious, 44–45; types of, 33–34; written vs. unwritten, 33–34
Norm compliance, 34–35, 264; devising

of systematic model, 31–32; effect of penalties on, 35; existentialist attack on, 91
"Normal," definitions of, 93–94
Normative anticipation, 87
Normative behavior, 6, 33, 36, 87, 237–238, 264
Normative kith and kin, 70
Normative sponsorship theory, 226
N-Square Factor and analysis, 219–220

"Officer Friendly" programs, 250, 255
On Aggression (Lorenz), 13
Operationalization, of research and planning, 11, 14, 149, 153, 219, 220
Operations research, 21
Opinion leaders, 71–72, 73, 76–77, 220–221
Ordinal measurement, 155–156
Organization power, 137, 138
Output, in analysis, 31, 183, 208, 211

Parable of the Spindle, 24–26, 51
Parties, political, 143
Pathology: physical, 95; psychological, 94
Pavlov, Ivan Petrovich, 90
Pearson correlation index, 154
Peirce, Charles, 78
Penalties, effect on compliance, 35. See also Punishment
Pentateuch, 139
People power, 136, 137
Performance measurement, 149, 166–167, 172–173
Personality, 85, 88–95, 96; abnormal, 94–95; antisocial, 98–99; components of, 40, 89, 164; deviant, 94; existential theories of, 91; normal, 93–94, 95; psychoanalytic theory, 89–90; self theories of, 91; S-R theories of, 90–91; term applied to groups, 96; tests, 92–93; trait theories of, 91–93, 99
Philosophy of History (Hegel), 5
Planning, 149, 158–165; evaluation criteria incorporated in, 170, 173; objectives to be stated clearly, 170; participants, 167–168; in PCR, 160–168, 219
Plato, 122
Pleasure principle (id), 40, 89
Pluralism, 145
Police: aggressive behavior of, 115–116; appeasement behavior of, 109–110, 116, 124, 207, 219, 220, 265, 266; attitudinal change in, 238; civilian complaints against, 116, 118, 239, 263; psychological tests for, 92; qualifications, 213, 238; training of, 213, 214–216, 218, 238
Police administrators, 23–24, 114, 209, 236–238; civilians as, 236, 239, 242, 253
Police athletic leagues, 107
Police brutality, 116, 263
Police-community relations (PCR), 198–199, 203, 207, 211–213; areas of effort, 213–214; avenues of "improvement," 218; centralization vs. decentralization, 231–232, 236, 240–241, 257–259; in Chicago, 245, 246–253; civilian heads of, 236, 239, 242, 253; communication with community, 216–217, 219–225; confrontations with citizens, 108–109, 113, 115–117, 207, 225–226; constitutional vs. crime-fighting requirements, 31, 45–46, 142; dealing with dissidents, 167–168, 226–228; elitism of, 238–239; generalization vs. specialization, 229–231, 236; in Los Angeles City, 256–257; in Los Angeles County, 253–256; measurement in, 152–153, 162–163, 196–198; in New York City, 242–245; operations, 240; organization structure, 232, 236, 237, 240–241, 242–259; press and information units, 78, 115; program development model, 269–270; program evaluation, 169–185, 214, 219; program implementation, 166–168, 219; program planning, 158–159, 160–168, 219; public reluctance to report suspicious occurrences, 180–181; research, 186–188, 191–193, 196–198; rumor-control centers, 78; in small communities, 265–266; special training for, 213, 214–216, 232–233, 238–239; specialized units for, 132, 212, 213, 214, 219–220, 229–259; support services, 240; systems approach, 209–211
Police departments, 97, 133; centralization vs. decentralization, 231–232, 236, 240–241, 245, 253, 257–259; information and press units, 78, 115; military vs. nonmilitary model, 234–236; organization structures and

charts, 132, 232, 240–259; relationship to local political leaders, 114; specialists, 230; specialized PCR units, 132, 213, 214, 219–220, 229–259

Policeman in the Community, The (Banton), 13

Policing arrangements, 204, 236–237, 264–265; devising of systematic model, 31–32; goal of, 6; as "holding actions," 50; normative structure, 236–237

Politeness, benefits of, 109–110, 116

Political candidates. *See* Candidates

Political democracy. *See* Democracy

Political leaders: "public burnings" of, 111; relationship to police departments, 114

Political models, 30, 41, 42–43

Politico-economic models, 41–43

Politics (Aristotle), 3, 125, 263

Poor Richard's Almanac (Franklin), 169, 206

Pope, Alexander, 203

Positive reinforcement, 90

Power, 135–137; Bible quoted on, 44–45; elements and sources of, 135–137; historical overview of, 138–140; influence of, 134; *vs.* influence, 135–136; limitations of 144–145; methods of, 138; as potential for use of force, 134–135; separation of (government), 141, 142; as sociological term, 32, 37–38, 134

Power groups, 49, 137

Practitioners, use of, 23–24

Pragmatism, 191

Precinct community councils, 240, 245

Prescriptive norms, 33, 34–35, 163

Presidency, 141

President's Commission on Law Enforcement and the Administration of Justice, 257

Press-information units, police, 78, 115

Primary drives, 40, 90

Primary traits, 93

Prior probability, 193

Private police, 42, 126, 133, 240

Probabilistic inference, 8–9, 11, 17–18, 191–193, 194; in communication theory, 54

Probability, 8–9, 17–18, 191; past, 191–193; prior, 193

Problem solving, 21–22

Program planning, evaluation, *etc. See* Evaluation; Planning; *etc.*

Proscriptive norms, 33, 34, 35

Psychoanalysis, 89, 100

Psychoanalytic model, 40, 164

Psychoanalytic theory, 89, 164

Psychological models, 39–41, 143

Psychological tests, 92–93

Psychology, 37, 39–40

Punishment, 90, 134; and norm compliance, 35, 264

"Quality of life," 122–124

Quantification, 14, 31, 32, 208, 211; examples, 138; how and when to use, 21, 22, 31–32, 171

Racism, 118–119

Randomization, 190

Range, index of, 15

Rank-ordering measurement, 155–156

Ratio-level measurement, 157–158

Reaction error, 180

Real-time measurement, 172–173

Reality anxiety, 89

Reality principle (ego), 40, 89

Rebellion, 162, 163

Rebels, 160–161, 163

Receivers, in communication theory, 52, 58, 60–61, 64–70; competition for attention of, 73–74; influence on, 70–77; selective perception by, 67, 73–74

Recommendations, 18, 171, 211, 219

Redundancy, in communication theory, 53, 56, 58, 59, 62–64, 68–69, 117, 123; types of, 63

Reinforcement: in communication, 77 (*see also* Redundancy); negative (punishment), 90; positive (reward), 90

Religion and religious freedom, 110–111, 205

Religious models, 30, 44–45

Reports, evaluative, 171, 174, 175, 185. *See also* Conclusions; Findings; Recommendations

Research, 152–153, 184, 186–199; basic *vs.* applied, 177; design, 179; empirical, 189, 220, 234; fallibility of, 194–196; methods, 190–194; into PCR, 186–188, 191–193, 196–198; scientific, 188, 189–190

Response, in S-R theory, defined, 90

Retreatism, 162, 163
Return of Sherlock Holmes, The (Doyle), 229
Reverse discrimination, 145, 205
Reward, 90; effect on value systems, 104
Riot behavior, 36. *See also* Looting
Ritualism, 162, 163
Rogers, Carl R., 142
Role, 36–37, 87–88, 96–97; defined, 37, 96; institutionalized, 37; overt, 97; prescribed, 97; subjective, 97
Role allocation, 87, 96–97
Role compliance, 87
Role conflicts, 6–7; in police-community situations, 41
Rome, ancient, 139–140
Roosevelt, Franklin D., 141
Rousseau, Jean Jacques, 140
Rumor-control centers, 78
Rumors: controlling, 78; diffusion of, 77

St. Paul, Epistle to the Hebrews, 51
Sample selection, 190; error typology, 179–180; randomization, 190
Sartre, Jean-Paul, 91
Scientific method, 189–190
Secondary drives, 40, 90
Secondary traits, 93
Seek and Find (Herrick), 186
Self-interest, 47
Self theories of personality, 91
Senior citizen escort services, 240, 245
Separation of powers, 141, 142
Set(s), in behavioral science, 102–103, 114; defined, 102; examples of, 103
Sexual deviation, 94, 98
Sidearms, 115–116
Simulations, 28
Slavery, 108
Slum population, alienation of, 104
Social choice, 134–135, 142, 144–145; legal restrictions to, 134, 145
Social engineering, 126
Social evolution, 145–146
Social force, 37–38, 134; defined, 134
Social groups, 130
Social movements, 127–129; characteristics, 127–128; strategic objectives, 128
Social power, 136–137. *See also* Power
Social problem, definition, 30
Social-psychological models, 39

Social psychology, 37, 39, 85, 96
Social sciences: concepts and terminologies of, 32–38; measurement in, 152–154, 158
Societal groups, 130
Society, American, contradictions and polarization, 110–111, 118
Sociological models, 30, 32–39, 143
Sociology, 32
Sociopathic personality disturbance, 98
Sociopolitical change: modes of adaptation, 145–146, 159–163; stages of, 164; time requirement, 164
Sociopolitical models, 143
Solitary confinement, 101
Spanish-Americans, 121
Specialization *vs.* generalization, 229–231, 236
Speech, in communication theory, 54–56, 58, 60–61
Spindle, Parable of, 24–26, 51
Sponsorship of programs, normative, 226
S-R (stimulus-response) theory, 90–91, 142
Staff analysis, 211
Statistical analysis, 14–16, 178, 211
Statistical groups, 130
Statistical regression, 180
Statistics, 14–15, 152
Status, 32, 36, 132; ascribed *vs.* achieved positions, 96; and authority, 38; defined, 36
Status sets, 96–97
Status systems, 96
Stimulus-response (S-R) theories, 90–91, 142
"Stop and frisk," 46
Strong police chief system, 114
Superego, 89–90; defined, 40, 89; development, as management goal, 233
Surveillance, 129
Symbolic association, 81, 100–102
Symbolic interaction, 100–102
Symbolism, in communication, 61, 81, 100, 101
Systematic models, 30–32
Systems analysis, 22, 31, 211
Systems approach, 22, 30–31, 208–211, 234

Tabulation of data, 10; frequency distribution, 15

Talmud, 136

Taylor, Frederick, 233, 234

Television, 50, 61, 72, 73; municipal use of, 62, 72; police and crime shows, 114

Tension, 112–114; analysis of, 225–226; community, indices of, 113; physiological syndromes, 113; psychological, 113

Terrorist groups, international, 224

Theology, 154

Think tanks, 161

Thinking and thought, 78–82

Thrift, in value systems, 205

Tillich, Paul, 91

Time-and-motion studies, 233

Tocqueville, Alexis de, 121

Traditions, as source of knowledge, 189

Trait theories of personality, 91–93, 99

Traits: primary *vs.* secondary, 93; scales and tests, of, 92–93, 197–198

Translations, 79–80

Transmitters, in communication theory, 52, 58, 60–61

Truman, Harry S, 174

Two-step flow of influence, 70–77, 164, 165, 220

Unrest, 36, 46, 61. *See also* Civil demonstrations; Looting

Urbanism, 104, 189

U.S. Congress, 141, 142

U.S. Constitution, 140, 141–142, 143, 205, 264. *See also* Constitutional rights

Value(s), 103; basic American, conflicts in, 110–111; defined, 102; historical perspective, 205–206

Value changes, effecting, 75–76

Value systems, 22, 44, 89, 188; effects of reward on, 104; examples of, 102

Value theory, 22

Variables, critically relevant, 5–7; "errors" as, 179; identification of, 6, 11, 13–14; measurement and quantification of, 13–14, 154–158, 196–198; in police-community relations, 6

Varieties of Police Behavior (Wilson), 13

Vietnam War, 137

Voltaire, 57

Volunteer services, 244–245

Von Neumann, John, 209

Watergate, 128, 141, 217

Watson, J. B., 90

Webster, Daniel, 61, 141

What Is a Minority? (Gough), 106

Whitman, Walt, 43, 141

Wilson, James Q., 13

Woman power, 49, 104

Words, 80–82, 100; symbolic associations, 81, 100

Wordsworth, William, 149

Work, as a value, 205, 206

World Bible Society, 44

World War II, Russia in, 137

Writing, in communication theory, 58, 60–61